P9-CQJ-695

WEST'S LAW SCHOOL
ADVISORY BOARD

JESSE H. CHOPER
Professor of Law,
University of California, Berkeley

DAVID P. CURRIE
Professor of Law, University of Chicago

YALE KAMISAR
Professor of Law, University of Michigan
Professor of Law, University of San Diego

MARY KAY KANE
Chancellor, Dean and Distinguished Professor of Law,
University of California,
Hastings College of the Law

WAYNE R. LaFAVE
Professor of Law, University of Illinois

ARTHUR R. MILLER
Professor of Law, Harvard University

GRANT S. NELSON
Professor of Law, University of California, Los Angeles

JAMES J. WHITE
Professor of Law, University of Michigan

West, a Thomson business, has created this publication to provide you with accurate and authoritative information concerning the subject matter covered. However, this publication was not necessarily prepared by persons licensed to practice law in a particular jurisdiction. West is not engaged in rendering legal or other professional advice, and this publication is not a substitute for the advice of an attorney. If you require legal or other expert advice, you should seek the services of a competent attorney or other professional.

Nutshell Series, In a Nutshell, the Nutshell Logo and West Group are trademarks registered in the U.S. Patent and Trademark Office.

COPYRIGHT © 1976, 1981, 1992 WEST PUBLISHING CO.
COPYRIGHT © 1999 By WEST GROUP
© 2004 West, a Thomson business
    610 Opperman Drive
    P.O. Box 64526
    St. Paul, MN 55164–0526
    1–800–328–9352

ISBN 0–314–15002–1

Carroll University Library
Waukesha,

TEXT IS PRINTED ON 10% POST
CONSUMER RECYCLED PAPER

∞

FEDERAL LAW OF EMPLOYMENT DISCRIMINATION

IN A NUTSHELL

FIFTH EDITION

By

MACK A. PLAYER
Professor of Law
Santa Clara University
School of Law

THOMSON

WEST

Carroll University Library
Waukesha, WI 53186

Mat # 40180377

*To
Jeanne*

PREFACE

True to its title, this work summarizes the federal law regulating invidious discrimination at the workplace. Key words are: "Federal," "Discrimination," and "Employment." The work should assist five groups: 1) students enrolled in university courses in employment discrimination 2), students taking survey courses in the broader areas of "employment law" or "labor law" who seek a supporting summary of the course's employment discrimination component, 3) attorneys not regularly working in this area of the law who need an overview or refresher, 4) non-attorney managers who seek introductory guidance, and 5) lay persons who want an overview of their rights and remedies.

As should be obvious, a "Nutshell" is NOT a reference book. For in-depth analysis, see Rothstein, Craver, Schroeder, & Shoben, EMPLOYMENT LAW (West 1999); Lindeman & Grossman, EMPLOYMENT DISCRIMINATION LAW (BNA, 1996). Nor should this summary be relied upon to provide legal advice. Persons pursuing legal rights should secure competent legal counsel.

a. Citations are sporadic and incomplete, used when it seemed helpful, but not simply to support the accuracy of each statement. Moreover, they often refer to the general topic area, and may be inserted for their dicta or because they provide a good summary of the issue. In short, case citations may not be an explicit, on-point support for the preceding sentence.

b. Divisions of authority are rarely noted. Chain citations are absent. A statement may reflect the weight of authority without it noting qualifications or a contrary view. Unfortunately, a reader may be in the jurisdiction that follows the contrary view.

c. Page citations for quotations are omitted. Statements are paraphrased, often omitting quotation marks.

d. Case citations in the text refer only to the court and date. A full citation is in the table of cases. Citations do not include largely irrelevant subsequent histories such as certiorari denied.

An apology—For examples, illustrations, terminology that suggest a lack of sensitivity, I apologize. Moreover, it is often difficult, without causing confusion, to identify groups as they would themselves prefer. I have done my best. Certainly, no insult or political statement was intended by my choice of words.

Thank You! Santa Clara University gave me the time, and the University of San Francisco gave me the place. My partner and co-participant in thinking about employment discrimination issues broadly, and in writing about them here and elsewhere, is Jeanne M.L.Player. To this particular endeavor Jeanne contributed ideas, text, corrective direction, and served as a final reviewer. Without Jeanne this work would not have been done. All errors are mine!

MACK A. PLAYER

March 2004

*

OUTLINE

Page

*

TABLE OF CASES

References are to Pages

XXVII

TABLE OF CASES

TABLE OF CASES

TABLE OF CASES

TABLE OF CASES

TABLE OF CASES

TABLE OF CASES

TABLE OF CASES

TABLE OF CASES

TABLE OF CASES

FEDERAL LAW OF EMPLOYMENT DISCRIMINATION

IN A NUTSHELL

FIFTH EDITION

*

PART I

CONTEXT AND OVERVIEW

CHAPTER 1

"EMPLOYMENT DISCRIMINATION" DEFINED

I—1.01 A Note on Scope

The law regulating the workplace can be divided into three categories: 1) Labor-management relations, 2) Employee protections, and 3) Non-discrimination. The employment law professional needs to be conversant with all three.

Statutes have long prohibited discrimination based on one's membership in a labor organization and protected the right to engage in concerted activities for mutual aid and protection. Labor relations law is a distinct area of the law. Internal union governance is also regulated by federal statutes and is considered elsewhere. Leslie, LABOR LAW IN A NUTSHELL (4th Ed. 2000)(West).

Social legislation protecting the economic and social interests of all workers, such as occupational safety, unemployment, compensation for work place injuries, minimum wage and overtime, worker privacy, pension integrity, and social security benefits are collected and segregated into broad employee rights surveys. Hood, Hardy, & Lewis, WORKERS COMPENSATION & EMPLOYEE PROTECTION LAWS IN A NUTSHELL (3rd Ed. 1999)(West); Covington & Decker, EMPLOYMENT LAW IN A NUTSHELL, (2nd Ed. 2003)(West).

The United States Constitution provides broad protections to individuals, including employees, against invidious discrimination by governments. It protects individual freedoms from government intrusion: speech, assembly, privacy, petition for redress of grievances and religion from government restraint and demands that governments provide "equal protection of the law" and accord individuals "due process of law." These important rights are thoroughly covered in courses in constitutional law. Barron & Dienes, CONSTITUTIONAL LAW IN A NUTSHELL (5th Ed. 2003)(West)

Making decisions—discriminating or selecting among alternatives—is inevitable. Employment discrimination law defines when a work place action (or "discrimination") is legally unacceptable. The focus is on distinctions deemed invidious in social terms and which generally are unrelated to job performance. Race, color, national origin, sex, religion, age, as well as mental and physical disability are the forms of discrimination proscribed by core federal anti-discrimination law. The proscriptions are not found in a single statute, but in a number of distinct federal statutes and programs each with its own language and history. The three core statutes,

Title VII of the Civil Rights Act of 1964, the Age Discrimination in Employment Act, and the Americans with Disabilities Act, limit their non-discrimination prohibitions to "employers", "employment agencies" and "labor organizations." A conclusion that a distinction does not involve "employment" and thus is outside of the scope of these statutory schemes does not necessarily mean that the distinctions are lawful. It means only that the victim must seek remedies elsewhere.

I—1.02   Federal and State Law

a.   Federal Law: The Necessary First Step

The focus is **federal** law. Yet federal employment discrimination law is not exclusive. The federal statutes neither preempt overlapping state law, nor preclude states from granting protections that go beyond those in the federal statutes. *California Fed. Sav. & Loan Ass'n v. Guerra* (S.Ct. 1987). Most states and many cities have codes of fair employment practices.

There is great substantive similarity between federal and state employment discrimination law. Virtually all state statutes were modeled after the federal statutes, frequently adopting identical language. State judicial and administrative interpretations often follow federal precedent. Federal law may provide stronger, or at least more settled, substantive rights. There may be procedural and remedial reasons for pursuing federal over state processes. Federal employees have no option; they must utilize federal law and follow distinct federal agency procedures.

b. State Fair Employment Statutes: A Key Second Step

The central importance of federal law does not depreciate the significance of state and local law. Many jurisdictions have added proscriptions not found in federal law. Discrimination on the basis of "marital status" or "sexual orientation," for example, is not proscribed by federal law, but is prohibited in a number of states. Some states define "disability" more broadly than does federal law. Even when state legislation is similar to the federal statutes, state enforcement agencies may have construed their legislation differently. An issue settled in federal law may be unresolved under state law, prompting a plaintiff to venture into state tribunals hoping for a favorable ruling. State law may provide wider coverage, reaching small employers not covered by federal statutes. Time limitations, remedies, and procedures may be more favorable to a party who invokes state law.

CHAPTER 2

THE COMMON LAW

I—2.01 What is "Common Law"?

Common law is the body of law that finds its source in judicial decisions, rather than in statutes or constitutions. While courts recognize a self-imposed obligation to respect judicial precedent (stare decisis), common law principles do evolve in light of changing social and economic conditions. The common law found its historical roots in England, and was transported to most British colonies, including the United States, where it remains as a basis of modern contract, tort, agency, and property law. Generally, common law evolves at the state level, not in federal courts. While there are significant similarities in the common law among the several states, the common law has evolved among them differently.

I—2.02 Why Common Law is Important

The common law provides the history and context of the statutes. Historical failure of the common law to provide meaningful protection to employees prompted the creation of the statutory schemes. Evolving tort and contract principles now provide substantive rights, (*e.g.*, "wrongful discharge" and breach of contract), as well as remedies not available under statutory law. A victim of sexual or racial harassment, for example, in addition to statutory claims, may also have state tort claims of assault, defamation, intentional infliction of harm, etc. Finally, in construing statutory terms courts rely on common law definitions. Common law concepts of agency, for example, guide the courts in determining what persons are "employees" for the purpose of determining coverage and scope of employer liability under the federal statutes. Common law standards for measuring damages are applied under the statutes.

I—2.03 "Employment At Will"

Historically, absent a formal document setting a fixed term for the employment, the relationship between an employer and employee was "at will" and could be terminated by either party for any reason, no reason, or even for reasons which were morally reprehensible. *Payne v. Western & A. R.R.* (Tenn. 1884). This laissez faire approach was uniformly adopted and regularly reaffirmed until the middle of the 20th Century. *Forrer v. Sears, Roebuck & Co.* (Wis. 1967).

The "at-will" rule permitted employers to refuse to hire women or racial minorities. Employers could, and did, segregate their work forces, assign unpleasant or dangerous tasks solely to racial minorities, and limited supervisory positions to white males. As employers were free to make any pay distinctions, they often set lower pay scales for women and minorities. Even well-meaning employers often based policies on stereotyped assumptions to the disadvantage of many groups.

I—2.04 Public Policy Exception: "Wrongful Discharge"

Today, most states subject the "at will" rule to a "narrow" and "tightly circumscribed" exception. If the discharge of an employee undermines public policy, the injured employee has a claim that the discharge was "wrongful." The narrowness of this exception is manifested in three ways:

a. Discharges Only

The exception applies only to discharges. Refusing to *hire* an applicant, regardless of the reason, continues to be "at will." *Sanchez v. Philip Morris, Inc.* (10th Cir. 1993). Retaliatory treatment, short of discharge, such as making transfers or denying promotions is not protected. *White v. State of Washington* (Wash. 1997). Harassment coupled with threats to discharge an employee, as opposed to the discharge itself, is not actionable. *Below v. Skarr* (Iowa 1997).

b. Preemption by Statutory Remedies

Claims of wrongful discharge may be preempted by available statutory remedies. *Dudewicz v. Norris–Schmid, Inc.* (Mich. 1993). For example, where state non-discrimination statutes proscribe race, sex, or age discrimination, the discharge of the employee on such grounds, may preclude an assertion of a common law "wrongful discharge".

c. *"Fundamental and Well Defined"*

The public policy undermined by the employee's discharge must be "fundamental and well defined." A discharge is not "wrongful" simply because it is "unfair." *Wilburn v. Mid–South Health Development, Inc.* (10th Cir. 2003)(Oklahoma). The problem is defining which public policies are "fundamental and well defined:"

—*Illegal Acts*: Virtually all states concur that to dismiss an employee because he/she refused to commit an illegal act at the behest of the employer is wrongful. *Petermann v. International Broth. Of Teamsters, Local 396* (Cal. App. 1959) (employee refused to commit perjury). It is "wrongful" to discharge an employee because the employee complied with a government subpoena. *Martin Marietta Corp. v. Lorenz* (Colo. 1992). It violates public policy to dismiss a lawyer, physician, accountant or pharmacist for refusing to violate defined and enforceable professional ethical obligations. *Shearin v. The E.F. Hutton Group, Inc.* (Del. 1994). Protection does not extend to an employee's personal ethical standards. *Pierce v. Ortho Pharm. Corp.* (N.J. 1980).

—*Invoking Statutory Protections:* Most states protect workers against dismissal for the exercise of statutory rights that exist for employee protection. For example where a statute grants compensation for job injuries, dismissal of an employee who asserts a statutory claim is "wrongful" in that the public policy to provide relief to injured employees is undermined. *Frampton v. Central Indiana Gas*

Co. (Ind. 1973). Many states protect employees from dismissal for exercising fundamental rights enjoyed as citizens. Accordingly, dismissing an employee because of his service on a jury or because she exercised the right to vote may be "wrongful." Courts are divided on whether amorphous rights protected in the constitution against governmental infringement or created by the common law, such as privacy or freedom of speech, are sufficiently "well defined" to be protected. *Prysak v. R.L. Polk Co.* (Mich. App. 1992)

—*Reporting Illegality: "Whistleblowers":* Many states protect employees who report their employer's violations of the law. This is based on a policy recognition that effective law enforcement requires communication to enforcement agencies by persons with access to information. *Harless v. First Nat. Bank in Fairmont* (W.Va. 1978). For example, it was wrongful to discharge an employee for reporting the employer's safety code violations. *Freund v. Nycomed Amersham* (9th Cir. 2003). A number of jurisdictions have codified this protection, and the "whistleblower" statute may provide the exclusive remedy for employees discharged for their reporting of illegal behavior. States which otherwise protect "whistleblowers" may limit protection to reporting: 1) conduct of the employer—as opposed to behavior of fellow employees—2) to "proper authorities"— which may not include internal complaints to management—3) that was illegal—as opposed to the employee's *belief* that it was illegal. *Geary v. United States Steel Corp.* (Pa. 1974).

d.   Remedies: Tort or Contract?

Most courts view wrongful discharge as a tort for which the employee may recover damages for foreseeable loses that include consequential injuries such as pain, suffering, emotional distress, and loss of reputation. *Cagle v. Burns & Roe, Inc.* (Wash. 1986). To punish, and thus to deter future wrongdoing, an employee may recover punitive damages for malicious misconduct. Some courts, however, view wrongful discharge as a contract breach, and limit damages to the "loss of bargain:" (*e.g.,* lost wages and related incidental economic loses). Punitive damages, as well as damages for non-monetary injuries such as pain, suffering, and humiliation are not generally recoverable for contract breaches. *Sterling Drug, Inc. v. Oxford* (Ark. 1988).

I—2.05   Implied Covenant of Good Faith and Fair Dealing

Modern law classifies the employment relationship as one based on contract (as opposed to a status), and "[e]very contract imposes on each party a duty of good faith and fair dealing in its performance and its enforcement." Rest. Cont.2d. Sec. 205. In theory, it would be a breach of the duty of fair dealing to discharge an employee except for reasons which are honest in fact, consistent with accepted norms of reasonableness, and germane to the expectations of the parties. *Monge v. Beebe Rubber Co.* (N.H. 1974) (duty breached where employee dismissed for refusal to have sex with a supervisor) The majority of American courts, however, either reject outright the implication of a covenant of good faith and fair dealing in employment contracts or limit its application to where the employer precludes the employee's receipt of expressly promised benefits, such as when an employee is fired to prevent him from securing accrued profit sharing benefits. *Mitford v. de Lasala* (Alaska 1983).

I—2.06 Contract Exception to "Employment at Will"

a. Traditional Restraint

Traditionally, employees had a heavy burden of proving the existence of a contract that limited the "at will" relationship. Even promises of "permanent" or "for life,"coupled with promises of yearly salary increases, did not establish a contract right against the employer. *Fisher v. Jackson* (Conn. 1955). The courts gave at least three reasons: 1) presumption of the "at-will" relationship, 2) lack of "mutuality" in that the employee was free to quit, and 3) Statute of Frauds requirement for a writing when the contract cannot be performed within one year.

b. Modern Contract Doctrines Applied to Employment Promises

Today, express contracts between the employer and employee can overcome the "at-will" presumption. While formal written contracts are usually found only with executives or professionals, less formal, but nonetheless enforceable, contracts can be formed through an exchange of letters, or by an "offer" letter from an employer that is "accepted" by the employee reporting to work. Binding contracts can even be made through unambiguous oral promises.

The person asserting contract rights must prove with reasonable certainty language that was "promissory" in nature, expressing what a reasonable person would perceive to be an intent to be bound. Expression of vague hopes or general expectations, such as "permanent" are not enforceable promises. *Rowe v. Montgomery Ward & Co., Inc.* (Mich. 1991). If the employer promised no specific duration, courts may consider the employment to remain terminable at the will, but enforce specific promises, such as benefits, working hours, and other conditions.

"Consideration" for the employer's promises is supplied by the employee beginning work for the employer or by continuing on the job after the employer expressed the promise. No additional, "mutually equal" consideration need be paid by the employee to support the employer's promises. *Thompson v. St. Regis Paper Co.* (Wash. 1984). If the employee changed position in a significant way in reliance on the employer's promises, such as by moving or by terminating employment elsewhere, such reliance makes the employer's promises binding (known as "promissory estoppel"). *Gorham v. Benson Optical* (Minn. App. 1995).

Most courts conclude that clear promises of employment for long or indefinite duration can be fully performed within a year, such as by the employee dying or quitting or by the employer going out of business, and thus are not subject to the requirement of a writing. *Kitsos v. Mobile Gas Serv. Corp.* (Ala. 1981)

I—2.07   Employment Manuals

a.   The Nature of Employment Manuals

Many employers promulgate detailed policy manuals that outline employee benefits and set workplace expectations. They may establish probationary periods during which new employee can be terminated for any or no reason, often with the express or implicit promise that thereafter employees can expect some measure of job security such as discipline only for "good cause." Manuals frequently contain statements indicating that the employer will not discriminate on the basis of race, color, sex, religion, national origin, age disability, or other classifications. Manuals commonly contain procedures for employees to direct grievances, often culminating in non-judicial resolution.

b.   Manuals and Contract Law

1.   Creating the Contract: If the terms of the manual, under all the circumstances, contain specific promises, they will be considered part of a contractual "offer" to the employee, which the employee "accepts" either by signing a document of acceptance or by beginning work. Internal operating directives, addressed to management and not widely communicated to employees, are not binding

promises. *Feges v. Perkins Restaurants, Inc.* (Minn. 1992).

Contract rights are determined by what a *reasonable person* would have understood to have been promised. The more precise and unqualified the language (such as by using "will" rather than "may"), the greater the likelihood that the language will be seen as contractual. *Woolley v. Hoffman–La Roche* (N.J. 1985). If the manual, reasonably read, merely articulates the employer's aspirations, with no expressed or implicit promise that such practices will be continued, the provisions will not be enforceable. *Toussaint v. Blue Cross & Blue Shield* (Mich. 1980). If the language is contractual in nature, the fact that the employee did not personally receive the manual or did not read or understand its terms will not relieve the employer from promises a reasonable person would have understood to have been made.

2. Disclaimers: Employers may attempt to insure that their manual is not considered a binding contract by including a disclaimer. In addition to a statement that the manual merely articulates "existing policies" with no obligation to continue those policies, the disclaimer may state that employment continues to be "at will." When given prominence and stated in terms that a reasonable person would understand, the disclaimer will be given effect. However, if a disclaimer is obscure or ambiguous in light of repeated and detailed specific promissory language found throughout the manual, the dis-

claimer will not be effective. *Jones v. Central Penin-sula Gen. Hosp.* (Alaska 1989).

3. Construing the Language: When a contractual obligation arises, the language must be construed. If a contract requires fifteen days notice prior to discharge, the employer who discharges the employee without notice must provide fifteen days of benefits. *Shivers v. John H. Harland Co., Inc.* (S.C. 1992). If certain procedures are required prior to discipline, such as notice, a hearing, and review by higher management, promised procedures will be enforced. When manuals set forth substantive grounds for discharge (*e.g.,* "just cause") or establish standards of performance (*e.g.,* "satisfactory"), the employee may be discharged only if a court finds that such reasons were present. *Cummings v. South Portland Housing Auth.* (1st Cir. 1993). What constitutes "just cause" or "unsatisfactory performance" is determined by the presumed intent of the parties. Past practices and general traditions in the industry play a key role in determining intent. See, 1985 Duke L.J. 594.

CHAPTER 3

THE STATUTES

I—3.01 The "Big Three" Generally

Title VII of the Civil Rights Act of 1964 (Title VII) proscribes discrimination based on race, color, national origin, sex (including pregnancy) and religion. The Age Discrimination in Employment Act of 1967 (ADEA), proscribes age discrimination. The Americans with Disabilities Act of 1990 (ADA) reaches mental and physical disabilities. While the operative language of the three is similar, and they have common analytical approaches, there are important substantive differences. Procedures and remedies, too, while having similarities, contain significant differences. The statutes are interpreted and enforced by the U.S. Equal Employment Opportunity Commission (EEOC).

I—3.02 Title VII of the Civil Rights Act of 1964 (Title VII) (42 U.S.C.A. 2000e)

Title VII was one title of a sweeping omnibus Civil Rights Act of 1964. Each title was essentially a distinct piece of legislation with its own language and legislative history. Title VII had a unique legislative history that resulted in few meaningful committee reports. The Senate adopted the original House passed version of the bill, but only after adding extensive amendments introduced and debated on the floor of the Senate. The Conference bill followed the Senate version, but produced no report. It was adopted by both houses without meaningful debate.

Title VII was first amended in 1972. The EEOC was authorized to file judicial actions. Time limitations were lengthened. Coverage was extended to public employers. In 1978 the Pregnancy Discrimination Act added a definition of "sex" to include pregnancy and childbirth. The Civil Rights Act of 1991 added extensive amendments, many of which were reactions to 1988–89 Supreme Court decisions. The 1991 amendments redefined the evidentiary burdens, defined liability in so-called "mixed motive" cases, prohibited adjustment of test scores, limited challenges to judicially approved affirmative action plans, authorized jury trials, redefined the time allowed to challenge seniority systems, and authorized limited recovery of compensatory and punitive damages.

I—3.03 The Age Discrimination in Employment Act of 1967 (ADEA) (29 U.S.C.A. 621)

In language similar (but not identical) to Title VII, the ADEA proscribes age discrimination against individuals age 40 and over. While Title VII was being debated in Congress, an amendment was proposed to make "age" a class protected by Title VII. Congress rejected the amendment, but directed the Secretary of Labor to study the problem of age discrimination and report to Congress. In response to that report Congress enacted a distinct statutory scheme that relied heavily, but not exclusively on Title VII language. Enforcement responsibilities, originally vested in the Secretary of Labor, were transferred to the EEOC in 1978.

The ADEA has been amended numerous times. In 1974, coverage was extended to public employers. In 1978 amendments expressly prohibited mandatory retirement and extended the protected age class from age 65 to age 70. Technical amendments in 1982 and 1984 attempted to reconcile ADEA obligations with employer obligations under Medicare and Medicaid. A 1986 amendment eliminated the upper age limit of protection. Special provisions in both 1986 and 1996 allowed states to retain age rules for hiring and retirement of police and firefighters. The Older Worker Benefit Protection Act of 1990 added a number of amendments. Differences in benefit plans had to be justified by their actual difference in costs, use of early retirement programs was clarified, and standards were adopted for employers to secure waivers of ADEA claims.

While the 1991 Civil Rights Act made extensive amendments to Title VII, changes to the ADEA were limited to relatively minor procedural points. This omission, along with unique provisions in the ADEA relating to executives, police officers and firefighters and special provisions for benefit plans result in differences between Title VII and the ADEA. Nonetheless, to the extent the ADEA draws operative language from Title VII, it is accorded similar judicial construction.

I—3.04　The Americans With Disabilities Act (ADA) (42 U.S.C.A 1201)

The ADA is broad statute addressing many aspects of discrimination against persons with disabilities. General definitions are applicable to all titles of the Act. Title I is applicable to employment. It broadly prohibits discrimination against qualified individuals with mental or physical disabilities in language similar to Title VII. It addresses other practices, such as failing to make reasonable accommodation for persons with disabilities, and it limits medical inquiries and examinations. The ADA adopts Title VII coverage, enforcement, and remedies provisions for non-federal employees. The ADA became applicable to employment in July 1992.

The direct ancestor of the ADA was the Rehabilitation Act of 1973. Coverage of the Rehabilitation Act was limited to federal employers and employers receiving federal financial assistance or which were performing service or supply contracts for the federal government. The ADA adopted substantive language similar to that of the Rehabilitation Act, and indicated that judicial and administrative interpretations of the Rehabilitation Act (which used the term "handicap") should guide interpretation of the ADA. The Rehabilitation Act, as amended, remains the source of protection against disability discrimination for federal employees and applicants.

I—3.05 Additional Protections

a. Equal Pay Act of 1963 (29 U.S.C.A 206(d)) (EPA)

The EPA was the first modern federal fair employment statute. Its scope is narrow. Men and women who perform "equal work" within an employer's "establishment" must receive "equal pay" unless the pay difference is attributable to a seniority system, a merit system, a system that measures quantity or quality of production, or "any other factor other than sex." The EPA was an amendment to the Fair Labor Standards Act, a 1938 statute that regulates minimum wages, overtime pay, and child labor. Accordingly, coverage and enforcement of the EPA are set by the Fair Labor Standards Act. Initial enforcement and interpretation was with the Secretary of Labor, but was transferred to the EEOC in 1978.

b. Civil Rights Act of 1866 (42 U.S.C.A. 1981)

Immediately after the American Civil War, federal legislation implementing the Thirteenth Amendment attempted to provide equal property and contract rights to the newly freed slaves. Section 1981 of title 42 drawn from the 1866 Civil Rights Act provides that "all persons [shall have] the same right to make and enforce contracts as is enjoyed by white citizens." As employment is a "contract," this Act prohibits discrimination on the basis of race in hiring or firing of employees. Amendments in 1991 specified that the "make and enforce contracts" language of the original Act included also all "benefits, privileges, terms and conditions of the contractual relationship." While the distinct history of 1981 limits it to "racial" discrimination, the concept of "race" includes ethnic identity. *St. Francis College v. Al–Khazraji* (S.Ct. 1987).

There is a substantive overlap between 1981 and Title VII's prohibition of race and national origin discrimination. However, as 1981 protects "all persons," its coverage is universal. Since it prohibits racial discrimination in "all contracts," it is not restricted to employment relationships. Finally, this Act imposes no administrative pre-requisites to suit, and allows damage remedies that are not subject to the limits imposed under Title VII.

c. *Executive Order 11246*

E.O. 11246 is the product of the constitutional power of the president to establish the terms and conditions by which the executive branch will do business with suppliers of goods and services. It has been re-promulgated by every president since Franklin Roosevelt.

The Order obligates service and supply contractors and subcontractors not to discriminate against employees or applicants on the basis of race, color, sex, religion, or national origin. To this extent the Order mirrors Title VII protection. Secondly, the Order directs contracting employers to undertake "affirmative action" in favor of identified "under represented classes," an obligation not imposed by Title VII. The Order delegates to the Secretary of

Labor the authority to define this affirmative action obligation. Regulations in place since the 1970s require employers with significant government contracts to: 1) evaluate their workforce to determine whether there is an underutilization of women and minorities within job categories, and 2) adopt specific plans to remedy any found underutilization. Those plans normally must include numerical goals and specific timetables cast in racial, ethnic, and gender terms.

Obligations under the Order are contractual in nature, and thus are enforced by the federal government through breach of contract actions against the offending employer. Remedies include enforcing the non-discrimination provisions or terminating the contract. In extreme cases the Secretary of Labor may issue an order baring the offending contractor from future government contracts. Private parties may not enforce obligations imposed by the Order or resulting affirmative action plans.

d. *Family and Medical Leave Act of 1993 (FMLA) (29 U.S.C.A. 2601)*

While the Family and Medical Leave Act is social legislation that is outside the scope of traditional employment discrimination law, obligations imposed by this Act often are tied to employee claims of disability, pregnancy, or age discrimination.

Eligible employees working for a *covered* employer are entitled to up to 12 weeks of *unpaid* leave during any 12 month period because of : 1) birth of a child, 2) adoption of, or providing foster care for, a child, 3) "serious health condition that makes the employee unable to perform the functions of the position", or 4) to care for a spouse, child, or parent who has a "serious health condition." Once leave is granted the employer is required to maintain the employee's existing health care benefits, and to restore the employee to the position at the end of the leave without reduction of benefits. Employees may not be retaliated against for asserting rights granted by the Act. *Infra,* 14.04.

Coverage is *not* coextensive with Title VII. Private party enforcement is through procedures and remedies which largely mirror those of the Fair Labor Standards Act. The Secretary of Labor has interpretative and enforcement powers.

I—3.06 Military Service

Job protection for members of the military goes back to World War II, and is somewhat outside the scope of "invidious discrimination." Nonetheless military service now receives protected status similar to that given by the core non-discrimination statutes: "A person who is a member of, * * * performs, * * * has performed, * * * or has an obligation to perform service in a uniformed [military] service shall not be denied initial employment, re-employment, retention in employment, promotion, or any other benefit of employment by an employer on the basis of that [military] membership, ... performance, ... or obligation." 38 U.S.C.A. 4311. Any person whose absence was necessitated by reason of service in the uniformed services is entitled to re-employment, with benefits and seniority that he/she would have held if the employment had not been interrupted by the military service. 38 U.S.C.A. 4312—4316. For up to one year the re-employed veteran may be dismissed only "for cause" which the employer must establish. 38 U.S.C.A. 4316(c). Thereafter, the employee may not be dismissed because of his/her past or anticipated military obligations. The plaintiff, however, would have the burden of proving that military service was **a** factor motivating the dismissal.

These rights are enforced by individual veterans who *may* file administrative claims with the Secretary of Labor, who in turn may request enforcement suits by the Attorney General. The individual may await the outcome of such proceedings. Alternatively, the veteran may simply file an enforcement suit in federal court. 38 U.S.C.A. 4323.

Title VII specifically preserves statutory veterans preferences, thus insulating employers against challenges that the preference has an adverse impact on one gender or particular ethnic group. 42 U.S.C.A. 2000e–11.

CHAPTER 4

THE EQUAL EMPLOYMENT OPPORTUNITY COMMISSION (EEOC)

I—4.01 The Commission

The EEOC is a five person, presidentially appointed independent commission. It has a presidentially appointed General Counsel. The Commission establishes broad policies, while the Office of General Counsel has enforcement authority. Regional offices of the EEOC are located in major cities throughout the country.

I—4.02 Functions

—*Investigation*: The EEOC may itself file charges of discrimination, a power rarely utilized. Charges of discrimination traditionally are filed by aggrieved individuals in a regional office of the agency and investigated by personnel in that office. The EEOC has broad pre-litigation subpoena power to compel disclosure of relevant information. *University of Penn. v. EEOC* (S.Ct. 1990) (EEOC could subpoena internal memoranda of a university tenure committee. Such memoranda were relevant to an investigation and were protected neither by a common law privilege nor by the First Amendment).

25

—*Conciliation*: Where the investigation discloses reasonable cause to believe that a violation has occurred, the EEOC is directed to undertake conciliation and attempt informal resolution of charges. If it is unable to do so, the EEOC notifies the charging party, who is free at this point to file a private judicial action.

—*Litigation*: The Office of General Counsel is authorized to file suit in the name of the EEOC on charges that have not been resolved. The EEOC may also intervene in litigation filed by a private party.

—*Interpretation and guidance*: The EEOC has issued a wide range of formal interpretations of the statutes known as "Guidelines." It has also issued less formal "Policy Statements" on common interpretative and enforcement questions. See, www. eeoc.gov. These published positions are not formal regulations that have the force and effect of law. Nonetheless, as they are based on the expertise of the agency charged by Congress with enforcing and interpreting the statutes, EEOC interpretations are entitled to "great deference" by the courts. The actual extent of judicial deference is uneven. The EEOC requires employers to post notices regarding the rights of employees, and it distributes publications outlining employee rights. The EEOC also conducts public outreach and informational programs.

—*Record Keeping*: Through formal regulations the EEOC requires employers to maintain employment records and to file statistical reports with the agency.

—*Resolution*: The EEOC differs from many other agencies (*e.g.*, the National Labor Relations Board) in that it does *not* make "final" adjudications of discrimination charges, subject to limited judicial review under the Administrative Procedures Act. EEOC findings of "reasonable cause" authorize the EEOC to file suit, but in no way does the finding, or lack thereof, bind or limit the charging party or require the respondent to provide a remedy. Enforcement requires an independent judicial action either by the EEOC or charging party. Trial court adjudication of facts and law is *de novo*.

Two exceptions: 1) Federal employees can have their claims heard by the EEOC, and findings against the employer can be enforced against the federal employing agency. 2) Charges made by high level state employees are resolved in a formal adjudicatory hearing conducted by the EEOC, which findings are "final" and subject to limited judicial review.

CHAPTER 5

THE CONSTITUTION

I—5.01 Constitutionality of the Statutes

The "Commerce Clause" (Art. I, Section 8, para. 3) gives Congress power to enact anti-discrimination statutes and to impose non-discrimination obligations on the state governments. *EEOC v. Wyoming* (S.Ct. 1983). Congress also has power under Section 5 of the Fourteenth Amendment to enact legislation prohibiting private and public discrimination rooted in race, ethnic origin, or gender distinctions. *Fitzpatrick v. Bitzer* (S.Ct. 1976) (race and Title VII); *Nevada Dept. Of Human Resources v. Hibbs* (S.Ct. 2003) (gender). But power under the Fourteenth Amendment cannot be the source of authority to regulate historically non-invidious distinctions. *Kimel v. Florida Bd. Of Regents* (S.Ct. 2000) (age); *Board of Trustees of Univ. of Ala. v. Garrett* (S.Ct. 2000) (disability). Finally, section 2 of the Thirteenth Amendment grants Congress power to enact legislation to remove the "badges and incidents of slavery." Legislation attacking racial and ethnic origin discrimination, such as the Civil Rights Act of 1866 (42 U.S.C.A. 1981), finds authority in the Thirteenth Amendment. *St. Francis College v. Al–Khazraji* (S.Ct. 1987).

I—5.02   Federalism: Balancing of Federal and State Powers

a.   State Sovereignty and Immunities

The Tenth Amendment to the Constitution reserves to the states powers not delegated to the national government by the Constitution. Notwithstanding the Amendment's sweeping language, federal statutes regulating employment actions by state governments are constitutional. *EEOC v. Wyoming, supra.* The Eleventh Amendment, however, prevents *private* suits seeking monetary relief in federal or state courts against state entities where the authority for the legislation being enforced was Congress' commerce power. *Kimel v. Florida Bd. Of Regents, supra,* (age); *Board of Trustees of Univ. of Ala. v. Garrett, supra* (disability). The Eleventh Amendment does not restrict suits against states when the legislation was enacted pursuant to the Fourteenth Amendment as in the case of race, national origin, and sex. *Fitzpatrick v. Bitzer, supra,*

The Eleventh Amendment does not preclude federal enforcement agencies from securing relief against state entities. Nor does the Eleventh Amendment preclude private parties from securing federal remedies against governmental entities other than the state. *Mt. Healthy City School Dist. Bd. of Ed. v. Doyle* (S.Ct. 1977).

b.   Federal Supremacy and Preemption

Article VI of the Constitution provides that federal law shall be supreme, thus supplanting *inconsistent* state law. In the employment discrimination area, federal legislation, with minor exceptions, does not pre-empt state regulatory schemes. While state law cannot restrict the application or enforcement of federal anti-discrimination law, it can and does mirror federal law, providing employees with an alternative remedy. Moreover, states are free to provide protections that *exceed* those granted by federal statutes. *California Federal Sav. & Loan Ass'n v. Guerra* (S.Ct. 1987).

I—5.03 Government as a Regulator

Statutes, programs, and judicial orders must be read in light of the Constitution. To the extent such programs conflict with the Constitution, they will be struck down.

a. *Imposing Race or Gender Distinctions: Affirmative Action*

Suspect or suspicious classifications such as race, ethnicity, or sex when used by government employers, imposed by a government on private employers, or utilized by courts as part of a judicial remedy are subjected to "searching" judicial scrutiny under Equal Protection and Due Process concepts, regardless of whether the governmental action benefits or harms traditionally disadvantaged minorities. *Adarand Constructors v. Pena* (S.Ct. 1995). This requires significant, if not "compelling," governmental interests for the classification, and a demonstration that the classification is narrowly tailored to achieve that interest. *Grutter v. Bollinger* (S.Ct. 2003), held achievement of a racially balanced student body is a compelling interest, and that the use of race as one of many factors in making admissions decisions was narrowly tailored to serve that interest. By contrast, *Gratz v. Bollinger* (S.Ct. 2003) held that the use of a fixed racial quota or points that give automatic advantage to every minority applicant was not sufficiently tailored, and thus was unconstitutional. See, *infra* 8.02(d) and 23.11.

b. First Amendment Freedom of Association and Religion

Statutes proscribe employer discrimination against employees on the basis of religion. This prohibition must be read in light of the First Amendment protection of the employer's "free exercise" of religion. Generally, a secular employer may not assert his personal religion as a basis for engaging in illegal discrimination. *EEOC v. Townley Engineering & Mfg. Co.* (9th Cir. 1988).

While religious organizations are permitted by Title VII to discriminate on the basis of religion, the statutes proscribe discrimination in employment by religions on the basis of race, color, sex, age, and disability. However, judicial enforcement of this prohibition against a religious organization may entangle the courts in the religion, perhaps in violation of both the "free exercise" and "establishment" clauses of the First Amendment. Compare *Combs v. Central Texas Annual Conf. of the United Methodist Church* (5th Cir. 1999) (selection of minister) with *Bollard v. California Soc'y of Jesus* (9th

Cir. 1999) (harassment of a novice). *Infra,* 7.01(e)(3).

Anti-discrimination statutes and their enforcement compel employment and thus force an association against the wishes of employers and fellow employees. Nonetheless, the statutes do not infringe the freedom of association taking place in a secular or commercial operation. But there are limits. *Boy Scouts of American v. Dale* (S.Ct. 2000) held that a state could not compel the Boy Scouts to accept a homosexual and avowed gay rights activist under state non-discrimination law because to do so violated the organization's First Amendment freedom of "expressive association."

I—5.04 Government as an Employer

a. "State Action"

The original United States Constitution and the first ten Amendments ("Bill of Rights") limited only the power of the national government. State powers were left largely unrestricted. The Fourteenth Amendment in 1868 prohibited *states* from depriving "any person of life, liberty, or property without due process of law" (Due Process Clause), and denying "to any person within its jurisdiction the equal protection of the laws" (Equal Protection Clause). The Constitution restricts only "state action," and thus applies only to governmental employers. *Rendell-Baker v. Kohn* (S.Ct. 1982).

b. "Right–Privilege" Doctrine

Until the mid–1950s the prevailing view was that government employment was a "privilege" not a "right." Public employment could be conditioned on grounds that would be impermissible if imposed on the public at large. *McAuliffe v. New Bedford* (Mass. 1892). Similar to employees in the private sector, government employees served "at will," and absent protective legislation, such as civil service laws, they could be hired and dismissed for any reason or no reason. In 1952 the Court recognized that governments could not allocate public employment using invidious classifications such as race. *Wieman v. Updegraff* (S.Ct. 1952). In 1968 the Court abandoned the "right-privilege" doctrine. Public employees may not be compelled to relinquish rights they enjoy as citizens, such as the First Amendment freedom to speak publicly on matters of public interest. *Pickering v. Board of Education* (S.Ct. 1968).

c. *The Analysis: An Overview*

The Fifth and Fourteenth Amendments broadly direct that a government's irrational or arbitrary treatment of individuals violates "Due Process" and "Equal Protection" of the laws. The Supreme Court developed a tiered approach for analyzing governmental action.

1. "Suspect:" Classifications against groups that have been subjected to a "history of purposeful unequal treatment or relegated to a position of political powerlessness" are "suspect" and subject to "strict judicial scrutiny." Strict scrutiny places on the government the "heavy burden" of establishing "compelling governmental interests" for mak-

ing such distinctions and proving that the classification narrowly serves that compelling interest. *San Antonio School Dist. v. Rodriguez* (S.Ct. 1973). The following classifications have been declared "suspect:"

Race: *Graham v. Richardson* (S.Ct. 1971). The burden is on the plaintiff/employee to establish a racial motivation behind the governmental decision or policy. Racial motivation will not be established simply by demonstrating that a policy may have an adverse effect on a particular race. *Washington v. Davis* (S.Ct. 1976).

Religion: *Sherbert v. Verner* (S.Ct. 1963). But see, *Goldman v. Weinberger* (S.Ct. 1986)(military regulation prohibiting Jewish officer from wearing yarmulke while on duty was sustained as being "reasonable," with special deference accorded to regulations of uniformed military services). See also, *Employment Div. Dept. of Human Resources v. Smith* (S.Ct. 1990), holding that religion-required practices cannot be basis for individual's failure to comply with criminal law of general application.

Alienage and National Origin: *Sugarman v. Dougall* (S.Ct. 1973). While aliens cannot indiscriminately be barred from state and local civil service jobs, state governments may exclude aliens from holding elective or important non-elective positions where they "participate directly in the formulation, operation, or review of broad public policy." Foley v. Connelie (S.Ct. 1978)(police officers); *Ambach v. Norwick* (S.Ct. 1979)(teachers). Federal government interest in regulating immigration and naturalization allows it to exclude aliens from the federal civil service. *Hampton v. Mow Sun Wong* (S.Ct. 1976).

Speech, Assembly and Privacy: *Pickering v. Board of Education* (S.Ct. 1968). Non-policy making, non-confidential employees are protected by the First Amendment from adverse employment decisions based on their public speech, rights to assembly, and political affiliation. *Rutan v. Republican Party* (S.Ct. 1990). The protection for speech extends only to the employee's discussion of issues of public concern, and not to public airing of internal job issues, particularly if such discussion undermines work-place discipline. Moreover, the government as an employer has interests in work place efficiency that permit it to limit employee speech at the work place during working hours. Privacy, likewise, is a constitutional right that governmental employees enjoy. But this right, too, is qualified by the government's interest as an employer to manage and secure the working environment.

2. Non–Suspect: Governmental distinctions along lines that have not been defined by a history of prejudice or of political impotence are subjected to less intense scrutiny. Such distinctions must have some rational basis, but, unlike suspect classification, it is the plaintiff/employee who must carry the difficult burden of proving government irrationality. The following are non-suspect classifications that will be sustained if not proved to be irrational:

Age: Age distinctions that force retirement have been routinely upheld as rational. *Massachusetts*

Bd. of Retirement v. Murgia (S.Ct. 1976) (age fifty retirement rational for police officers); *Gregory v. Ashcroft* (S.Ct. 1991)(age seventy for judges).

Disabilities: *Cleburne v. Cleburne Living Center, Inc.* (S.Ct. 1985) (nonetheless, the zoning ordinance disadvantaging the disabled was struck down as being irrational). *Contractors Ass'n of Eastern Pa. v. City of Philadelphia* (3rd Cir. 1993) upheld regulations *favoring* applicants with disabilities as being "rational" in light of the history of the economic and social disadvantage of persons with disabilities.

3. "Suspicious:" There is a mid-tier category between the extremes of "strict scrutiny" and "rational basis." Distinctions against groups that have not been politically disenfranchised nor subjected to a long history of official discrimination, but nonetheless have experienced societal prejudice and frequently are victims of stereotyped assumptions, are "suspicious" and subjected to a heightened scrutiny. Such distinctions require the government employer to establish "important governmental objectives" that are "substantially achieved by the use of the classification."

Sex/Gender: *Craig v. Boren* (S.Ct. 1976). An overly broad use of gender as a proxy for more narrow and germane classifications that could equally serve identified and otherwise legitimate government objectives violates "equal protection," as will the blanket exclusion of women from certain governmental jobs, and the use of gender to allocate employment benefits. See, *United States v. Virginia*

(S.Ct. 1996) (exclusion of females from state military academy violated the Equal Protection Clause).

Sexual Activity: Until recently, discriminating against gay or lesbian persons was evaluated in terms of its "rational basis." *Padula v. Webster* (D.C.Cir. 1987) (FBI refusal to employ homosexuals not subjected to heightened scrutiny and being found rational, upheld). *Lawrence v. Texas* (S.Ct. 2003), placed this authority in doubt. After noting the long history of discrimination against homosexuals, the international rejection of legal restraints against sexual orientation, and the increasing legal and societal acceptance of private, consenting homosexual activity, the Court concluded that a Texas criminal prosecution of private homosexual activity between consenting adults violated privacy rights protected by the Fourteenth Amendment. The Court's rationale suggests that if a person were a victim of discrimination by a government employer based on sexual orientation, that discrimination would be reviewed under the heightened level of review given gender distinctions, if not the strict scrutiny accorded intrusions on fundamental liberties. Even if not subjected to heightened scrutiny, it may not be difficult for a plaintiff to establish the irrationality of a governmental employer discriminating on the basis of sexual orientation or for one's private, lawful sexual behavior. For example, *Schroeder v. Hamilton School Dist.* (7th Cir. 2002), rejected a heightened scrutiny standard in reviewing harassment of a gay teacher, but noted that liability could be established if the employer ignored a gay teacher's complaints about harassment and failed to take steps to protect the employee.

d.   Procedural Due Process

1.   "Property" and "Liberty:" The Due Process Clauses of the Fifth and Fourteenth Amendments require due process of law for governmental "takings" of "liberty" and "property." But unless the government employee can establish a liberty or property interest in the job, the constitutional obligation to provide "due process" is not triggered. Generally, an applicant has no "property" interest in a vacant position and no "liberty" is infringed by his being denied employment. In short, the Constitution does not require procedural (as distinguished from substantive) fairness in filling vacancies.

An employee will have a "property" interest in *continued* employment, protected against undue "taking," when the employee has a "legitimate claim of entitlement" to the position. A mere hope or generalized expectation of continued employment does not suffice. "Property" requires de facto, enforceable, tenure-like policy assuring ongoing employment. *Board of Regents v. Roth* (S.Ct. 1972).

Even in the absence of "property," an employee will have a "liberty" interest infringed if an adverse action stigmatizes the employee's reputation so that pursuit of similar employment is substantially hindered. An accusation of dishonesty or immorality infringes that "liberty," and thus requires procedural due process. *Putnam v. Keller* (8th Cir. 2003). Dismissal for failure to perform up to the employer's expectations is not sufficiently stigmatizing to deprive the employee of a "liberty." *Bishop v. Wood* (S.Ct. 1976).

2. The "Process" "Due:" If the employee establishes a property or liberty infringed by the employer's action, the employee is entitled to receive notice of the reasons for the discipline and before the action is taken, a reasonable opportunity to be heard. A pre-dismissal hearing need not be elaborate or provide full rights of confrontation. At some point, however, an employee being deprived of liberty or property in the job is entitled to confront the evidence against him, present his evidence and arguments, and have a final decision made by an unbiased person. *Cleveland Bd. Of Educ. v. Loudermill* (S.Ct. 1985).

*

PART II

COVERAGE AND SCOPE OF THE CORE STATUTES

CHAPTER 6

SCOPE

II—6.01 Employer "Discrimination": Adverse Action "Because of"

The statutes reach: 1) failure or refusal to hire, 2) discharge, or 3) discriminating "against any individual with respect to compensation, terms, conditions or privileges of employment." In addition, employers may not "limit, segregate, or classify employees or applicants for employment in any way which would tend to deprive any individual of employment opportunities or otherwise adversely affect [his/her] status as an employee." The statutory language is "not limited to economic or tangible discrimination, but strikes at the entire spectrum of disparate treatment." *Meritor Savings Bank v. Vinson* (S.Ct. 1986). Nonetheless, differences in treatment that neither affect a tangible benefit nor create an abusive working environment are outside the scope of the statutes. *Oncale v. Sundowner Offshore Services, Inc.* (S.Ct. 1998). Routine management and

41

scheduling decisions and differences in office equipment or aesthetics are not "terms and conditions of employment." *Markel v. Board of Regents, University of Wis.* (7th Cir. 2002). Criticism and unfavorable evaluations become adverse actions only upon the employer taking tangible action based thereon. *Tademe v. St. Cloud State Univ.* (8th Cir. 2003). Even transferring an employee to a different location is not an adverse action if salary, benefits, seniority, title, and responsibility are not altered. *Spears v. Missouri Dep't of Corr. & Human Res.* (8th Cir. 2000).

The statutes do not require employers to act fairly or rationally. No matter how high handed a practice or how arbitrary or mistaken a decision, the law does not interfere unless the action is "because of": 1) race, 2) color, 3) religion, 4) sex, 5) national origin, 6) age, or 7) disability.

II—6.02   The Employment Relationship

a. Generally

Actions taken by an employer not directed toward employment, such as investment decisions, treatment of shareholders, plant location, and product marketing, are not within the scope of the core statutes.

As the statutes prohibit "employer" discrimination against "individuals" regarding "employment," they reach acts that interfere with an individual's employment at the covered employer and employment elsewhere. Thus, an "employer" that provides unfavorable references concerning a former employee to a prospective employer is subject to the statutes. A hospital that discriminated in referral of nurses to patients was accountable for its acts of discrimination even though patients, not the hospital, were the actual employers of the nurses. *Sibley Memorial Hosp. v. Wilson* (D.C.Cir. 1973).

b. Non-employment Relationships

1. Partners and Directors: Inclusion in, or exclusion from, partnership or shareholder status generally are not acts of employment. Nonetheless, where management control is centralized in a small number of managing partners, an employer may not evade the statutes simply by labeling those who work for it as "partners." Thus, non-managing, but technical "partners" are statutory "employees." *Clackamas Gastroenterology Assoc. v. Wells* (S.Ct. 2003). Denial of an equity, but non-management partnership, in a large accounting firm is an employment decision. *Price Waterhouse v. Hopkins* (S.Ct. 1989).

2. Independent Contractors: Services for an employer, such as maintenance, repair, janitorial or security, even selling the employer's product, may be performed by contractors distinct from the employer's employees. Treatment of independent contractors, or employees of an independent contractor, is not one of employment. Traditional common law principles of "master/servant" are applied to distinguish between "employees" who are protected by the statutes and independent contractors who are not. *Clackamas Gastroenterology Assoc. v. Wells*, *supra*. The greater the employer's "right of control"

over the time, means, and manner of the work to be performed, the more likely the relationship will be one of "employment." *Nationwide Mut. Ins. Co. v. Darden* (S.Ct. 1992) (ERISA) (insurance salesman). Other factors are: who furnishes the equipment, where is the work performed, the method of payment, retirement and Social Security withholding, how the parties defined the relationship, length of time of the relationship, and whether the work is an integral part of the employer's business (such as a salesperson) or provides collateral support (such as janitorial or security service). *Spirides v. Reinhardt* (D.C.Cir. 1979).

3. Licensing Authority: Issuance of licenses or professional certification is not, standing alone, employment even though a license may be necessary to secure employment. Professional tests, such as a bar examination or a medical board examination, are not subject to the statutes. *Woodard v. Virginia Bd. of Bar Examiners* (4th Cir. 1979). However, where a state teacher certification examination qualified teachers to teach in public schools, this was an employment act because, in addition to the challenged test, the state exercised pervasive control over the operation of public school employers. *Association of Mexican–American Educators v. California* (9th Cir. 2000) (en banc).

4. Students: Where the thrust of a relationship is "educational," as where individuals are student teachers or are working in a supervised clinic for which they receive academic credit, the student will not be considered an "employee" even if financial support is provided in terms of a scholarship or fellowship. *Pollack v. Rice Univ.* (S.D.Tex. 1982).

5. Volunteers: While charitable organizations can be "employers," persons whose services are not compensated and are based solely on the worker's charitable impulses are not employees.

6. Prisoners: Those incarcerated by law and performing jobs while incarcerated are not employees unless they are specifically employed and paid distinct wages.

7. Military: Members of the uniformed military services are not in an employment relationship.

Caveat: 42 U.S.C.A 1981, which prohibits racial discrimination in the making or enforcing of *contracts,* is violated by all race based contract discrimination. Constitutional protections also are applicable to the treatment of prisoners, students in state schools, and military personnel. Other statutes prohibit discrimination in education, housing, health care, etc.

c. *Joint Employment*

1. Horizontal—Employees of Contractors and Contingent Workers: One entity may engage another to perform services on its premises in an independent contractor relationship (e.g., janitorial and security services companies contracting with a building occupant). The occupant of the premises may have input on which workers are acceptable as well as directing where and how the work is performed. Where responsibilities are shared more or less equally, the worker may be an employee of *both* employers. *Redd v. Summers* (D.C.Cir. 2000). This is often the case with contingent workers. A large number of potential workers are engaged by firms

which, in turn, provide temporary staffing for numerous clients. The staffing firm selects potential workers, enters into a contract with these workers, and refers workers to clients. The EEOC indicates that *both* the staffing firm and the client firm *can* be "employers." The client firm will be an "employer" through its exercise of day-to-day supervisory control over the individual's work. The staffing firm may also be an "employer" where it initially selects the worker, retains an ongoing relationship with the worker with authority to terminate the relationship, and is in some way responsible for benefits provided the worker.

2.   Vertical—Parents and Subsidiaries: A parent company is not an employer of individuals working for a legally distinct subsidiary based solely on the parent's ownership. However, the parent will be deemed a joint employer with the subsidiary if there is an interrelationship of operations, common management, and centralized control of labor relations. *Romano v. U–Haul Int'l* (1st Cir. 2000). An employer association that did not direct or encourage discrimination is not liable for acts of its members. *Anderson v. Pacific Maritime Ass'n* (9th Cir. 2003).

II—6.03 Labor Organizations

The statutes proscribe three categories of discrimination by labor organizations: 1) Internal union affairs: excluding or expelling from membership or "otherwise discriminating" in the internal operation. 2) Representation: failing or refusing to refer for employment, or classifying its membership or applicants in any way which would tend to deprive an individual (whether or not a union member) of employment opportunities. 3) Causing illegal acts by the employer or others.

Segregating the union along racial and gender lines is both discriminating in the internal affairs of the union and classifying members in a way that tends to deprive them of employment opportunities. *EEOC v. International Longshoremen's Ass'n* (5th Cir. 1975). In addition to Title VII constraints, unions certified as bargaining representatives have a duty of fair representation imposed by the National Labor Relations Act that prohibits negotiation of discriminatory contractual terms. *Steele v. Louisville & N.R. Co.* (S.Ct. 1944). Unions also must process and pursue employee grievances in a nondiscriminatory fashion. *Goodman v. Lukens Steel Co.* (S.Ct. 1987). While they may not encourage illegal action, unions have no affirmative duty to challenge discrimination. *EEOC v. Pipefitters Ass'n, Local 597* (7th Cir. 2003).

II—6.04 Employment Agencies

Employment agencies may not fail or refuse to refer for employment or otherwise discriminate against or classify any individual because of race, sex, national origin, religion, age or disability. It may not honor discriminatory requests by employers. It may not maintain segregated files that permit others to discriminate. However, so long as the agency refers applicants on a non-discriminatory basis, it has no obligation to police the hiring practices of the employer to which it refers individuals. *Kaplowitz v. University of Chicago* (N.D. Ill. 1974).

CHAPTER 7

COVERAGE

II—7.01 "Employer"

a. Generally

In addition to satisfying the common law concept of being an "employer," the core statutes require the entity to meet additional statutory standards. Title VII and the ADA have identical coverage. The ADEA differs only in the number of employees required. The Equal Pay Act and the Family and Medical Leave Act have different standards.

b. "Persons Affecting Commerce"

An "employer" must be a "person" in an industry "affecting commerce." "Person" includes any legal entity. "Affecting commerce" is the outer limit of Congressional authority to legislate under its commerce powers. Therefore, virtually any "person", even local, non-profit enterprises, with the requisite number of employees will have sufficient impact to "affect commerce." *Johnson v. Apna Ghar, Inc.* (7th Cir. 2003). "Commerce" does not mean commercial; the statutes apply to charitable organizations. *Martin v. United Way of Erie County* (3rd Cir. 1987).

c. Number of Employees

To be an "employer" under Title VII and the ADA, the "person" must have *fifteen* or more employees. The ADEA requires *twenty* or more employees. Individuals not in an employment relationship to the "person" are not "employees" for the purposes of determining coverage. Thus, independent contractors, shareholders, managing partners, and corporate directors are not counted as "employees." *Clackamas Gastroenterology Assoc. v. Wells* (S.Ct. 2003). (See *supra* 6.02(b)).

d. Period of Time

To be an "employer" the person must employ the requisite number of "employees" "each working day for *twenty* or more calendar weeks in the current or previous calendar year." The twenty weeks of employment need not be consecutive. When the requisite number of employees has been employed for the necessary twenty weeks, all employment decisions in that year and the *next* calendar year are covered regardless of downward fluctuation in the number of employees. Whether an employee is employed on "each working day" is determined by the employer's payroll for the week, not upon whether the employees were physically present on each of the working days of the week. *Walters v. Metropolitan Educ. Enterprises, Inc.* (S.Ct. 1997).

e. Special Types of Employers: Some Inclusions and Exclusions

1. Governments: State and local governmental units that employ the necessary number of employees within a discrete agency are "employers" subject to substantive prohibitions identical to those imposed on private employers. While the federal government is excluded as an "employer," distinct provisions of Title VII and the ADEA prohibit discrimination by the executive departments in terms similar to those applicable to other employers. The federal government's treatment of individuals with disabilities is governed by the Rehabilitation Act, which reaches outcomes similar to the ADA.

The Congressional Accountability Act of 1995 made the substantive prohibitions of Title VII, the ADA, the ADEA, the Equal Pay Act, the Family and Medical Leave Act, the Employee Polygraph Protection Act, and the Veterans Employment and Reemployment Act applicable to the legislative branch of the Federal government. 2 U.S.C.A. 1301. Enforcement procedures prescribed for legislative employees differ markedly from procedures for executive branch employees.

2. Indian Tribes: Title VII specifically excludes "Indian tribes" from the definition of "employer." This exclusion applies to the tribe's semi-sovereign, governmental functions and to commercial activity undertaken by the tribe. The ADEA does not expressly exclude Indian tribes from coverage, but the statute cannot be applied to the tribe's non-commercial, sovereign, governmental work. *EEOC v. Fond du Lac Heavy Equipment Co.* (8th Cir. 1993).

3. Religious Organizations: Churches and religious organizations with the requisite number of employees are defined "employers." Nonetheless, Title VII allows religions and religious educational institutions to discriminate on the basis of *"religion or religious belief or practice."* This exemption is applicable to all activities of the religion, including its secular, profit-making commercial activity. *Corporation of the Presiding Bishop v. Amos* (S.Ct. 1987). *Infra* 19.04. The exemption for religious organizations is limited to discrimination on the basis of religion. Religious organizations may *not* discriminate in employment because of race, color, ethnic origin, sex, age or disability.

It is constitutional to impose laws of general application on religious organizations. *Employment Div., Dept. of Human Resources v. Smith* (S.Ct. 1990). Nonetheless, the Constitution's protection of the free exercise of religion must be considered. Application of the statutes to those performing *secular* work for the religion (*e.g.*, clerical, maintenance, custodial) is constitutional. *Weissman v. Congregation Shaare Emeth* (8th Cir. 1994). It violates the First Amendment, however, to apply the statutes in a way that challenges selection, assignment, pay, or dismissal of those whose duties are central to the religious activity of the church (*e.g.*, pastors, priests, rabbis, teachers). *Combs v. Central Texas Ann. Conf. of the United Methodist Church* (5th Cir. 1999). The distinction between secular and religious is not always clear. A church's music director and music teacher could not constitutionally assert a claim of sex discrimination against the church employer. *EEOC v. Roman Catholic Diocese of Raleigh* (4th Cir. 2000). However, duties of an editorial secretary at a church publishing house were sufficiently secular to allow a Title VII claim. *EEOC v. Pacific Press Pub. Co.* (9th Cir. 1982). Greater judicial intrusion is likely where the discrimination is in the form of harassment which the church itself forbids. *Bollard v. California Soc'y of Jesus* (9th Cir. 1999).

4. Membership Clubs: Excluded from the Title VII and ADA definition of "employer" are bona fide private membership clubs (other than labor organizations) which are exempt from taxation under the Internal Revenue Code. To be a defined "club", the organization must have defined social or recreational purposes that promote a common literary, scientific, or political objective and impose meaningful conditions of membership. Athletic and country clubs meet this definition; credit unions, nursing homes, and hospitals do not. *Quijano v. University Federal Credit Union* (5th Cir. 1980). The ADEA has no specific exclusion for membership clubs. Note: the issue is not the club's *membership* practices, which are outside the scope of the statutes, but whether the club is an "employer," and thus may not discriminate against its employees and job applicants.

5. American Employers Abroad: The statutes do not apply to *aliens* employed and working outside the United States. The statutes do apply to American companies operating abroad, as well as their foreign subsidiaries, in their treatment of *citizens* of the United States, provided that compliance with

American law is not made unlawful under the law of the host country.

6. Foreign Employers in the United States: Foreign companies doing business in the United States are subject to the statutes. Foreign governments operating in their sovereign capacity within the United States, such as embassies and consulates, are immune from general employment laws of the United States. *McCulloch v. Sociedad Nacional de Marineros de Honduras* (S.Ct. 1984). However, commercial activity of foreign governments, such as national airlines and banks, are subject to the statutes. *Wickes v. Olympic Airways* (6th Cir. 1984).

Treaties of friendship, commerce, and navigation between the United States and the guest nation may exempt certain employment activities of companies from the guest nation, generally by allowing companies of the guest nation to hire executives, managers, experts, and similar professionals "of their choice." Such treaties have been construed to permit the guest employer to prefer its own nationals, but not to authorize race, sex, or age discrimination. *MacNamara v. Korean Air Lines* (3d Cir. 1988).

Treaties typically apply only to companies incorporated in the guest nation. Companies incorporated in the United States, even if wholly owed by foreign nationals, are "companies of the United States" and outside any exemption provided by the treaties. *Sumitomo Shoji America, Inc. v. Avagliano* (S.Ct. 1982). *CF., Papaila v. Uniden Am. Corp.* (5th Cir. 1995)(U.S. subsidiary can invoke treaty where preference for nationals is dictated by its foreign parent)

II—7.02 "Labor Organization"

A labor organization is an association which exists in whole or in part to deal with employers concerning employee grievances, labor disputes, and terms or conditions of employment. To be covered, the labor organization must be "engaged in an industry affecting commerce." This occurs if the union maintains a hiring hall or has *fifteen* or more members (*twenty-five* under the ADEA), *and* is certified or recognized by a defined "employer" as the exclusive bargaining representative, is actively seeking to represent such employees, or charters an organization which represents or seeks to represent employees.

Unions representing governmental employees are covered even though they may not fall literally within the statutory definition of being in an "industry affecting commerce."

II—7.03 Employment Agencies

The statutes define "employment agency" as "any person regularly undertaking, with or without compensation, to procure employees for an employer." Coverage is tied to securing employees for "employers." The size or number of employees of the agency is irrelevant. State and local employment services are "employment agencies." *Pegues v. Mississippi State Employment Serv.* (5th Cir. 1983).

Entities at which the agency seeks to place employees must have enough employees to be defined "employers." Thus the agency may have fifteen or more employees, thus itself meeting the definition of "employer," but it will be covered in its referral activity only if it regularly refers individuals to statutory "employers." Consequently, an agency that limits itself to providing baby-sitting, home care, or nurse referral services to individuals is not an "employment agency" because the persons to whom employees are referred have fewer than fifteen employees.

The organization also must satisfy a non-statutory, common sense conception of the term in that the primary purpose of the organization must be procurement of employees. While state licensing authorities, professional certification boards, and newspapers (running help wanted advertisements), to some extent "procure employees," as this is not their primary purpose, they are not "employment agencies." *Brush v. San Francisco Newspaper Printing Co.* (N.D.Cal. 1970). Because its primary purpose is education, a university is not an employment agency. *Cannon v. University of Chicago* (N.D.Ill. 1976). However, a university placement service, whose purpose is to procure employment, may be an employment agency. *Kaplowitz v. University of Chicago* (N.D.Ill. 1974).

PART III

"DISCRIMINATION BECAUSE OF:" BASIC MODELS OF PROOF

CHAPTER 8

FACIAL CLASSIFICATIONS

III—8.01 "Equal Treatment" Principle

a. Individual vs. Class

Distinctions are illegal if made *"because of"* race, color, religion, national origin, sex, age, or disability. Defendant's motive is key, but is obvious when the employer utilizes facially discriminatory policies, such as not hiring members of protected classes (e.g., male food servers or bus drivers over age 55). The focus is on treatment of the *individual*. In *City of Los Angeles Dep't of Water and Power v. Manhart* (S.Ct. 1978) the employer's retirement system provided similarly situated male and female employees the same stipend upon retirement. However, based on the statistical reality that women live longer than men, and thus, as a class would collect their pensions for more years, the employer required female employees to make greater periodic payments into the system. As a result, the take home pay of male employees was higher than identically situated female employees. In economic terms men and women as *classes* were treated equally:

> The question, therefore, is whether the existence or non-existence of 'discrimination' is to be determined by class characteristics or individual characteristics. * * * The statute's focus on the individual is unambiguous. It precludes treatment of individuals as simply components of a racial, religious, sexual or national class. * * * Even a generalization about the class is an insufficient reason for disqualifying an individual to whom the generalization does not apply.

Thus, paying each woman a lesser amount than a similarly situated man was discrimination "because of *her* sex." *Infra,* 14.01 discusses pension and benefit plans.

b. Sex or Race "Plus" a Legitimate Factor

It is illegal to combine a legitimate factor with a proscribed classification. The statutes do not require discrimination to be based *"solely"* on proscribed grounds. In *Phillips v. Martin Marietta Corp.* (S.Ct. 1971), the employer did not exclude women—indeed 75% of its employees were women—but it refused to employ women with pre-school aged children. Men with pre-school aged children were not disqualified. The lower court held that this was not "sex" discrimination because the distinction was based on sex *"plus"* the legally permissible factor of pre-school aged children. The Supreme Court reversed: "The Court of Appeals erred in * * * permitting one hiring policy for women and another for men." Consequently, it is sex discrimination to deny jobs to fertile women that are available to men regardless of their fertility. *UAW v. Johnson Controls, Inc.* (S.Ct. 1991). It is sex discrimination to reject married females while hiring married men. *Sprogis v. United Air Lines, Inc.* (7th Cir. 1971). Women or older workers may not be required to take and pass tests not imposed on younger men. *EEOC v. Brown & Root, Inc.* (5th Cir. 1982).

c.   *"Good Cause"*

The ADEA states that it is not unlawful for an employer "to discharge or otherwise discipline an individual for good cause." 29 U.S.C.A. 623(f)(3). The same concept is implicit in Title VII. Nonetheless, differential treatment based on race, gender, or age is not justified simply because there was "good cause" for the discipline of an individual. The employer in *McDonald v. Santa Fe Trail Transp. Co.* (S.Ct. 1976), discharged a white employee for theft, while similarly situated black employees were retained. The Court held:

> While [the employer] may decide that participation in a theft of cargo may render an employee unqualified for employment, this criterion must be applied alike to members of all races. * * * [W]hatever factors the mechanisms of com-

promise may legitimately take into account in mitigating discipline of some employees, under Title VII, race may not be among them.

Differences in discipline between employees of different classes must be based on differences in their conduct, culpability, or work history. *Gray v. Toshiba America Consumer Products, Inc.* (6th Cir. 2001).

d. *"Good Faith"*

If a defendant uses a proscribed classification, defendant's underlying good faith in doing so is irrelevant. In *Goodman v. Lukens Steel Co.* (S.Ct. 1987), a labor union refused to process grievances of black workers that charged the employer with racial discrimination. The Court accepted that union "leaders were favorably disposed toward minorities" and that the union's decision not to process the discrimination claims may have been a good faith attempt to better serve all workers, including the minorities, by not antagonizing the employer. Nonetheless, refusal to file race discrimination grievances of black workers was "because of" race and proscribed by Title VII.

III—8.02 Defenses and Justifications

a. *The Bona Fide Occupational Qualification (BFOQ)*

1. Generally

Title VII provides:

It shall not be an unlawful employment practice * * * to hire and employ * * * on the basis of religion, sex, or national origin in those certain instances where religion, sex, or national origin is a bona fide occupational qualification reasonably necessary to the normal operation of that particular business or enterprise. 42 U.S.C.A. 2000e–2(e)

The ADEA has a similarly worded BFOQ defense to age distinctions.

Because Title VII defines "sex" to include pregnancy and childbirth, pregnancy distinctions will be allowed if they satisfy the BFOQ defense. "Race" is *not* included as a BFOQ, which raises the question of how to address rare cases where race might be critical to job performance (e.g., actors, models, undercover police). *Knight v. Nassau County Civil Serv. Comm'n* (2d Cir. 1981)(black employee cannot, against his wishes, be assigned to minority recruiting).

BFOQ is a true defense in that defendant has the burden of establishing its elements. It is narrow, and its requirements are strictly construed. Defendant may not justify sex, national origin, religious, or age classifications by using an alternative, but less demanding justification, such as "business necessity." 42 U.S.C.A. 2000–2 (k)(2).

2.   Elements of a BFOQ

(a) *"Business"*: The BFOQ only allows use of sex, national origin, religious or age qualifications that affect an employee's *ability to do the job*. The defense cannot be invoked to justify broader societal goals, such as protecting the health of unborn children. *UAW v. Johnson Controls* (S.Ct. 1991).

(b) *"Essential"*: The statute uses the phrase "reasonably necessary." This requires defendant to establish that *"all or substantially all"* members of the excluded class cannot safely and effectively perform job duties *"essential"* for the safe and effective operation of the employer's business. An inability of the excluded class to perform peripheral, or nonessential, duties does not meet the statutory standard. For example, even if females provide a more soothing atmosphere than would men during an airplane flight, a "soothing atmosphere" is tangential to the primary duty of flight attendants to insure the safe and efficient transport of passengers. Accordingly, the female gender is not a BFOQ for the job of flight attendant. *Diaz v. Pan American Airways, Inc.* (5th Cir. 1971). Even if females could not fully perform the intimate search aspects required for guard duty at a county jail facility, occasional guard duty may not be essential to the work of a deputy sheriff. If not, gender is not a BFOQ. *Hardin v. Stynchcomb* (11th Cir. 1982).

—*"Costs"*: Financial burdens of hiring persons from different genders, such as providing separate bathrooms, changing areas, or distinctive clothing do not go to the essence of one's ability to perform the job, and thus cannot serve as a BFOQ. *UAW v. Johnson Controls, Inc. supra.*

—*"Paternalism"*: "Protecting" women by denying them the opportunity to work in dangerous jobs such as police officers, firefighters, prison guards, or mine workers, cannot be a BFOQ even if women might be subjected to heightened dangers, such as assault, because of their gender. *Weeks v. Southern Bell Tel. & Tel. Co.* (5th Cir. 1969).

A BFOQ can be established, however, where: 1) there is a significant risk to the employee because of their gender, religion, or national origin, and 2) should the employee be harmed, third persons would be placed at risk or essential activities of the employer would be undermined. In *Dothard v. Rawlinson* (S.Ct. 1977), women were denied guards positions in an all male maximum security prison that did not segregate its sex offenders. The Court accepted the assertion that there was a greater possibility that women guards would, because of their sex, be subjected to physical assaults by inmates. Emphasizing that concern for the safety of the female guards alone could not justify exclusion of women, the Court held that the threat of an increased number of attacks on women posed a significantly increased risk to other guards, to inmates, and to the general security of the prison. On these narrow, perhaps unique, facts the male gender was a BFOQ.

—*Customer and Co-Worker Preferences*: Preferences of customers or co-workers for employees of a particular gender, ethnic origin, religion, or age rarely go to the essence of the ability of the worker to fulfill job requirements. Men may not be denied the job of airline flight attendant merely because a majority of passengers may prefer or expect female attendants. *Diaz v. Pan Am. World Airways, Inc.* (5th Cir. 1971). Women may not be denied a job on a ship or an off shore oil rig merely because the male employees prefer male co-workers. A female health club could not limit its instructor positions to females. *EEOC v. Sedita* (N.D. Ill. 1991)

At some point, customer preference may be so pervasive that one's gender may deprive the worker of the ability to perform core duties. If so, the BFOQ would be established. For example, modesty concerns of geriatric or maternity patients may make intimate care by those of the opposite sex so upsetting that it would endanger the health of the patient. If so, a BFOQ for intimate care nursing is established. *Fesel v. Masonic Home of Delaware* (D.Del. 1978). Women inmates or patients who have suffered abuse from men may not respond well to male counselors, thus making the female gender necessary for successful performance as a counselor. *Torres v. Wisconsin Dep't of Health & Social Services* (7th Cir. 1988). The absence of pregnancy may be a BFOQ for the position of counselor at a girls club that is attempting to encourage young women not to become pregnant prior to marriage. *Chambers v. Omaha Girls Club* (8th Cir. 1987). The EEOC has indicated that a current, authoritative, and factual basis for a belief that *foreign* business persons would not do business with a woman may justify not placing a woman in that position. Cf, *Bollenbach v. Board of Educ.* (S.D.N.Y. 1987) where Hasidic Jews objecting to female bus driver for male students would not make gender a BFOQ.

—*"Authenticity"*: Employers may desire to use male models to display male clothing or to utilize

actresses for female roles in dramatic productions
(and vice versa). The EEOC, supported by legislative history, recognizes that "authenticity" may be
necessary for such jobs. 29 CFR 1604.2. The limit of
acceptable "authenticity" depends on the essence of
the product being sold. Restaurants generally cannot establish gender as a BFOQ for food service
employees, in that the essence of the job is serving
food, which can be performed equally well by both
sexes. This is true even if the employer is attempting to use sex as a marketing tool to attract certain
customers. For example, an airline that used sexually explicit advertisements to attract predominately
male business travelers could not invoke a BFOQ
defense to hiring only female flight attendants. The
essence of the airline business was safe travel, not
sexual entertainment. *Wilson v. Southwest Airlines
Co.* (N.D.Tex. 1981). By contrast, where the establishment is selling "sex," as in the case of exotic
dancers, who, incidentally, may serve food and
drinks to customers, gender is a BFOQ. Thus, the
male gender may be a BFOQ for a server at a
restaurant emulating "old world traditions." *EEOC
v. Joe's Stone Crab, Inc.* (11th Cir. 2000). To create
the atmosphere of an ethnic dining experience, restaurants can prefer service personnel from that
ethnic background.

—*Lesser Discriminatory Alternatives*: The policy
excluding all members of the protected class is not
"necessary" if there is a reasonable alternative to
the exclusionary policy. Accordingly, employers
must provide *reasonable* restructuring of the job as

an alternative to excluding all members of the class. However, it is unreasonable for the employer to restructure jobs or move employees into a wholly different job that requires different skills and training. To illustrate, the job of prison guard requires intimate searches and observing of inmates while showering and using the toilet. Privacy interests of the inmates preclude members of the opposite sex from performing these intimate duties. If these duties could be realigned and performed only by employees of the same sex as the inmates without unduly disrupting the employer's normal operation or imposing significant burdens on fellow employees, gender would not be a BFOQ for a prison guard. *Hardin v. Stynchcomb* (11th Cir. 1982). By contrast, if an employee were hired as a flight attendant, and because of her pregnancy could no longer perform flight duties, she need not be reassigned as a ticket agent. *Levin v. Delta Air Lines, Inc.* (5th Cir. 1984).

(c) *"All or Substantially All"*: To establish a BFOQ, defendant must have a reasonable basis for concluding that "all or substantially all" persons in the excluded class cannot perform "essential" job functions. In a job that requires physical prowess such as strength, an employer could not exclude women simply because men as a class are stronger, and thus more likely to have the necessary strength. Assuming that some women possess the necessary strength, the employer may not use gender as a proxy for measuring the strength qualification. Accordingly, a BFOQ cannot be based on statistical premises or stereotyped assumptions as to group abilities.

There is a qualification. A BFOQ can be established if the employer proves: 1) that some members of the excluded class present a substantial risk to the employer or to third parties, and 2) that it is impracticable to reduce this risk to acceptable levels though individual evaluations of fitness. In *Western Air Lines, Inc. v. Criswell* (S.Ct. 1985), an airline forced retirement of flight engineers (the third person in the cockpit) at age 60. While accepting that aging increased the risk of cardiovascular events in persons over age 60, which events could disable the employee, the Court held that such a possibility alone was insufficient to establish "under age 60" as a BFOQ for an engineer. First, the airline failed to show the "substantial" nature of the risk to the airline or its passengers if engineers over age 60 were retained. Secondly, the airline failed to establish that it was impracticable to reduce any increased risk to acceptable levels by conducting a physical evaluation of each engineer.

Pregnancy at some point limits the physical activity of many women, and virtually all women will be incapacitated at the point of delivery. However, even though incapacity to perform essential job duties may eventually occur, in most jobs that will take place without significant risk *to the employer* or third persons. Moreover, even elevated risks usually can be reduced to acceptable levels through individual physical evaluations, disqualifying only those pregnant women who can no longer perform or whose conditions impose unacceptable risks on others. Thus, non-pregnancy is not a BFOQ for most jobs. In some jobs, such as airline flight crews or public safety officers, the threat of incapacity may present an unacceptable risk of harm to others that cannot be predicted through individual physical evaluations, and in such cases non-pregnancy would constitute a BFOQ. *Burwell v. Eastern Air Lines, Inc.* (4th Cir. 1980).

b. Special Defenses under the Age Act

1. Law Enforcement and Fire Fighters: Prior to 1996 amendments, maximum hiring age and mandatory retirement of law enforcement officers and firefighters were addressed under the BFOQ defense and produced inconsistent results. The ADEA now permits a State or political subdivision to refuse to hire or to discharge any individual because of age as a firefighter or law enforcement officer if the employer adopted job performance tests through which older workers are entitled to demonstrate their fitness for duty and the individual has attained the age of hiring or retirement under applicable law. If applicable law was enacted after September 30, 1996, that age must be at least 55. Or age may be used as the basis for hiring or retirement pursuant to a bona fide hiring and retirement program that is not a subterfuge to evade the purposes of the ADEA.

2. Bona Fide Executives: The ADEA permits the compulsory retirement of persons who: 1) are at

least age 65, 2) have been bona fide executives for at least two years preceding the retirement, and 3) are entitled to an immediate, non-forfeitable annual retirement of at least $44,000 from this employer. Retirement benefits from sources other than the employer such as Social Security, personal savings, or benefits from other employers are not counted toward the $44,000 minimum. *Passer v. American Chem. Soc.* (D.C. Cir. 1991).

c. *Affirmative Action*

1. Definition and Sources: "Affirmative action" historically referred to outreach attempts to recruit women and minority applicants, re-evaluation of selection devices, special training programs or "make whole" relief to actual victims of discrimination. By the 1970s "affirmative action" included undertakings to remedy unbalanced workforces, whatever the cause of the imbalance, through express consideration of race, national origin, and gender. Such affirmative action may be voluntary, as where the employer's program was a product of social consciousness, community pressure, or to avoid the appearance of illegal discrimination. It may be compelled, as where an employer is ordered by the court or governmental agency to use race, gender or national origin in making future decisions. Finally, private employers may be directed by a government to undertake affirmative action as a condition of receiving a government contract. In particular, a directive of the President of the United States imposes an "affirmative action" obligation on employers with federally financed construction

and significant service or supply contracts. *Supra,* 3.05(c).

2. Statutory Provisions

(a) Indians and Indian Reservations: Title VII allows businesses on or near an Indian reservation to follow a publicly announced practice of giving preferential treatment to an individual because he/she is an Indian who lives on or near a reservation. 42 U.S.C.A. 2000e–2(I)

(b) "Preferential Treatment" Proviso: Apart from the above, affirmative action has no statutory authority. On the contrary, a Title VII proviso could be read to preclude the use of race, ethnic background, or gender to remedy existing work imbalances:

> Nothing in this title shall be interpreted to require * * * preferential treatment to any individual or to any group because of race, color, religion, sex or national origin * * * on account of an imbalance which may exist with respect to the total number or percentage of persons of any race, color, religion, sex or national origin employed * * * in comparison with the total number or percentage of persons of such race, color, religion, sex or national origin in any community * * * or in the available work force * * *. 42 U.S.C.A. 2000e-(2)(j).

3. "Voluntary" Affirmative Action Under Title VII: *United Steelworkers of America v. Weber* (S.Ct. 1979) held that notwithstanding the "preferential treatment" proviso, properly circumscribed affirma-

tive action did not violate Title VII. In *Weber* the employer was located in an area where 39% of the population, but less than 2% of the employer's skilled work force, was black. While there had been no judicial finding of illegal discrimination, the under-representation of blacks in the skilled work force could be traced historically to racial policies of the craft unions. To comply with obligations under E.O. 11246, the employer and union entered into a collective bargaining agreement which provided that 50% of persons admitted to a jointly administered apprenticeship program would be black until the proportion of black skilled workers at the plant approximated the black population in the area. Pursuant to this plan, seven black and six white employees were selected. Plaintiff, a white man, was rejected notwithstanding the fact that he had greater seniority than some of the selected black employees. Plaintiff would have been selected had he been black.

Weber first read the Title VII "preferential treatment" proviso (see above), as prohibiting only "required" use of race, sex, or national origin; it did not prohibit "voluntary" use of such factors. (The Court assumed that complying with E.O. 11246 was "voluntary.") Moreover, the statutory prohibition against *forced* preferential treatment implicitly permits *voluntary* preferential treatment. As to why the express prohibitions against race discrimination did not apply, the Court reasoned that Title VII could not be read literally, nor legislative debates taken at face value. Looking to the "spirit" of the statute, the Court concluded that voluntary attempts to remedy "conspicuous racial imbalance in traditionally segregated job categories" could not be "race" discrimination in light of the broad purpose of Title VII to promote equal employment of under-represented racial minorities.

In response to proof that race, ethnic origin, or sex was used to make a decision, the employer may present its affirmative action plan and establish that the challenged decision was made pursuant to that plan. To prevail, plaintiff must establish that the plan does not meet the *Weber* standards.

4. *Weber* Standards

(a) Justification: Private employers may adopt affirmative action plans only to remedy "conspicuous imbalances in traditionally segregated job categories." The "imbalance" must be based on a documented comparison of workers in relevant job categories of the employer to the percentage of women and minorities in the area work force *qualified* to hold the jobs. *Cygnar v. Chicago* (7th Cir. 1989). An imbalance may be "conspicuous" even if it is less glaring than that required to establish a prima facie case of illegal motivation. The "conspicuous imbalance" must be in a "traditionally segregated job category." "Traditionally segregated" suggests that while the imbalance need not be a product of past illegal behavior, it must have been in place for a significant period time. Presumably, adoption of an affirmative action plan for white males, even if they are currently under represented, cannot be justified in that it is unlikely that white males have been "traditionally segregated" out of the job.

(b) Reasonableness: The plan must be fixed, detailed, and presumably written. It must be more than the employer's general desire to increase diversity, and then use race or gender in ad hoc decision-making. Plans must set a goal in terms of percentages where the employer's work force would roughly equal the racial and gender make-up of the qualified population. A goal that *exceeds* the percentage of qualified women and minorities in the surrounding area workforce is unreasonable.

The means of achieving the goal will be unreasonable if it "unduly trammels" opportunities of white male employees or applicants, such as by refusing to consider white male applicants or reserving certain positions for minority applicants only. *Hill v. Ross* (7th Cir. 1999). The Court has sanctioned two methodologies: ratio and "plus." *Weber* sustained a 1–1 black/white hiring ratio. *Johnson v. Transportation Agency, Santa Clara County* (S.Ct. 1987), upheld a plan directing decision-makers to consider race or sex of the applicant in an under represented group as a "plus" factor in selecting between qualified applicants, with decision-makers being evaluated by superiors on the progress being made toward reaching the plan's defined numerical goal.

Hiring criteria such as education or experience can be modified in a way that favors minority applicants, but a plan is unreasonable if it directs the hiring of minority applicants who cannot perform job duties. The 1991 Civil Rights Act also makes it an unlawful employment practice "to adjust the scores of, use different cutoff scores for, or otherwise alter the results of, employment related tests on the basis of race, color, religion, sex or national origin." 42 U.S.C.A. 2000e–2(*l*).

Layoffs based on race or gender "unduly trammel" the interests of white, male employees. Race or gender may not be used to maintain current ratios, even if the ultimate goal is yet to be achieved. In determining the order of layoff the employer must utilize neutral factors such as seniority or performance evaluations. Where employees are otherwise identical, the plan may not allow race to be a "tiebreaker." *Taxman v. Board of Educ. of Twsp. of Piscataway* (3rd Cir. 1996).

As affirmative action is remedial, plans must be temporary. Once the stated goal is achieved, continued use of race or gender to maintain a balance creates an improper quota. *Johnson v. Transportation Agency, Santa Clara County, supra* (the plan need not have specific termination language if there was an understanding that it was "temporary" and would expire once the imbalance was rectified).

5.　Affirmative Action by Governmental Employers: Similar to private employers, governmental employers have adopted voluntarily affirmative action programs. Governments are subject not only to Title VII but also to the restraints of the Constitution which imposes different, and presumably more stringent, standards. Equal Protection concepts direct that suspect classifications, such as race or ethnicity, or suspicious classifications, such as sex, when used by government employers, are subjected to a "searching" judicial scrutiny even when used "benignly" to remedy racial imbalances. This requires governmental employers to carry the burden of establishing "compelling" governmental interests for the classification and demonstrating that the use of the classification serves in the most narrow way the achievement of the governmental interests. *Gratz v. Bollinger* (S.Ct. 2003).

A government has a compelling interest in remedying its own discrimination. *Cotter v. City of Boston* (1st Cir. 2003). But whether a government employer has a "compelling" interest to remedy a racial and gender imbalance brought about by societal discrimination has not been resolved. Compare, *Wygant v. Jackson Board of Education* (S.Ct. 1986)(maintaining a racially balanced *faculty* at a school not "compelling") with *Grutter v. Bollinger* (S.Ct. 2003)(securing and maintaining racially balanced *student body* in a university is "compelling").

If the compelling nature of the classification is established—as in the case of remedying past illegal conduct—the method of achieving the goal must be narrowly tailored. Compare, *Grutter v. Bollinger* (S.Ct. 2003)(use of race as *one* of many factors to achieve student body diversity was "narrowly tailored") with *Gratz v. Bollinger* (S.Ct. 2003)(granting numerical bonus that gave all minority applicants distinct advantage over all nonminority applicants was not sufficiently tailored). In this regard, constitutional standards for the plan resemble those articulated under Title VII by *Weber* and *Johnson*. Consequently, departing from strict ranking in order to promote three fully qualified black officers out of 36 promotions, without denying any promotion to white officers, was a "narrowly-tailored means of addressing demonstrated past discrimination." *Cotter v. City of Boston* (1st Cir. 2003). Like Title VII, the remedy must be temporary in that once the identified under representation no longer exists, race or gender conscious hiring practices must be discontinued. *Quinn v. City of Boston* (1st Cir. 2003).

6. Imposing Affirmative Action: Affirmative action programs imposed by governments, requiring employers doing business with the government to utilize race and ethnicity in making hiring decisions, such as E.O. 11246, are analyzed under a "strict scrutiny" standard. *Adarand Constructors v. Pena* (S.Ct. 1995). Dramatic under-representation plus a specific legislative or administrative finding of past illegal behavior by the employer or in the industry probably establishes a "compelling governmental interest" to remedy the possible illegality. Imposition of a plan to remedy the found pattern would be sufficiently tailored to sustain its constitutionality if it imposed standards valid under Title VII. *Legal Aid Socy. v. Brennan* (9th Cir. 1979).

CHAPTER 9

DISPARATE TREATMENT: PROVING MOTIVE

III—9.01   Motivation vs. Impact

In addressing challenges to hiring, promotions, and discharges based on ostensibly neutral policies or decisions:

> The Court has consistently recognized a distinction between claims of discrimination based on disparate treatment and claims of discrimination based on disparate impact. * * * Disparate treatment is the most easily understood type of discrimination. Liability * * *depends on whether the protected trait actually motivated the employer's decision. By contrast, disparate-impact claims involve employment practices that are facially neutral in their treatment of different groups but that in fact fall more harshly on one group than another and cannot be justified by business necessity. * * * Courts must be careful to distinguish between these theories. *Raytheon Co. v. Hernandez* (S.Ct. 2003).

> "[A] disparate treatment claim cannot succeed unless the employee's protected trait actually played a role in that process and had a determinative influence on the outcome." *Hazen Paper Co. v.*

Biggins (S.Ct. 1993). Motive is an issue of fact, to be treated no differently than other fact questions. *U.S. Postal Service Bd. of Governors v. Aikens* (S.Ct. 1983). Plaintiff carries the ultimate burden of proving proscribed motive. *Texas Dept. of Community Affairs v. Burdine* (S.Ct. 1981). In cases involving hiring, promotion, and discharge, motive may be proved through: 1) direct or verbal evidence, 2) circumstantial evidence that allows inferences to be drawn from surrounding objective facts, and 3) statistical patterns. Some cases have elements of all three. Differences in "terms and conditions of employment," such as compensation and harassment, trigger distinct models of proof. See, *infra,* Part IV.

III—9.02 Direct or Verbal Evidence

a. "Direct" Evidence Defined

The classical definition of direct evidence is that which, if believed, suffices to prove the issue without inference, presumption, or resort to other evidence. *Shorter v. ICG Holdings, Inc.* (10th Cir. 1999). A statement must reflect *directly* on the alleged discriminatory animus and *bear squarely* on the contested decision. *Taylor v. Virginia Union Univ.* (4th Cir. 1999)(en banc). For example, when an applicant is told at the time of his rejection, "We wanted a younger man for the job," this is direct evidence of age motivation in that there is an unavoidable evidentiary link between the comment and the decision. *Schnidrig v. Columbia Mach., Inc.* (9th Cir. 1996). If additional inferences are required to prove motive, courts may classify the verbal evidence as "circumstantial" and either deny its admissibility—labeling it as a "stray remark"—or require additional supporting evidence.

A broader approach considers *any* words indicative of a decision maker's motivation, and excludes from evidence only "statements made by non-decision makers or statements by decision makers unrelated to the decisional process itself." *Price Waterhouse v. Hopkins* (S.Ct. 1989) (O'Connor concurring). Statements which, more likely than not, indicate proscribed motive, are admitted, with the issue going to their weight. *Costa v. Desert Palace, Inc.* (9th Cir. 2002)(en banc). For example, obscene racial insults such as managers regularly referring to blacks as "niggers" or labeling Mexicans as "wet backs" indicate a pervasive class prejudice that will support, if not require, a finding that the expressed animus infected decisions concerning members of the defamed group. *Brown v. East Miss. Elec. Power Assn.* (5th Cir. 1993). Evidence of illegal motive can also flow from an employer's articulated use of stereotypes such statements that a woman being considered was too "macho" and that a "lady" should not be such using foul language. *Price Waterhouse v. Hopkins, supra* (S.Ct. 1989).

b. Prove the Words Were Said!

The critical issue is whether the terms were used. If the purported speaker denies the words were spoken, plaintiff carries the burden of persuading the fact finder otherwise. A failure to find that the words were spoken ends the inquiry.

c. *"Evaluative" vs. "Descriptive"*

Reference to one's membership in a protective class to *describe* the individual carries no inference of illegal motivation. For example, in reviewing an incident, the supervisor alluded to plaintiff's "strut" and described him as a "large, strong, muscular black man" who was attempting to intimidate "three smaller white men." This described the incident, and carried no inference of racial motivation. *Evans v. McClain of Georgia, Inc.* (11th Cir. 1997). Similarly, describing a younger employee as a "bright, intelligent, knowledgeable *young* man" carried no inference of age motivation. *Merrick v. Farmers Ins. Group* (9th Cir. 1990). Even pejorative references may be seen as "colloquialisms" and not evidence of illegal animus, as where employers stated that they wanted to get rid of "deadwood" or the "old boy network." *Pottenger v. Potlatch Corp.* (9th Cir. 2003). Referring to a group of men as "little old ladies" *(Haskell v. Kaman Corp.* (2d Cir. 1984)), or calling a female employee a "bitch" *(Neuren v. Adduci, Mastriani, Meeks & Schill* (D.C. Cir. 1995)), were seen as "personal opinions," not expressions of gender or age prejudice.

By contrast, language evincing an *evaluative* prejudice is evidence of motive. Stating that plaintiff was "so old he must have come over on the Mayflower" is evaluative language indicative of age motivation. *Reeves v. Sanderson Plumbing Products*

(S.Ct. 2000). Evaluative judgment was found in the comments, "Older workers have problems adapting to changes" *(Beshears v. Asbill* (8th Cir. 1991)), and "Two chinks (referring to Asians) in the department is more than enough." *Chuang v. University of California Davis, Bd. of Trustees* (9th Cir. 2000).

d.　Causation Link—*"Stray Remarks"*

Evaluative language must be made by, or attributed to, the decision maker. Racist, ageist, or sexist comments by co-workers or supervisors not involved in the decision have little probative value. *Girten v. McRentals, Inc.* (8th Cir. 2003). Evaluative comments of a decision maker also must be linked logically in context and in time to the challenged decision. This is accomplished when the expressed animus occurs simultaneously with the decision or evinces the existence of a discriminatory policy or mind-set. *Schnidrig v. Columbia Mach., Inc.* (9th Cir. 1996). When an employer expresses a general opinion that "women are not good sailors" shortly before or after the employer rejects a specific female applicant as a sailor, the expressed prejudice against women for this kind of job has a logical connection to the employer's rejection of this woman sufficient to support a finding of illegal motivation. *Fisher v. Pharmacia & Upjohn* (8th Cir. 2000)("We need to get rid of the old guys."). However, the comment about women sailors, while offensive, has little probative value in establishing defendant's motive if a female applicant is denied an office position.

The length of time between the evaluative remarks and the decision is critical. At some point the
lapse of time will be so great that the inflammatory
impact of the remark will exceed its probative value. Accordingly, isolated insults, boorish comments
or behavior (such as a sexist or racist joke at a local
pub), or an expression of stereotyped notions removed in time or context from the employment
decision are labeled "stray remarks" and may be
excluded from evidence. *Manning v. Chevron Chemical Co., LLC* (5th Cir. 2003) (use of term "nigger"
four years earlier)

e.   *Strength of the Inference*

Verbal or "direct" evidence statements fall into
one of four categories: 1) Inadmissible: The probative value of the comment is so weak that it is
outweighed by the inflammatory prejudice it would
engender, as where the remarks were not made by a
decision maker or were made at a time or in a
context remote from the decision. 2) Insufficient:
The remark has probative value that outweighs its
inflammatory impact—and thus is admissible—but
it does not alone support a finding of illegal motive.
To avoid summary judgement, plaintiff must present additional evidence of motive. 3) Sufficient: The
nature and circumstances of the remarks are strong
enough *to permit* a finding of illegal motivation.
However, the fact finder remains free to conclude
that defendant was not illegally motivated. 4) Compelling: The nature and circumstances of the statement definitively establish defendant's motive. The

fact finder *is required* to find illegal motivation. Such would be the case where the motive is expressed simultaneously with the decision or where the decision maker has regularly and recently used odious pejorative language to describe plaintiff's race, sex, age, or ethnic origins. *Brown v. East Miss. Elec. Power Assn.* (5th Cir. 1993).

III—9.03   Unexplained Disparate Treatment

a. The "Three Step Minuet": The McDonnell Douglas Model

Plaintiff may establish motive though circumstantial evidence. Step 1: Plaintiff establishes that he/she was treated differently than a person of another class. Step 2: If plaintiff demonstrates differential treatment, defendant must "articulate a legitimate, non-discriminatory reason" for plaintiff's treatment. Defendant's failure to articulate a legitimate reason for its action leaves unrefuted an inference of illegal motive that requires a judgment for plaintiff. Step 3: If defendant "articulates a legitimate, non-discriminatory reason" for its treatment of plaintiff, the initial inference disappears, and burden shifts back to plaintiff to present evidence of the pretextual nature of defendant's articulated reason. If plaintiff presents no evidence of pretext or illegal motivation, defendant is entitled to a judgment. *McDonnell Douglas Corp. v. Green* (S.Ct. 1973). If the plaintiff presents additional evidence that could persuade a fact finder that a discriminatory reason may have motivated the employer or that the defendant's proffered explanation is unworthy of credence, the fact finder, evaluating all the evidence, must resolve the issue of defendant's motivation. Plaintiff carries the burden of proof. *Texas Dept. of Community Affairs v. Burdine* (S.Ct. 1981). This model is neither rigid nor absolute, but is a guide to judicial thinking. It is not normally presented to the jury in instructions. *Brown v. Packaging Corp. of America* (6th Cir. 2003).

b.   Step 1: The Prima Facie Case

1.   Hiring and Promotion. Plaintiff creates an initial inference (or prima facie case) of illegal motivation by establishing six elements. (i) plaintiff was within a class protected by the statutes; (ii) there was a vacancy for which defendant was seeking applicants; (iii) plaintiff applied for the position; (iv) plaintiff was qualified; (v) plaintiff was denied the position, and (vi) the employer continued to seek applicants of similar qualifications or filled the position with a person from a different class. *McDonnell Douglas Corp. v. Green, supra* (S.Ct. 1973).

(i) *"Protected Class"*: A plaintiff first identifies that he/she is a member of a traditionally disadvantaged racial or ethnic minority protected by Title VII, is a female, is at least age 40, or meets the statutory definition of being a "qualified individual with a disability." Whites and males are protected by Title VII under the same standards as are women and minorities. *McDonald v. Santa Fe Trail Transp. Co.* (S.Ct. 1976). Nonetheless, to present a prima facie case of race or sex motivation a white male plaintiff must "establish background circumstances that support an inference that the defendant is one of those unusual employers who discriminate against the majority." *Mattioda v. White* (10th Cir. 2003). "Special circumstances" include a statistical pattern of favoritism toward minority workers, plaintiff having qualifications clearly superior to the minority person selected, verbal expressions of animus against males or whites, or evidence of an ill defined *ad hoc* "affirmative action" goal. *Sutherland v. Michigan Dep't of Treasury* (6th Cir. 2003).

"Special background circumstances" are also required if the plaintiff's protected class is religion. *Shapolia v. Los Alamos Nat. Laboratory* (10th Cir. 1993). As the religion of the plaintiff and the favored employee often is not obvious, plaintiff must establish the employer's knowledge of plaintiff's religion. Moreover, in many situations courts would not infer religious motivation from a mere difference in affiliation. That plaintiff was a Baptist and the person favored was a Lutheran, without more, does little to suggest that the employer was illegally motivated. "Special circumstances" suggesting religious motivation might arise, however, if plaintiff was of an historically victimized faith (Jews) or is of a faith subject to possible political prejudice (Muslims). "Special circumstances" could include evidence of defendant's strongly held and openly manifested religious beliefs that conflicted with plaintiff's or a pattern of favoritism toward those of a particular faith.

(ii) *"Vacancy"*: Plaintiff must prove that the employer had an opening that it desired to fill. This can be established through job postings, advertisements, or evidence that applicants were informally solicited.

(iii) *"Application"*: Plaintiff must apply or make reasonable efforts to convey to the employer a specific interest in the vacancy. Informal inquiries do not suffice. Formal application may be excused if plaintiff made it clear to an employer with an informal hiring process that he was interested in being informed of vacancies as they arose. *Lockridge v. Board of Trustees, Univ. of Ark.* (8th Cir. 2003). Application may not be required if the employer has created a pervasive atmosphere of discrimination making it understood that applying would be fruitless. *International Broth. of Teamsters v. United States* (S.Ct. 1977).

(iv) *"Qualified"*: A person who possesses posted job credentials is "qualified." Conversely, failure of the plaintiff to establish that she has the required experience, training, education (e.g., high school diploma) or certification (e.g., driver's license) or a passing score on a uniformly required test precludes a finding that she is "qualified," even if plaintiff proves that she could actually perform the job. Where no job qualifications are announced, plaintiff proves that she is "qualified" by demonstrating possession of necessary skills or knowledge.

Plaintiff need not show that her qualifications were *superior* to those of the person selected. *Pat-*

terson v. McLean Credit Union (S.Ct. 1989). That the person selected for the job was more qualified in the objective terms of education, skill, or experience or that the employer had subjective reasons for rejecting the plaintiff, such as inferior interpersonal skills, all are relevant reasons to be articulated by defendant. But plaintiff's relative ability or potential should play no role in plaintiff's prima facie showing. *Turner v. Honeywell Federal Mfg. & Tech.* (8th Cir. 2003).

(v) *"Rejected"*: It must be shown that plaintiff will not receive an offer. This is established by proof that her application was formally rejected, that the employer hired another applicant into the vacancy, or that the employer continued to recruit for the position over a significant period of time.

(vi) *"Disparate Treatment"*: *McDonnell Douglas Corp. v. Green, supra,* (S.Ct. 1973) indicated that disparate treatment was needed to create an inference of illegal motive. This is accomplished by showing that a person from another class was hired into the vacancy or that the employer continued to seek applicants *after* plaintiff was rejected. Selection of a similarly qualified applicant from the same class as plaintiff at or near the time of plaintiff's rejection tends to preclude an inference that plaintiff's class membership motivated the decision maker. *Jones v. Western Geophysical Co.* (5th Cir. 1982).

In age discrimination cases, plaintiff creates a prima facie case of illegal motive if the favored person is "significantly younger" than the qualified plaintiff who is over age 40, even if the favored person is also over age 40. *O'Connor v. Consolidated Coin Caterers Corp.* (S.Ct. 1996). It is not clear what age difference is "significant". *Balderston v. Fairbanks Morse Engine* (7th Cir. 2003)(10 year difference is "significant"; 6 year difference is not).

2.   Discipline and Discharges: Differential treatment of current employees requires modification of the *McDonnell Douglas* model. Plaintiff establishes a prima facie case by showing that: (i) she was a member of a protected class, (ii) up to the point of the employer's action plaintiff's performance was at or above legitimate expectations, (iii) adverse action was taken against the plaintiff, and (iv) the employer sought a replacement for plaintiff or there was evidence that persons of a different class were treated more favorably. *Moore v. City of Charlotte* (4th Cir. 1985).

Plaintiff's adequate performance up to the point of dismissal can be proved by defendant's records or through qualified expert testimony comparing the employer's expectations to expert evaluation of plaintiff's performance. Adequacy of performance cannot be established through plaintiff's self-evaluation or by lay testimony of co-workers. *King v. Rumsfeld* (4th Cir. 2003).

Some courts have imposed on plaintiff a heightened burden of proving performance at a level that "rules out the possibility that he was fired for job performance" and that the employer either retained an employee under "comparable circumstances" or sought a replacement for plaintiff who had "roughly equivalent qualifications." *Benoit v. Technical Mfg. Corp.* (1st Cir. 2003). For example, a black plaintiff who was discharged for alleged misconduct, pointed to a white co-worker who was retained despite engaging in similar misconduct. Nonetheless, because the evidence disclosed that the retained employee had an overall better job performance ratings and less tardiness, plaintiff failed to establish a *prima facie case. Knight v. Baptist Hosp. of Miami, Inc.* (11th Cir. 2003).

3. Reductions in Force: The model is further modified when plaintiff is laid off as part of a general reduction-in-force, and thus the employer is hiring no replacements. After establishing that plaintiff is a member of a protected class, was laid off notwithstanding adequate performance while persons in other classes in the job category were retained, plaintiff must also prove that some of the retained persons of another class were performing at a level *lower* than plaintiff. *Mitchell v. Data General Corp.* (4th Cir. 1993). Alternatively, plaintiff may establish a prima face case with evidence that defendant did not uniformly apply the criteria, that the process or the data used for selection were manipulated, or that the force reduction itself was a pretext to eliminate workers in a protected class. *Beaird v. Seagate Technology* (10th Cir. 1998).

Note: The Worker Adjustment and Retraining Notification Act of 1988 (29 U.S.C.A. 2101) requires large employers to give employees 60 days advance notice of plant closings and mass layoffs not caused by natural disasters or unforseen circumstances, except where the employer is a "faltering company" seeking financing. Failure to provide the required notice obligates the employer to provide wages for the period in which notice was required but not provided.

4. Compensation: A difference in pay rates between persons of different classes who perform substantially equal work can create an inference that the difference was motivated by class membership. *Bazemore v. Friday* (S.Ct. 1986). Compensation discrimination follows different proof models discussed *infra*, Chapter 13.

c. *Step 2: "Legitimate, Non–Discriminatory Reason"*

If plaintiff creates a prima case, defendant *must* "articulate" a "reason" for its treatment of the plaintiff. Defendant's denial of invidious motivation will not suffice, nor will proof that the employer has a balanced work force. There must be a "reason," and that reason must be supported by evidence. Assertion in pleadings, arguments of counsel, or speculations of the trial court do not suffice. *Texas Dept. of Community Affairs v. Burdine* (S.Ct. 1981).

The reason must be "legitimate" and "non-discriminatory." This burden is not heavy. "Legitimate" does not require that the reason be job related. *McDonnell Douglas Corp. v. Green* (S.Ct. 1973). A reason does not lack legitimacy simply because it produces an adverse impact on plaintiff's class or because the defendant could have used alternatives that would have had a less negative impact on plaintiff's class. *Furnco Const. Corp. v.*

Waters (S.Ct. 1978). A reason that violates the law would seem, by definition, to lack "legitimacy." Nonetheless, *Hazen Paper Co. v. Biggins* (S.Ct. 1993), held that articulation of a reason that would violate the federal ERISA statute was sufficient to rebut a plaintiff's prima facie case of age discrimination.

To accord defendant an opportunity to address whether the articulated reason is a pretext, defendant's reason should be "clear and reasonably specific." *Texas Dep't of Community Affairs v. Burdine, supra,* (S.Ct. 1981). Length of service, performance evaluations, education, technical training, experience, references, test scores, work history, and misconduct all are legitimate reasons. *McDonnell Douglas Corp. v. Green, supra* (S.Ct. 1973). By contrast, totally nebulous reasons or reasons so bizarre or idiosyncratic that plaintiff would have no basis for rebutting them are not "legitimate." Some subjectivity is legitimate in evaluating management and professional positions. Nonetheless, as subjectivity provides a ready mechanism for discrimination that can cloak, or be a proxy for, illegitimate motive, subjective conclusions should be as specific as circumstances allow. *Robbins v. White–Wilson Medical Clinic, Inc.* (5th Cir. 1981) ("yucky attitude" not legitimate). "Qualifications" should specify which qualifications the employer actually relied upon. "Personality" should identify the traits the employer found objectionable. "Conflict" should include some details of the disagreement. "Appearance" should outline the aspects of plaintiff's appearance which defendant disliked. *Chapman v. AI Transport* (11th Cir. 2000)(en banc).

Nonetheless, while giving lip service to the proposition that subjectivity requires "close judicial scrutiny" courts have accepted as "legitimate" extremely subjective conclusions. *Brooks v. Ameren UE* (8th Cir. 2003)(plaintiff scored lower during interviews on "people skills", "leadership", and "decision-making"); *Manning v. Chevron Chemical Co., LCC* (5th Cir. 2003) (plaintiff not "best qualified."). One court stated that reasons will be "legitimate" even if "foolish, trivial, or baseless," and defendant may carry its burden by stating that the supervisor fired the plaintiff because he "did not like him." *Balderston v. Fairbanks Morse Engine* (7th Cir. 2003). Incompetence of the decision maker was held to be a legitimate reason for plaintiff's rejection. *Hill v. Mississippi State Employment Serv.* (5th Cir. 1990).

Seniority is a legitimate basis for making promotion decisions or in selecting employees to lay off, but a seniority system cannot be a legitimate reason to force the retirement of an individual because of age. 29 U.S.C.A. 623(f)(2)(A). An "employee benefit plan" cannot "excuse the failure to hire any individual" because of age nor "require or permit the involuntary retirement" of any such individual. 29 U.S.C.A. 623(f)(2)(B)(ii).

d. *Step 3: Pretext Evidence*

If, but only if, defendant presents a legitimate, non-discriminatory reason for its treatment of plaintiff, the burden reshifts to plaintiff to present additional evidence of defendant's illegal motive. The evidence must be of sufficient strength to *permit* a fact finder to find in plaintiff's favor.

In *St. Mary's Honor Center v. Hicks* (S.Ct. 1993), the employer articulated legitimate reasons for plaintiff's dismissal: violating a work rule and threatening a supervisor. Plaintiff countered with evidence that the incident was manufactured to provoke plaintiff's outburst. The trial court found as a matter of fact that defendant's articulated reasons (rule violation and threat) were not the "real" reasons for plaintiff's discharge. The "real" reason, the trial court found, was a non-racial personality conflict between plaintiff and the supervisor. Since plaintiff failed to carry the ultimate burden of proving racial motivation, the trial court rendered judgment for defendant. The court of appeals reversed holding that disbelief of the articulated reason *required* a judgement for the plaintiff. The Supreme Court reversed the court of appeals. When a fact finder does not accept defendant's articulated reason, it does not follow *as a matter of law* that plaintiff *must* prevail on the ultimate issue of illegal motive. However, a prima facie showing of disparate treatment coupled with a fact finder's conclusion that defendant's articulated reason was not the real reason for plaintiff's dismissal are sufficient to *permit* a fact finder to conclude that defendant was improperly motivated. No additional or direct evidence was required to support a verdict for plaintiff. *Reeves v. Sanderson Plumbing Products, Inc.* (S.Ct. 2000).

Defendant's proof that it honestly believed in the truth of the articulated reason at the time of the decision undermines the inference that the reason, although false, was used as a pretext. *Smith v. Chrysler Corp.* (6th Cir. 1998). Nonetheless, if the employee in fact did not commit the infractions as articulated, this *permits* the fact finder to draw an inference that the employer did not *believe* that the employee committed the infractions, and thus the fact finder could accept that the articulated "rule infraction" was a pretext to hide discriminatory motive. *Hernandez v. Spacelabs Medical, Inc.* (9th Cir. 2003).

Evidence that the articulated reason was not applied equally suggests pretext, as does changing, inconsistent, or contradictory reasons for the treatment of plaintiff. Even an employer's general lack of candor and truthfulness suggests that the articulation lacks credibility. *Applebaum v. Milwaukee Metro. Sewerage Dist.* (7th Cir. 2003). Other factors that suggest pretext include plaintiff's overall superior qualifications and higher performance ratings than the favored employee of another class (*Aka v. Washington Hosp. Center* (D.C.Cir. 1998)(en banc)), and the presence of alternative, less discriminatory devices that would have better served the employer's business. *Furnco Const. Corp. v. Waters* (S.Ct. 1978). Racist/sexist/ageist insults, statistical patterns, or incidents of discriminatory behavior that, standing alone, would not support a finding of illegal motive, when combined with other evidence, may permit a finding that an articulated reason was a pretext.

e. Defendant's Counter–Step

Defendant may present evidence suggesting absence of illegal motive. That persons of plaintiff's class were regularly hired and promoted by the decision maker suggests benign motivation. While a balanced work force is no substitute for defendant articulating a legitimate reason, a balanced work force, as well as evidence that defendant has undertaken special efforts to recruit and retain persons of plaintiff's class, supports defendant's position that an articulated reason was not a pretext. *Rivera-Aponte v. Restaurant Metropol #3, Inc.* (1st Cir. 2003) (That 2/3 of the male employees were over age 45 "is not the hallmark of an employer who discriminates against older workers."). That the supervisor who discharged plaintiff recently hired her suggests that the articulated reason, rather than plaintiff's class, motivated the decision. *Grady v. Affiliated Cent., Inc.* (2d Cir. 1997).

f. End of the Dance: Plaintiff's Ultimate Burden

The fact finder weighs the evidence. To prevail, plaintiff must convince the fact finder by a preponderance of the evidence that it is more probable than not that defendant was motivated by factors made illegal by the statutes. *U.S. Postal Service Bd. of Governors v. Aikens* (S.Ct. 1983). Such a finding, for or against plaintiff, is one of fact, and subjected to limited appellate review. *Anderson v. City of Bessemer* (S.Ct. 1985).

III—9.04 "Mixed Motives": Legitimate and Illegitimate Factors

In *Price Waterhouse v. Hopkins* (S.Ct. 1989), plaintiff presented verbal evidence that sexual stereotyping played a role in her being denied a promotion. Defendant countered with evidence that legitimate factors (plaintiff's personality) played a key role in the decision, and argued that even if sex bias was a factor in the decision, the employer would have denied the promotion to plaintiff based solely on legitimate reasons. The Court held that once plaintiff proved that illegal factors "played *a* motivating part" in the employment decision, the employer is presumptively liable. However, "defendant may avoid *liability* by proving by a preponderance of the evidence that it would have made the same decision had it not taken the plaintiff's [protected class] into account."

The 1991 Civil Rights Act altered the liability aspects of *Price Waterhouse* by providing: "An unlawful employment practice is established when the complaining party *demonstrates* that race, color, religion, sex, or national origin was a motivating factor * * * even though other factors also motivated the practice." 42 U.S.C.A. 2000e–2(m). "Demonstrates" means meeting both the burden of producing evidence and convincing the fact finder. 42 U.S.C.A. 2000e(m). Thus, defendant is liable anytime a plaintiff succeeds in convincing the fact finder that a forbidden factors was *"a"* motivation for the treatment of plaintiff. However, if defendant "demonstrates that [it] would have taken the same action in the absence of the impermissible factor" the court shall not award back pay, damages, or the hiring or reinstatement of plaintiff. Thus, while defendant's proof that it would have made the same decision on legitimate grounds does not negate its liability, it does limit plaintiff's remedies to prospective injunctive relief and the recovery of attorneys fees and court costs.

Some lower courts had held that plaintiff could prevail in such a "mixed motive" case only if plaintiff established defendant's liability with "direct evidence." *Desert Palace, Inc. v. Costa* (S.Ct. 2003) rejected the distinction between "direct" and "circumstantial" evidence. Regardless of the nature of the proof, if plaintiff convinces the fact finder that defendant was motivated by *a* forbidden factor, liability is established.

III—9.05   After Acquired Evidence

In *McKennon v. Nashville Banner Pub. Co.* (S.Ct. 1995), after plaintiff filed suit alleging age discrimination the employer discovered that before plaintiff was discharged she had copied and removed confidential documents. Defendant asserted that it should not be liable for age discrimination because had it known of plaintiff's improper conduct it would have made the same decision on these legitimate grounds. The Court held that the mixed motive analysis of *Price Waterhouse* and the 1991 Civil Rights Act response were inapposite. If defendant was motivated *at the time it dismissed plaintiff* solely by illegal considerations, defendant is liable. Moreover, defendant could not avoid back wages and damages solely by proving that had it known of the misconduct it would have dismissed plaintiff for the misconduct. At least for the period running from the unlawfully motivated action until the point the evidence of the wrongdoing was uncovered, the successful plaintiff is entitled to back pay. To avoid further back pay responsibility and a duty to reinstate the plaintiff, defendant must "establish that the wrongdoing was of such severity that the employee in fact would have been terminated on those grounds alone if the employer had known of it at the time of the discharge."

When employees have made misstatements in their original application employers have argued that had the employee been truthful they would have not been hired, and thus a discharge upon discovery of the "resume fraud" is warranted. However, proof that the plaintiff would *not have been hired* had the truth been known will not reduce defendant's liability. The employer must prove that it would have *dismissed* plaintiff once the misstatement was uncovered. Defendant will not carry this burden unless it can demonstrate that regardless of how long individuals have been employed and regardless of their subsequent job performance, it consistently *dismissed* similarly situated employees for application inaccuracies. *Shattuck v. Kinetic*

Concepts, Inc. (5th Cir. 1995). Even if the employer proves that application misstatements have resulted in offending employees being dismissed, minor inaccuracies or those *not material to job performance* (such as age, marital status, or number of dependents) may not serve as a basis for denying full relief to victims of illegal discrimination. See, *Calloway v. Partners Nat'l Health Plans* (11th Cir. 1993).

If defendant proves that it would have dismissed the plaintiff once the material misstatement was discovered, defendant will not be liable for subsequent back pay or be ordered to reinstate the plaintiff. Based on its discriminatory motive for the treatment of plaintiff, defendant will be liable for back wages up to the point that the misstatements were discovered and for the payment of costs and plaintiff's attorneys' fees. *Wallace v. Dunn Const. Co., Inc.* (11th Cir. 1995).

III—9.06　Past Motive Perpetuated

Current distinctions neutral on their face and neutral in terms of current motivation that perpetuate distinctions that at one time were invidiously motivated are discriminatory. For example, prior to being covered by Title VII an employer paid a discriminatory wage rate to black employees. It continued to use those rates to set annual salary increases. Because of the *past* racially motivated decisions, similarly situated employees *currently* received different salaries "because of" their race. *Bazemore v. Friday* (S.Ct. 1986). An employer once segregated employees by race or gender giving white male employees the more desirable jobs. Acting in good faith using reasonable business judgment the employer adopted a rule that prohibits employees from transferring from one unit to another. If the no-transfer rule is the basis for denying a woman or black employee a requested transfer, the denial is "because of" their protected class. *Jones v. Lee Way Motor Freight* (10th Cir. 1970).

III—9.07　Identical Treatment—Improper Motivation

An employer engages in illegal discrimination if it uses a device objective on its face, such as a test or a seniority system, which was adopted for the purpose of discouraging or screening out members of a protected class. Use of a pen and paper test implemented for the purpose of disproportionately disqualifying minority applicants, is discrimination "because of race" when a black applicant is not hired because of his low test score. *Albemarle Paper Co. v. Moody* (S.Ct. 1975). A seniority system modified to disadvantage employment units dominated by female employees is sex discrimination against women discharged pursuant to the system. *Lorance v. AT & T Technologies* (S.Ct. 1989). A compensation system established so that workers in job categories dominated by females would be paid less than job categories dominated by men is sex discrimination. *County of Washington v. Gunther* (S.Ct. 1981).

CHAPTER 10

SYSTEMIC PATTERNS

III—10.01 Statistics and Burdens: The *Teamsters* Model

International Broth. of Teamsters v. United States (S.Ct. 1977) held that illegal motive can be proved through employment patterns that indicate a systemic practice of discrimination. In *Teamsters*, the plaintiff demonstrated that in some geographic areas where blacks constituted over 30% of the population, defendant employers had virtually no minority workers. Nationwide, in the more desirable job of "line driver," 0.4% were black and 0.3% were Hispanic. Relying on the Title VII proviso which prohibits "preferential treatment" based "solely" on racial imbalances (42 U.S.C.A. 2000e–2(j)), defendant argued that data comparing the employer's work force with area population could not establish liability. The Court held, however, that judicial acceptance of statistical data was appropriate and did not require employers to grant "preferential treatment;" the data merely provided evidence of illegal motivation.

[I]mbalance is often a telltale sign of purposeful discrimination; absent explanation, it is ordinarily expected that nondiscriminatory hiring practices, will, in time, result in a work force more or less representative of the racial and ethnic composition of the population in the community from which employees are hired.

The initial burden is upon the plaintiff to demonstrate through accepted statistical methodologies that there is an under-representation of a protected class in the employer's work force, or division thereof, which cannot be explained as a product of chance. If plaintiff establishes a statistically significant imbalance, the burden shifts to the defendant to demonstrate that plaintiff's statistics were unreliable, or failing this, to present a non-discriminatory explanation for the apparently discriminatory pattern. Assertions of good faith or of hiring only the most qualified applicants do not refute a statistical demonstration of under-representation.

Plaintiff's demonstration of an unexplained imbalance, supported by anecdotal incidents of disparate treatment, established a pattern of illegal motivation, which, in turn, created an inference that each hiring decision was infected by illegal motivation. The litigation now proceeds to a remedy stage. To secure a remedy for individual claimants, plaintiff must prove that the individual member of the victimized class applied for a position or was deterred from applying because of defendant's discriminatory practices. Once plaintiff establishes "applicant" status for a claimant, the burden shifts back to the employer to prove that the "applicant" was not hired for legitimate reasons such as lack of a vacancy or superior qualifications of the person selected. Defendant's burden at this point is one of persuasion, to prove that the legitimate reason actually motivated each "applicant's" rejection. *International Broth. of Teamsters v. United States, supra,* (S.Ct. 1977).

III—10.02   Refining *Teamsters*

a.   Statistical Methodology

Hazelwood School Dist. v. United States (S.Ct. 1977) refined the *Teamsters* model. The Court first sanctioned use of statistical doctrines, in particular the "rule of exclusion" or standard deviation analysis. Standard deviation analysis states the probability that an observed outcome was the product of chance or random selection. It has four steps: (1) identifying an expected outcome, (2) observing the actual outcome; (3) determining the difference between the expected and actual outcomes, and (4) applying mathematical formulae to calculate the probability that the difference between the expected and the observed outcomes was a product of chance.

To illustrate, a balanced coin fairly flipped has a 50% probability of landing heads. Consequently, if flipped 100 times, the most likely, or *expected* outcome is 50 heads and 50 tails. Measuring the *actual* outcome is accomplished by flipping the coin 100 times, and counting the number of times heads actually occurs. We know that a fair coin, fairly flipped 100 times would not always result in 50 heads. Random chance could produce an actual outcome on either side of 50 (*e.g.*, 51 or 49). However, as the actual outcome approaches the "inexorable zero" of either 0 or 100 heads, we can assume, without a formula, that something other than chance influenced the observed outcome. It might have been the wind, a weighted coin, or a clever flipper. But we are virtually certain that an observed outcome of 3 or 4 heads from 100 flips was not produced by chance. However, if the 100 flips produced 38 heads, such an outcome is neither obviously random nor obviously non-random. Chance is a possibility. Standard deviation formulae provide the mathematical probabilities that chance produced the observed outcome.

Statisticians and courts agree that if a result could be the product of chance only one time in 100 (0.01 "confidence level"), chance cannot be relied upon as an explanation. A confidence level of 0.01 is reached when the observed outcome differs from the expected outcome by 2.57 standard deviations. Disproving the hypothesis of random selection does not prove that the flipper was crooked; it merely eliminates mathematically an hypothesis of random selection or an assertion by the flipper of simple "bad luck." The coin flipper remains free, however, to explain the outcome in terms other than chance (*e.g.*, wind or weighted coin). If neutral explanations are not forthcoming, an observer has little choice but to conclude that the flipper was dishonest.

In the employment context, assume over time an employer filled 100 vacancies drawing from a pool of potential workers that was 50% male and 50% female. The *expected* mix (or outcome) of employees would be 50/50 male/female. If the employer has 48 female workers, (the *observed* outcome), we intuitively know that random selection remains a viable explanation. However, if there are only 15 women employees, standard deviation formulae would demonstrate that such an outcome would happen so rarely that chance is not an hypothesis. Something other than luck or random selection produced the outcome. The burden is on the employer to identify that "something else." If defendant fails, particularly if plaintiff also presents non-statistical direct or circumstantial evidence of illegal motive, a finding that defendant was illegally motivated is required.

b.   Key Statistical Elements

1.   Expected Outcome: Determining the percentage of employees one would *expect* in defendant's workplace, or unit thereof, by race or sex requires first identifying the geographical area from which the employer draws its workers. In *Hazelwood*, defendant asserted that the suburban district where defendant was located, excluding the City of St. Louis, was the appropriate area. In this suburban area, 5.7% of the teachers were black. Plaintiff asserted that the larger metropolitan St. Louis City and County was more appropriate. In the broad metro area, 15.4% of the teachers were black. Consequently, *if* the school district selected its teachers from the suburban district, the expected percentage of black teachers in the Hazelwood schools would be 5.7% *If* the broader metropolitan area was used to

establish the expected percentage of black teachers at Hazelwood, that number would be 15.4%. Determining the appropriate geographical pool will depend largely upon where the employer draws or seeks to draw its workforce. The Court remanded the case to the trial court to make this factual determination.

Measuring an expected outcome also requires a determination of the extent qualifications of persons in the appropriate geographical area match the qualifications required by the employer. If the skill "involved is one that many persons possess or could readily acquire"—such as driving a truck in *Teamsters*—one would expect the employer's work force to mirror the general, unrefined racial, ethnic, and gender population of the relevant geographical area. However, when the job requires special training or skill, a certain level of education, or a professional certification, population data must be refined to reflect that qualification. *Hazelwood* involved employment of teachers. Consequently, the percentage of certified *teachers* by race in the area—as opposed to the general racial mix of the population—provides the accurate expected number. Consideration of differences in interest of various classes in certain jobs may require refinement of raw population data. Proof that women as a class disproportionately do not seek out high pressure commission compensated positions required plaintiff to refine snapshot data to account for those different interests. *EEOC v. Sears, Roebuck & Co.* (7th Cir. 1988).

2. Actual Outcome and Measuring the Difference: The employer's actual experience is accomplished by counting the percentage of women or minorities in an appropriate segment of the employer's workforce. In *Hazelwood*, the plaintiff presented a simple "snapshot" of the number of teachers by race in the employer's work force, without regard to when they were hired. This demonstrated that 1.8% of the *current* teachers were black. The employer countered with a data demonstrating that 3.7% of the *recently hired* teachers were black. The difference was critical. If the 1.8% "snapshot" of *current* teachers presented by plaintiff is the expected outcome, it is sufficiently below the teacher population of both the suburban area (5.7%) and the metro area (15.4%) that chance would be eliminated as an hypothesis. However, if the 3.7% *recent hire* is the experience to be compared, the difference between the 3.7% experience and a 5.7% (suburban area) expected outcome is sufficiently close that chance would not be eliminated as an hypothesis. The Court remanded this question for a determination of which actual outcome should be used for the mathematical comparison.

3. Different Approaches: Pool vs. Flow *Hazelwood* illustrates applicant pool analysis where the expected value is a "snapshot," frozen in time. The population demographics in the relevant geographical area are compared with a "snapshot" of the employer's outcomes (either overall workforce or recent hiring experience).

Applicant flow analyzes the employer's actual decision-making experience. The percentage of applicants actually hired by the employer is established. If 500 people applied and 100 were hired, the over-all hiring rate is 20%. This establishes an expected outcome of 20%. Next, the actual hiring rates of particular classes are calculated. Assume that of the 500 applicants, 200 were minority applicants and 40 were hired. This produces a hiring rate, or outcome, of 20% for minority applicants. As the expected and observed outcomes are the same (20%), no discriminatory motive can be inferred. However, if of the 200 minority applicants only 25 were hired, this produces a hiring rate of 12.5%. Here the difference between the *expected* outcome of 20% and the *observed* outcome of 12.5% raises the mathematical question of whether chance can be eliminated as an explanation for the difference.

As flow data reflects the actions of current decision makers, it tends to be a more reliable indicator of current motivation. However, if the employer's practices discourage minority persons from applying, or, conversely, if affirmative action efforts have produced disproportionately high numbers of minority applicants who might be marginally qualified, and thus might be rejected at a higher rate for legitimate reasons, flow data may be skewed, rendering snap shot comparisons more reliable.

Statistical reliability requires a reasonably sized sample. The precise number needed for reliability varies with the degree of difference between the expected and observed outcomes. If the sample size is so small that the outcome will be changed by adding or subtracting a few more experiences, the courts will reject as unreliable conclusions drawn therefrom.

c. *Statistics and Individual Disparate Treatment*

While the statistical model is most commonly employed in class actions or pattern and practice suits filed by government agencies, statistics can establish prima facie motivation in individual disparate treatment cases. *Davis v. Califano* (D.C.Cir. 1979). If the sample size is small or otherwise inconclusive, data may be admitted to buttress verbal or circumstantial evidence of illegal motive. Conversely, an employer may present favorable statistical data as evidence that it did not discriminate against the individual plaintiff. *Ortega v. Safeway Stores, Inc.* (10th Cir. 1991).

d. *Force Reductions*

Statistics that demonstrate a "stark pattern of discrimination unexplainable on grounds other than age" can establish age motive in selecting employees for layoff. Two variables are key, the age of the employees at the time of the force reduction, and whether the employees were laid off. If other variables are available, such as performance evaluations, education, and experience, they must be utilized to refine plaintiff's data. Failure of the plaintiff to use available data raises questions as to the viability of an otherwise stark comparison. *Pottenger v. Potlatch Corp.* (9th Cir. 2003). Plaintiff's data must focus on the part of the company where plaintiff was employed and the force reduction that affected the plaintiff. Data from other force reductions, other units, or different decision makers are not probative. *Balderston v. Fairbanks Morse Engine* (7th Cir. 2003). If plaintiff establishes a statistical pattern that eliminates chance as an hypothesis, the employer will avoid liability to individual claimants only by proof that the particular decision was attributable to a legitimate reason such as plaintiff's poor work history or his relative lack of skill.

CHAPTER 11

DISPARATE IMPACT: LIABILITY IN THE ABSENCE OF MOTIVE

III—11.01 Impact Analysis: Griggs v. Duke Power Co.

Claims of disparate treatment may be distinguished from claims that stress 'disparate impact'. The latter involve employment practices that are facially neutral in their treatment of different groups but in fact fall more harshly on one group than another and cannot be justified by business necessity. Proof of discriminatory motive * * * is not required under a disparate impact theory. *International Broth. of Teamsters v. U.S.* (S.Ct. 1977).

In *Griggs v. Duke Power Co.* (S.Ct. 1971), the employer required applicants to possess a high school diploma and make a passing score on two professionally developed tests purporting to measure general intellectual ability. The lower court read Title VII language ("because of") to require invidious intent, and found that the employer acted in good faith in adopting and applying the selection devices. The Supreme Court reversed, stating:

The Act proscribes not only overt discrimination but also practices that are fair in form but discriminatory in operation. The touchstone is business necessity. If an employment practice which operates to exclude Negroes cannot be shown to be related to job performance, the practice is prohibited. * * * [A]bsence of discriminatory intent does not redeem employment procedures or testing mechanisms that operate as 'built-in headwinds' for minority groups and are unrelated to measuring job capability.

The Civil Rights Act of 1991 codified impact analysis under Title VII. The Act defines "demonstrate" to mean "meets the burden of production and persuasion," (42 U.S.C.A. 2000e-(m)), and makes it an unlawful employment practice if plaintiff *"demonstrates"* that a particular practice causes a disparate impact on a protected class, and the respondent fails to *"demonstrate"* that "the challenged practice is job related * * * and consistent with business necessity." 42 U.S.C.A. 2000e-(2)(k).

Impact analysis involves three steps: 1) Plaintiff must identify the device that resulted in his/her exclusion and establish the disparate impact of that device on the class to which he/she belongs. 2) If impact is "demonstrated," the employer avoids liability only by proving that the challenged device is "job related" and "consistent with business necessity." 3) If defendant "demonstrates" the "business necessity" of the challenged device, plaintiff may establish that the device was adopted to achieve discriminatory purposes. *Albemarle Paper Co. v. Moody* (S.Ct. 1975); 29 CFR 1607.3B.

Impact analysis may be applied to all classes protected by Title VII. *Dothard v. Rawlinson* (S.Ct. 1977)(sex). The Americans With Disabilities Act adopts impact analysis. *Infra,* 21.10. Courts are divided on whether impact analysis is available under the Age Act. *Adams v. Florida Power Co.* (11th Cir. 2001). *Infra,* 20.04. The 1866 Civil Rights Act requires proof of racial motivation. *General Bldg. Contractors Ass'n v. Pennsylvania* (S.Ct. 1982).

III—11.02 The Testing Proviso: More on *Griggs*

Title VII reserves the right "[to use] professionally developed ability tests not designed, intended or used to discriminate." 42 U.S.C.A. 2000e–2(h). In *Griggs v. Duke Power Co. supra* (S.Ct. 1971), the employer had utilized a "professionally developed ability test" to select employees that the lower courts found was not "designed, intended or used" to discriminate. The Court reversed. A test that has an adverse impact on a protected class and is not proved by defendant to be job related is being *"used to discriminate"* and is not preserved by the proviso. Ability tests are subject to impact analysis.

III—11.03 Subjective Selective Systems: *Watson*

In *Watson v. Fort Worth Bank & Trust* (S.Ct. 1988), a black employee repeatedly had been denied promotions. The employer justified each of its decisions through subjective comparisons between plaintiff and the successful candidates. Plaintiff alleged that the subjective promotion system adversely affected black workers. The lower courts held that impact analysis was applicable only to identified objective devices, such as tests or educational credentials. The Court reversed, holding that unstructured subjective systems could be subjected to impact analysis. *Wards Cove Packing Co. v. Atonio* (S.Ct. 1989), confirmed *Watson,* but emphasized that the impact of a subjective system is not established by a showing of racial imbalance in the employer's workforce. (Data showing statistically significant work force imbalances can, however, establish prima facie case of improperly *motivated* decision making, thus shifting to defendant the burden to explain the disparity in neutral terms. *Supra,* Chapt. 10.)

III—11.04   Plaintiff's Case: Proving Impact

a.   Generally: Nature of the Proof

"Plaintiff * * * is responsible for isolating and identifying the specific employment practices that are alleged responsible for any observed statistical disparities. Once the employment practice at issue has been identified, causation must be proved; that is the plaintiff must offer statistical evidence of a kind and degree sufficient to show that the practice in question has caused the exclusion of applicants for jobs or promotions because of their membership in a protected group.

Watson v. Fort Worth Bank and Trust, supra (S.Ct. 1988).

New York City Transit Auth. v. Beazer (S.Ct. 1979), emphasized that the impact of the challenged device must be proved with precision. Plaintiffs challenged a rule denying employment to persons enrolled in a methadone-based drug rehabilitation programs. Plaintiffs' data demonstrated that 81% of all employees referred to the employer's medical director for drug abuse were black or Hispanic, and that 63% of persons receiving methadone maintenance from *public* programs were black or Hispanic. This data was inadequate. First, the rule being challenged was disqualification of persons *enrolled* in drug rehabilitation programs, not persons *referred* to the employer's medical director for current drug abuse. Second, data showing the high percentage of minorities in *public* programs failed to include racial data from *private* treatment programs which conceivably rendered plaintiffs' data unreliable. Third, many persons in drug rehabilitation programs presumably were not otherwise qualified for employment with defendant. Given these flaws, plaintiffs failed to prove the impact of the challenged rule on their group.

Specific proof of impact is not required if the impact of a device is *inevitable*. Where medical evidence established that substantially all pregnant women would be advised not to lift 150 lbs, plaintiff need not present statistical evidence of the extent that such a lifting requirement excluded pregnant

women. *Garcia v. Woman's Hospital of Texas* (5th
Cir. 1996). Nonetheless, impact will not be assumed
simply because impact is logical or even likely.
While early authority assumed that informal word
of mouth recruiting in a predominately white male
work force would produce an adverse impact on
minorities *(Barnett v. W.T. Grant Co.* (4th Cir.
1975)), later decisions demand proof that informal
recruiting in fact is producing such an impact.
Holder v. City of Raleigh (4th Cir. 1989). It is
logical to assume that a rule prohibiting the employment of spouses would fall more heavily on
women, who generally earn less and have less seniority than their husbands. Nonetheless, supporting data is needed showing that significantly more
women than men in fact resign when a no spouse
rule is invoked. *Thomas v. Metroflight, Inc.* (10th
Cir. 1987).

"[P]laintiff's burden to establish a prima face
case [of impact] goes beyond the need to show that
there are statistical disparities in the employer's
work force." *Watson v. Fort Worth Bank and Trust,
supra* (S.Ct. 1988). An unbalanced workforce could
be the product of legitimate factors: geography,
cultural differences, or the lack of unchallenged
qualifications for the jobs. A simple demographic
imbalance that does not account for these possibilities says very little about whether a particular
device *caused* the imbalance. *Wards Cove Packing
Co. v. Atonio., supra* (S.Ct. 1989) held that a high
percentage of nonwhite workers in low paying can-
nery jobs compared to a low percentage of such
workers in higher paying, more desirable non-can-

nery jobs did not establish that the employer's selection system for the non-cannery jobs had an adverse impact on plaintiffs' class. Thus, a "snap-shot" that compares the percentage of males vs. females *hired* over a limited period of time does little to prove that a particular practice was responsible for the hiring disparities. Such disparity could be attributable to a low number of women applicants. *EEOC v. Joe's Stone Crab, Inc.* (11th Cir. 2000) (108 men and 0 women). However, "flow" data demonstrating a significant disparity in the percentage of male and female *applicants* hired would have been strong evidence that the subjective system was causing the observed difference. *Watson v. Fort Worth Bank and Trust, supra* (S.Ct. 1988). *Infra,* 11.04(c).

b. Applicant Pool

Applicant pool analysis determines the percentages of persons in this pool, by class, who possess the challenged criteria. *Griggs v. Duke Power, supra* (S.Ct. 1971) accepted that requiring a high school diploma had an adverse impact on black applicants based on census data from the state where defendant was located (North Carolina) which disclosed that 34% of white males had high school diplomas compared to only 12% of black males. *Dothard v. Rawlinson* (S.Ct. 1977) held that a minimum height of 5'-2" and a minimum weight of 120 lbs for jobs as prison guards had an adverse impact on women, based on *national* data which demonstrated the height and weight minima would exclude 41.13% of women but less than 1% of the male population. A rule that disqualifies those with criminal records was shown to have an adverse impact on minority applicants by comparing the percentage of minorities to non-minorities in the community who have criminal conviction records. *Green v. Missouri Pacific R.R. Co.* (8th Cir. 1975).

Applicant pool analysis requires plaintiff to identify the geographical area from which the employer would be expected to draw its workers. *Griggs* accepted the *state* percentage, based on an assumption that the relative percentage of high school graduates in the "pool" from which the employer selected its workers would not differ significantly from state percentages. *Dothard v. Rawlinson* (S.Ct. 1977) accepted *national* height and weight data based on an assumption that height and weight of men and women in Alabama was similar to the height and weight of men and women nationally. Moreover, *Dothard* did not require plaintiff to account for the possibility that a significant proportion of women under 5′–2″ and weighing less that 120 lbs would not be interested in, or "otherwise unqualified" for, the job of prison guard.

Later decisions were more demanding. Plaintiff's data must account for unchallenged qualifications and relative interest in the job. In *Wards Cove Packing Co. v. Atonio* (S.Ct. 1989), plaintiff challenged the educational criteria for office workers in Seattle. The percentage of persons by race in rural Alaska who lacked the challenged criteria failed to demonstrate the impact of the educational criteria. The Court reasoned that as defendant drew its office workers primarily from the Seattle area, many minority persons living in Alaska would not be interested in office work in Seattle, and thus plaintiff's data which focused on Alaska lacked probity. Accordingly, where the racial composition of the particular community from which the employer is shown to secure its applicants differs markedly from the racial composition of broader city or state populations, the broader city or state data will not suffice. *Bennett v. Roberts* (7th Cir. 2002)(data that included large metro areas, such as Chicago, not reliable when employer is located in a rural community, and state wide data unreliable where employer hired nationally). A showing that persons of a particular gender were disproportionately interested in a particular type of job made unreliable data that did not account for this relative lack of interest. *EEOC v. Sears, Roebuck & Co.* (7th Cir. 1988).

New York City Transit Auth. v. Beazer (S.Ct. 1979) rejected plaintiffs' evidence comparing minority and non-minority participation in drug rehabilitation programs as showing the racial impact of refusing to employ persons in such programs. The Court assumed that many of those in the general population pool in drug rehabilitation programs would not be *otherwise qualified* for the position in that they might have disqualifying criminal records or lacked unchallenged educational or physical requirements for the job.

c. Applicant Flow

"Flow" data examines the employer's actual experience using the challenged device. The percentage of actual applicants, by gender or ethnic class, who pass the employer's test are compared. A significant difference, by class, between those applicants who pass and those who do not establishes the impact of the test. *Griggs v. Duke Power Co. supra* (S.Ct. 1971) accepted the impact of the employer's use of standardized tests established by an EEOC study conducted at *another employer* that used similar tests showing that 58% of the whites passed compared to 6% of the blacks. Plaintiffs challenging an employer's promotion standards often rely on applicant flow data that compares the percentage by class of employees applying for the promotion to the percentage by class of those actually offered promotion. *Malave v. Potter* (2d Cir. 2003).

The difference in the flow rates between classes must be "significant." "Significance" is best determined by the mathematical doctrine of the "rule of exclusion" or standard deviation analysis. This doctrine identifies a difference between an expected and an observed outcome, and states the mathematical probability that the difference was a product of chance. When chance is eliminated as an hypothesis for the different selection rates, the device is seen as causing the difference, and of having an adverse impact on the class. *Supra*, 10.02.

Based on the assumption that a devise without impact will have essentially the same flow rates

within each class, the *overall* pass/fail rate of all
takers provides the expected outcome. If an employer gives an objective test to 150 applicants, 100 of
whom pass, this establishes a pass flow rate of 2/3
or 66.6%. The expected outcome, or passage rate,
for *each class* taking the test would be 66.6%. The
effect of the device on each class is accomplished by
calculating its particular pass/fail rates. If each class
passes at or very near a rate of 66.6%—the expected
outcome—the test is not adversely affecting any
group. If differences approach the "inexorable zero"
no mathematical analysis is needed to demonstrate
their impact, as, for example in *Griggs*, where the
passage rate of whites was nearly 10 times greater
than the passage rate of minorities. However, when
the difference between observed and expected outcomes is not dramatic, statistical analysis is necessary.

Assume that within the 150 applicants who had
an overall passage rate of 66.6%, 100 were white,
and 50 were black. Seventy-five of the white applicants passed, giving white applicants a pass rate of
75%. Of the 50 minority applicants, 25 passed,
giving them a 50% pass rate. The mathematical
question is whether the difference between the expected outcome—66.6%—and the observed outcome—50%—is great enough that chance can be
eliminated as an hypothesis. If chance is mathematically ruled out as an explanation, courts conclude
that the device produced an adverse impact on
plaintiff's class. (Application of the standard devia-

tion formula demonstrates that in this hypothetical, chance would have produced the observed outcome approximately one time in 100, thus satisfying most courts that chance is not a viable hypothesis.)

The EEOC provides an alternative "rule of thumb" known as the "Rule of 4/5ths." A device will have a presumed adverse impact if it produces "[a] selection rate for any race, sex, or ethnic group * * * less than 4/5ths (80%) of the rate for the group with the highest rate." 29 CFR 1607.3. In the above hypothetical, minority applicants had a passage rate of 50%. Whites—"the group with the highest rate,"—passed at 75%. Eighty percent of the white applicant passing rate of 75% = 60%. Thus a minority passing rate of less than 60% establishes the adverse impact of the device. As the minority passage rate in fact was 50%, the "Rule of 4/5ths" demonstrates the adverse impact of the defendant's test.

Meaningful results require an adequate sample size. Courts reject conclusions if a minor change in the raw numbers would make significant changes in the percentages. See *Harper v. Trans World Airlines, Inc.* (8th Cir. 1975), where a no-marriage rule which disqualified four women and one man was insufficient to prove the impact of the rule.

d. A "Bottom Line" Defense: Where Flow is Measured

Where is flow measured when more than one selection devise is used? Title VII, 42 U.S.C.A. 2000e–2(k)(1)(B), provides:

[T]he complaining party shall demonstrate that each particular challenged practice causes a disparate impact, except that if the complaining party can demonstrate to the court that the elements of a respondent's decisionmaking process are not capable of separation for analysis, the decisionmaking process may be analyzed as one employment practice.

In *Connecticut v. Teal* (S.Ct. 1982), each applicant was given an objective screening test. Those who failed to make a minimum score on the test were eliminated from further consideration. Those who passed the test were then evaluated using additional criteria. Eighty percent of the white applicants, but only 54% of the black applicants, passed the first test, a difference sufficient to establish the adverse effect of the test on black applicants. However, when other factors were used to evaluate applicants who survived the screening test, 22.9% of the initial black applicants ultimately were hired, compared to 13.5% of the white applicants. Thus the "bottom line," or ultimate selection rate, showed no impact on black applicants. The Court held, however, that the focus must be on the initial screening test.

If components are related and combined for a single score with no discrete performance disqualifying applicants, such functionally integrated devices are analyzed as a single employment practice. Thus, a multiple choice objective examination which provides a final numerical score would be analyzed as a single device, and it would be inappropriate to analyze relative performance on each question. In *Teal,* had all candidates been allowed to participate in every aspects of the selection process, with scores on each component being integrated into a single final ranking, the final combined score, not the various components, would be analyzed for impact. *Stout v. Potter* (9th Cir. 2002).

e.   Flow or Pool?

Flow data generally provides stronger evidence of impact in that it measures the actual effect of the challenged device. *Malave v. Potter* (2d Cir. 2003). This generalization is true only if the presence of the challenged device does not discourage or encourage applicants. For example, the announced policy of requiring a college degree would discourage from applying those who did not have a degree. True impact of the requirement could not be measured by flow data. Similarly, advertised height and weight minima would self-select, in that only the persons who met the standards would apply.

Flow data may also be unreliable where the employer has a vigorous affirmative action recruiting program that is producing an unusually high number of minority applicants, many of whom may lack the training or language skills to perform well on the challenged selection test. Flow data also may unjustifiably demonstrate the absence of impact where the employer has a reputation for discriminating against women and minorities to the point that few bother to apply.

III—11.05 Defendant's Burden: "Business Necessity"

a. Toward a Definition of "Business Necessity"

Griggs v. Duke Power Co., supra (S.Ct. 1971) held that once plaintiff established the adverse impact of the device the burden was on the defendant to demonstrate the "business necessity" of the device. The Court also stated that exclusionary devices would be justified when "manifestly related" to job performance. *Wards Cove Packing v. Atonio, supra* (S.Ct. 1989) attempted a more precise definition:

> [T]he dispositive issue is whether the challenged practice serves, in a significant way, the legitimate goals of the employer. * * * A mere insubstantial justification in this regard will not suffice. * * * At the same time, though, there is no requirement that the challenged practice be "essential" or "indispensable" to the employers' business to pass muster.

The 1991 Civil Rights Act restated the original *Griggs* terminology. Once plaintiff demonstrated impact, defendant's burden was to demonstrate that the practice was "job related" and consistent with "business necessity." 42 U.S.C.A. 2000e-(2)(k). Legislative history indicates that the "business necessity" standard should be that which was defined by the courts *prior* to *Wards Cove Packing*. This leaves three possibilities:

—*Necessity:* In requiring that "job relatedness" must also be *consistent* with "business necessity" the statute suggests that defendant must prove that the device should be "necessary,"—meaning "compelling" and "without workable alternatives." *Bradley v. Pizzaco* (8th Cir. 1993).

—*Legitimacy:* Based on a premise that *Wards Cove Packing* restated prior authority, "business necessity" would require only that defendant prove that "the challenged practice serves in a significant way the *legitimate* goals of the employer." Only "insubstantial justifications" fail to meet the employer's burden.

—*Business Legitimacy:* If Congress rejected the *Wards Cove Packing* articulation of "business necessity," as legislative history suggests, courts must search for the "business necessity" definition that existed *prior to Wards Cove Packing*. Unfortunately, that standard never was definitively articulated. *Dothard v. Rawlinson* (S.Ct. 1977), stated that a discriminatory employment practice must be *"necessary to safe and efficient job performance." New York City Transit Auth. v. Beazer* (S.Ct. 1979), indicated that the employer's burden is met if the practice *"significantly serves"* the employer's *"legitimate business goals* of safety and efficiency," suggesting that while the employer's goal must be a specific *"business"* purpose, it need not be "essential." Thus it unclear whether the device need be "necessary" or only serve "legitimate business" purposes. *Lanning v. South Eastern Penn. Transp. Auth.* (3d Cir. 1999).

b. Lesser Discriminatory Alternatives

Proof that an employer had available alternatives that served business needs equally as well as the challenged device, but without the discriminatory effect, would establish that the challenged device is not "necessary." Thus, if true "necessity" is required, plaintiff's proof of a lesser discriminatory alternative would deprive the defendant of the business necessity defense. However, if "business necessity" is established by defendant's demonstration that the device serves its legitimate business purposes, existence of a lesser discriminatory alternative does not destroy the "necessity" for defendant's use of the device. Lesser discriminatory alternatives would only be some evidence of defendant's unlawful *motive* in adopting the device. *Albemarle Paper Co. v. Moody* (S.Ct. 1975).

The 1991 Amendments added to this uncertainty by making it an "unlawful employment practice" where plaintiff demonstrates that an identified practice produces an adverse impact on a protected class and that there is an alternative employment practice which produces a less discriminatory impact that the employer has refused to adopt. 42 U.S.C.A. 2000e–2(k). This suggests that the employer must have been aware of the efficacy of the alternative device and its lack of impact, and suggests further that defendant must have "refused" suggestions to adopt the alternative. It is unclear whether Congress made this the sole basis for analyzing alternatives, or whether it was creating a distinct form of liability.

c. A Sliding Scale?

If unsuccessful job performance jeopardizes the health or safety of other employees or the general public, courts are deferential to employer use of rational selection devices. In *Spurlock v. United Airlines, Inc.* (10th Cir. 1972) the prerequisites to admission into an airline pilot training program were a college degree, a commercial pilot's license, and 500 hours of flight time. In sustaining these devices notwithstanding their impact on protected classes, the court stated:

> When a job requires a small amount of skill and training and the consequences of hiring an unqualified applicant are insignificant, the courts should examine closely any pre-employment standard or criteria which discriminate against minorities. In such a case, the employer should have a heavy burden to demonstrate * * * that his employment criteria are job related. On the other hand, when the job clearly requires a high degree of skill and the economic and human risks involved are great, the employer bears a correspondingly lighter burden to show that his employment criteria are job related.

When validating scored tests, as opposed to evaluating credentials, courts may refuse to give special deference to selecting applicants for safety-sensitive jobs. *Lanning v. South Eastern Penn. Transp't. Auth., supra* (3d Cir. 1999)(running speed test for selecting transit police officers must be validated).

III—11.06   Scored Tests: *Griggs,* and *Albermarle Paper*

a. *The General Command*

Griggs v. Duke Power Co., supra (S.Ct. 1971) stated that even if tests are "professionally developed" they cannot "operate as 'built-in headwinds' " for minority groups:

> What Congress has forbidden is giving these devices and mechanisms controlling force unless they are demonstrably a measure of job performance. * * * What Congress has commanded is that any tests used must measure the person for the job and not the person in the abstract.

The Uniform Guidelines on Employee Selection Procedures, 29 CFR Part 1607, adopted soon after *Griggs*, required that scored tests having an adverse impact must be "validated" according to standards of the American Psychological Association. *Albemarle Paper Co. v. Moody, supra* (S.Ct. 1975) held that these Guidelines are entitled to great judicial deference, and should be applied to establish the "business necessity" of testing devices. The Court emphasized:

> [D]iscriminatory tests are impermissible unless shown, by professionally acceptable methods, to be predictive of or significantly correlated with important elements of work behavior which comprise or are relevant to the jobs for which candidates are being evaluated.

Albemarle Paper held that the general reputation, widespread use, or casual reports of reliability could not be accepted in lieu of actual documentation. Even expert conclusions as to a test's reliability, unsupported by documented studies, do not suffice. Detailed, precise statistical validation as set forth in the Guidelines is required. Tests validated by other employers can be used by a defendant only if job duties at the two locations are the same. Test validation thus requires closely monitored studies conducted by testing experts.

b. Test Validation

There are three methods by which the job relatedness of tests are validated: 1) content, 2) criterion and 3) construct.

1. Content: A test that replicates major or essential portions of the job has "content validity" (*e.g.*, typing speed and computer literacy test to select secretarial support persons, a driving test to select cab drivers, or a welding test used to select welders). Where central aspects of the job require a level of physical performance (*e.g.*, strength and agility for firefighters) tests that measure that performance have "content validity."

The test need not replicate the entire job as long as it measures major components of a required skill or ability. For example, in qualifying police officers, a test that measures level of running speed and stamina had content validity even though officers perform many duties that do not involve running or require stamina. *Blake v. Los Angeles* (9th Cir.

1979). A test is not valid if it only measures minor, insignificant elements of the job. Measuring typing skills as the test for selecting police officers would lack content validity because typing is a minor aspect of an officer's duties.

Griggs teaches that general intelligence tests do not have content validity. Even though intelligence may be said to be an element in the successful performance of any job, the relationship between job content and performance on a general intelligence test is too attenuated.

Pen and paper tests lack content validity for jobs that require a particular skill or physical activity. However, where the job requires specific knowledge, such as teachers for the subject matter taught, pen and paper tests that measure critical knowledge are content valid. *United States v. South Carolina* (D.S.C. 1977). Tests that measure reading and expression will have validity where reading and expression skills are a key part of the job. *Association of Mexican–American Educators v. California, supra* (9th Cir. 2000)(en banc)(teachers).

When an absolute standard is required for successful job performance, a test is not valid if used to select candidates based on *relative* ability. Thus, if the job regularly requires a worker to lift 75 lbs, a test that eliminates those who cannot lift that amount will have content validity. But the test will not be validated if it is used to prefer applicants who can lift 100 lbs over those who can only lift 75 lbs. Selection according to relative rank on test scores is valid, however, where test scores vary with the level of job performance. Thus, a word processor who can type 50 words per minute on a test is presumably more efficient than one who can type only 40 words per minute, and thus may be preferred over a competent but slower performer.

A minimal passing score, particularly on tests of knowledge, will be valid if set at "reasonable" levels. The precise cut off point for "passing" need not be separately validated. Thus, on a test measuring basic reading, writing, and mathematics a professional estimate that a "passing" score on 12 of 16 questions was reasonable was upheld. *Association of Mexican–American Educators v. California, supra* (9th Cir. 2000)(en banc).

2. Criterion or "Predictive Validity": Criterion-related validity establishes that a test *predicts* job performance by demonstrating a statistically significant correlation between test scores and scored job performance. Unlike content validity, a predictive test need not, and often does not, have components that resemble job duties. For example, *if* persons who perform well on a music appreciation test in fact can be shown to perform well as bricklayers, the music test may be used to hire bricklayers.

Defendant first must establish a positive correlation between test performance and job performance, and second, must prove that the positive correlation is statistically significant. The correlation between test performance and job performance requires an analysis of major or key job components—criteria—and an objective method to evaluate performance on those criteria. Subjective, generalized evaluations by supervisors, without objective benchmarks, do not suffice. While the criteria being measured need not encompass the entire job, they must measure significant, major, or critical aspects of the job. *Albemarle Paper Co. v. Moody, supra* (S.Ct. 1975). The job performance being evaluated must be that which the test taker would assume immediately upon being employed or very soon after a brief orientation. A test may not be used to select entry level workers simply based on a correlation to job performance measured long after employment or for jobs duties the employee might be promoted into at a future time. Performance in training, as opposed to actual job performance, may be used as a criterion measure if the training program has a content relationship to the future job. Thus, a test was validated by comparing test scores with performance in the police academy, rather than on-the-job performance as an officer. *Washington v. Davis* (S.Ct. 1976).

The next step is to give the test to a significant number of workers. Test performance and job performance are then plotted to secure a "correlation coefficient" between test scores and job performance ratings. A positive practical correlation exists when the data demonstrates that persons who do well on the test also tend to do well in performing job criteria, and conversely, those who do poorly on the test tend to perform less well on job criteria. A practical, predictive correlation does not require 100% correlation. Outliers are inevitable even in tests having a high level of predictive value. Expert analysis is required.

If there is a positive correlation between job and test performance, the employer must then demonstrate mathematically that it is unlikely that the observed positive correlation could have been a product of chance. A test will be validated if defendant shows that the positive practical correlation could occur by chance, or randomly, in no more than 1 time in 20 (or a "significance" of 0.05 or lower). This, too, requires analysis by statisticians or testing experts.

Validation studies should include an investigation of test "unfairness" or possible cultural bias. "Unfairness" is an hypothesis, not uniformly accepted by experts, that a test predicting job performance of white male employees may not predict job performance of persons from different cultures. To insure against "unfairness," separate or "differential validation" is conducted. That is, the test and job performance of white males are separately analyzed from the test and job performance of distinct racial or gender groups. The EEOC does not require differential validation where not technically feasible, provided there is no specific evidence of cultural bias in the test and the sample used in the validation study included a representative cross section of all classes.

The preferred method of conducting a validation study, and one requiring for reliability the fewest number of participants, is a "predictive" study. All, or a representative sample, of the employer's applicants are given the test before they begin work. The applicants are hired without regard to their test score. Job performance is measured soon after the employee is hired. To insure that test results do not corrupt subsequent job performance evaluations, test scores must not be available to those evaluating job performance. This method is more precise because it measures job performance against the full spectrum of test performances.

A second method is "concurrent" validation. A representative sample of current employees are given the test. The test scores are compared to existing or subsequent job performance evaluations of the tested workers. Concurrent validation has three major problems: 1) significant length of employment may influence test performance, 2) job performance may have been evaluated among experienced employees for a test that selects new employees, and 3) applicants who were rejected because they failed this or a similar test will not be included in the study. These problems are not necessarily fatal if identified and accounted for by the testing expert. 29 CFR 1607.14C.

3. Construct: A third, largely theoretical, method of validation identifies a psychological trait or characteristic ("construct") which is necessary for job performance. The test measures the presence and degree of that characteristic. For example, "leadership" would be a construct for a fire captain; "patience" for a teacher; "compassion" for a nurse. Construct validation requires a showing not only

that the construct is a foundation for the job and that the test accurately measures the construct, but also that there is a statistical correlation between the identified construct and job performance using standards similar to those involved in a criterion validity study. 29 CFR 1607.14D.

c. *Avoiding   Validation   by   Avoiding   Impact: "Norming"*

Where impact can be eliminated, there will be no need to validate the device. Eliminating impact of scored tests can be accomplished by using "within group scoring" to adjust raw scores based on performance within ethnic or gender groups. For example, on a physical test, women with 50 points may receive the same rank, or adjusted score, as men who have 60 points, and by this adjustment eliminate impact of the test on women. Needing ten new employees, the employer ranks white applicants and minority applicants separately, and regardless of raw scores selects the top five scoring white applicants and the five top minority applicants. While such adjusted scoring, or "norming" may eliminate the impact of the test, it does so by utilizing facial classifications. Employees will be rejected because of their race or sex. Absent a legitimate affirmative action plan, the legality of such racial or gender based adjustments is doubtful. *United Steelworkers of America v. Weber* (S.Ct. 1979). Moreover, amendments to Title VII provide:

It shall be an unlawful employment practice for respondent * * * to adjust the scores of, use different cutoff scores for, or otherwise alter the results of employment related tests, on the basis of race, color, religion, sex, or national origin. 42 U.S.C.A. 2000e–2(*l*)

III—11.07 Objective, Non–Testing Devices

Non-testing devices need not be "validated" along the lines required for scored tests. *Hawkins v. Anheuser–Busch, Inc.* (8th Cir. 1983). The "job relatedness" of such devices is more intuitive. *Griggs v. Duke Power Co. supra* (S.Ct. 1971) recognized that an educational credential, such as a high school diploma, will not be assumed to be job related simply because it is rational. Rarely can such credentials be a "business necessity" for selecting employees to fill lower level or semi-skilled jobs such as laborers, clericals, or factor workers. However, if the job requires a skill closely related to the content of the educational credential, it will be sustained as a "business necessity." Thus, a valid drivers license is "necessary" for taxi or truck drivers. A library can require a library science degree for professional librarians. General educational minima, such as a bachelors degree, have been sustained for executives or professionals. *Hawkins v. Anheuser–Busch, Inc., supra* (8th Cir. 1983). For positions that place the public at a high level of risk from unsuccessful performance, such as pilots, police officers, and firefighters, reasonable general educational credentials are often, but not uniformly, sustained. *Davis v. Dallas* (5th Cir. 1985).

Height and weight minima or maximums rarely are "necessary" for successful job performance (*e.g.,* height needed to reach airplane controls), and cannot serve as a proxy for a particular physical requirement such as strength. Individual evaluations of each applicant's fitness usually is a more reliable indication of the necessary ability. *Dothard v. Rawlinson* (S.Ct. 1977). Specific abilities, such as to lift certain weights or run timed distances, must be validated according to professional testing standards. *Lanning v. South Eastern Penn. Transp't Auth.* (3d Cir. 1999)(running speed test used to select transit police).

Requiring experience, such as prior supervisory responsibility or one year's experience in the job before promotion to a supervisor will not likely be a "business necessity" unless the supervisor's job is highly skilled or the economic or human risks involved in hiring an unqualified individual are great. *Walker v. Jefferson County Home* (11th Cir. 1984).

Disqualifying persons with criminal convictions can be a "business necessity" if the position being filled requires trust and integrity, as do jobs that provide access to valuable property or where the aggressive nature of the past crime suggests that the applicant would present a risk of harm to customers or fellow employees. However, if the employer or third persons are placed in little risk from recidivist behavior, for example in an outdoor maintenance job, the exclusion of persons with minor or distant criminal records would not be a business necessity. *Green v. Missouri Pac. R. Co.* (8th Cir. 1977). Reliance on *arrest* records rarely would be "job related." Similarly, it would be difficult for an employer to demonstrate that having poor credit ratings or being a defendant in civil litigation was "job related." (Note: firing an employee because of a garnishment for a single indebtedness or discrimination because of one's bankruptcy may violate other federal statutes. 15 U.S.C.A. 1674, 11 U.S.C.A. 1525. Use of credit information in making adverse employment action requires notification of the individual of the reasons and source of the information. 15 U.S.C.A. 1681).

Employers often favor friends or relatives of current employees. Such nepotism tends to perpetuate the current racial composition of the work force, or, if not, it may be shown through flow data to have an adverse impact on a protected class. *Thomas v. Washington County School Bd.* (4th Cir. 1990). To some courts nepotism is not a "business necessity." *Bonilla v. Oakland Scavenger Co.* (9th Cir. 1982). Some employer's refuse to employ spouses or relatives of current employees. Even if plaintiff can demonstrate the adverse impact of an anti-nepotism policy, courts see strong job related interests in not having relatives working in the same unit. *EEOC v. Rath Packing Co.* (8th Cir. 1986).

Failure to provided sanitary facilities for workers or separate facilities for women, might be shown to adversely affect women. If so, the failure cannot be justified as a necessity solely because it adds a cost to the employer. *DeClue v. Central Ill. Light Co.* (7th Cir. 2000). If the employer's bathroom facilities are so unsanitary that female employees are subjected to a higher level of health risks than male employees, this establishes an adverse effect on women. Toleration of unsanitary conditions is not a business necessity. *Lynch v. Freeman* (6th Cir. 1987).

III—11.08 Subjective Systems

If plaintiff proves impact of a subjective selection system—usually through applicant flow data measuring the outcome of such a system on women or minority applicants—it will be difficult for defendant to prove the business necessity of using subjective judgements to fill unskilled or semi-skilled jobs, particularly if objective criteria are available. *Rowe v. Cleveland Pneumatic Co.* (6th Cir. 1982). However, when used in a way that guards against unconscious prejudice, subjectivity will be "necessary" where objective devices do not measure the qualities needed for successful job performance, as in the case of managers, supervisors, academics, artists, or professionals. *Watson v. Fort Worth Bank and Trust, supra* (S.Ct. 1988).

III—11.09 Seniority

a. Seniority Proviso and Teamsters

Title VII preserves the right to apply different terms or conditions "pursuant to a bona fide seniority system * * * provided that such differences are not the result of an intention to discriminate be-

cause of race, color, religion, sex, or national origin." 42 U.S.C.A. 2000e–2(h). *International Broth.
of Teamsters v. United States* (S.Ct. 1977) construed
this proviso to protect bona fide seniority systems
notwithstanding the impact of seniority on a protected class. The employer had two seniority units:
one for intercity drivers; another for local drivers.
The intercity jobs were more desirable. By virtue of
pre-Act segregation, most intercity drivers were
white, while many local drivers were ethnic minorities. Defendants utilized seniority within each unit
to determine promotions and layoffs within the
unit. Consequently, drivers with substantial seniority in the local unit could not use their seniority to
bid into the desirable vacancies in the intercity unit.
The Court recognized that were it not for the proviso, the seniority system would violate the Act. It
perpetuated the employer's segregation of minorities into the less desirable local driver unit, virtually reserving the more desirable jobs for white employees, and the employer could not establish that
unit seniority was a business necessity. Nonetheless, the Court concluded:

> [T]he unmistakable purpose of [the statutory se-
> niority proviso] was to make it clear that the
> routine application of a bona fide seniority system
> would not be unlawful under Title VII. * * *
> [T]his was the intended result even where the
> employer's pre-Act discrimination resulted in
> whites having greater existing seniority rights
> than Negroes. * * * [A]n otherwise neutral, legit-
> imate seniority system does not become unlawful

under Title VII simply because it may perpetuate pre-Act discrimination.

b.   Teamsters Extended

Prior to *Teamsters*, the Court had held that where a victim of discrimination has *filed a timely charge* of discrimination, the court, as a remedy, should order defendant to "make whole" the plaintiff, which generally requires the employer to hire the victim into the job illegally denied him with full seniority running from the date of the illegal treatment, even when to do so diluted the seniority of incumbent workers. *Franks v. Bowman Transp. Co.* (S.Ct. 1976).

In *United Air Lines, Inc. v. Evans* (S.Ct. 1977), plaintiff, a married female, had been discharge by defendant pursuant to a no-marriage rule. She did not challenge the dismissal. Years later, after the employer had revoked the rule, plaintiff was re-hired. The collective bargaining agreement between the employer and the union provided that employees lost accumulated seniority if there was a significant break in service. A reduction-in-force resulted in plaintiff being laid off because of her lack of seniority. Plaintiff argued that since the break in service, which caused her loss of seniority, was the result of the employer's *illegal* sex discrimination, the provision in the seniority system that caused the loss of previously earned seniority was not saved by the statutory proviso. The Court saw no meaningful way to distinguish *Teamsters*. The seniority system, with its break-in-service provision, was upheld stating:

> [A] challenge to a neutral [seniority] system may not be predicated on the mere fact that a past event which has no present legal significance has affected the calculation of seniority credit, even if the past event might at one time have justified a valid claim against the employer.

On its face, the proviso only permits the employer "to apply" different standards pursuant to a bona fide seniority system, leaving the possibility that the proviso does not protect *adoption* of seniority systems that perpetuate prior discrimination. *American Tobacco Co. v. Patterson* (S.Ct. 1982) rejected such a reading, holding that the proviso protected both good faith *adoption* of new systems, as well as good faith *application* of existing systems

c. *What is "Seniority"; When is there a "System?"*

Seniority is "a scheme that, alone or in tandem with non-'seniority' criteria allots to employees ever improving employment rights or benefits as their relative lengths of pertinent employment increases." *California Brewers Ass'n v. Bryant* (S.Ct. 1980). The system need not be enshrined in a formal collective bargaining agreement, promised in an employee handbook, or directed by an internal operations manual. Well established traditions of the shop, systematically followed with some precision will establish that the employer's use of service length was part of a "system." Nonetheless, "system" presupposes that decisions be more than an informal, ad hoc process that took into account in some imprecise way the employee's length of service. *Williams v. New Orleans S.S. Ass'n* (5th Cir. 1982). Because "seniority" presupposes benefits *increasing* with the passage of time, a system of "reverse seniority" whereby benefits *decrease* with length of service is not a "seniority system".

d. Non–Time Aspects: California Brewers

While "the principal feature of any and every 'seniority system' is that preferential treatment is dispensed on the basis of some measure of time served in employment" nonetheless,

for a seniority system to operate at all, it has to contain ancillary rules that accomplish necessary functions, but which may not themselves be directly related to length of employment. For instance, every seniority system must include rules that delineate how and when the seniority time clock begins ticking, as well as rules that specify how and when a particular person's seniority may be forfeited. Each seniority system must also have rules that define which passages of time will 'count' toward the accrual of seniority and which will not. * * * Rules that serve those necessary purposes do not fall outside the [seniority proviso] simply because they do not, in and of themselves, operate on the basis of some factor involving the passage of time. *California Brewers Ass'n v. Bryant, supra* (S.Ct. 1980).

International Broth. of Teamsters v. United States, supra (S.Ct. 1977) recognized that limiting the use of seniority within a narrow unit, and not allowing unit seniority to be used for jobs in other units, was part of the "system." *United Air Lines, Inc. v. Evans, supra* (S.Ct. 1977) held that a provision mandating a loss of seniority through a break in service was ancillary to the system and protected by the proviso. *California Brewers Ass'n v. Bryant, supra* (S.Ct. 1980) addressed a rule which required an employee to work a minimum of 45 weeks per year to be considered "permanent" and thus receive competitive benefits over "temporary" employees, even though many "temporary" employees had more years of total service than "permanent" employees. Such a practice was part of a "system" protected by the proviso.

A seniority system does not lose its protection simply because it includes additional subjective factors that modify strict length of service such as providing that the most senior person "qualified" for the position will get the job, or allowing seniority to be controlling unless the junior person is substantially more qualified. *Zambetti v. Cuyahoga Community College* (6th Cir. 2002). However, a system may not "depart fundamentally from commonly accepted notions concerning acceptable contours of a seniority system, simply because those rules were dubbed 'seniority.'" Educational requirements or successful completion of a test could not be imposed as a condition on the operation of the seniority system and receive the protections of the seniority proviso. *California Brewers Ass'n v. Bryant, supra* (S.Ct. 1980). An absolute prohibition against employees transferring between departments, even if written into a seniority contract, may not be a protected ancillary to the seniority system. *Hebert v. Monsanto Co.* (5th Cir. 1982).

The ADEA specifically states that a seniority system shall not require or permit the involuntary retirement of any individual because of age. 29 USCA 623(f)(2)(A).

e. Bona Fides of the System

A seniority system will not be protected if its adoption or application is not bona fide or is the "result of an intention to discriminate." If the employer articulates the seniority system as the reason for plaintiff's treatment, the burden is upon the plaintiff to prove lack of bona fides or the illegal motive in defendant's adoption or application of the system. *Pullman-Standard v. Swint* (S.Ct. 1982).

The first focus is upon the origins of the system. In *Teamsters,* while the employer had engaged in racial discrimination in making initial job assignments, there was no evidence that the seniority system itself was a product of that segregation. Had the seniority system been drawn along racial lines, or if it was initiated as a way to deprive women or minorities of job opportunities, the proviso would not have protected it. For example, altering the system in a way that provided greater job security to units that were predominately male soon before a wide-spread layoff was announced suggests illegal motivation for that implementation. *Lorance v. AT & T Technologies* (S.Ct. 1989).

Critical also is whether the seniority system was applied equally to all persons in a color-and gender-blind fashion. In *Teamsters* it was. The white drivers in the city units were treated the same as minority drivers. Had this not been true, if white drivers in the city unit had been granted waivers, this would have been strong evidence of discrimination in the application of the system. Sporadic, hit and miss, or imprecise application of length of service suggests its lack of legitimacy. *Williams v. New Orleans S.S. Ass'n* (5th Cir. 1982).

The system's rationality is important. Systems that are irrational, idiosyncratic, or consist of gerrymandered units suggest improper motive in their creation. In *Teamsters* the units were drawn along rational lines, followed industry practice, and were consistent with National Labor Relations Board certifications, all factors supporting the conclusion that the system was adopted and applied in good faith.

f. Timing the Challenge

The time to challenge a seniority system commences with: 1) its adoption, 2) the day the individual becomes subject to the system, or 3) the day when the system is applied to the injury of the plaintiff. 42 U.S.C.A. 2000e–5(e)(2).

III—11.10 Two Exclusions from Impact Analysis

a. Security Clearance

Requiring persons to have a security clearance might adversely affect those of certain national origins. Nonetheless, Title VII provides that it does not violate the Act for an employer to refuse to hire or to discharge an employee because the position requires such a clearance and the individual is unable to secure the necessary clearance pursuant to any statute or Executive order of the President. 42 U.S.C.A. 2000e–2(g).

b. Veterans' Preferences

Even if providing preferences for veterans were shown to have an adverse impact on women or a racial minority, Title VII provides that "Nothing contained in [the Act] shall be construed to repeal or modify any Federal, State, territorial, or local law creating special rights or preferences for veterans." 42 U.S.C.A. 2000e–11. This protection is limited to lawfully required preferences, and does not preserve from scrutiny the impact of a veteran's preference voluntarily undertaken.

CHAPTER 12

ADVERTISEMENTS AND INQUIRIES

III—12.01 Title VII and the ADEA

a. Advertisements

Title VII and the Age Act make it illegal for covered entities to "print or publish, or cause to be printed or published any notice or advertisement relating to employment * * * indicating a preference, limitation, specification or discrimination based on [a proscribed class]". 42 U.S.C.A. 2000e–3(b). This restriction does not infringe the free speech guarantees of the First Amendment. *Pittsburgh Press Co. v. Pittsburgh Comm'n on Human Relations* (S.Ct. 1973). Terms in advertisements that suggest age or gender preference, such as advertisements for "boys and girls," "students" or "recent graduates" are suspect. 29 CFR 1625.4(a). Improper advertisements also provide direct evidence of discriminatory motive when someone in the class excluded by the advertisement is not hired.

b. Interviews

Title VII and the ADEA do not proscribe making uniform inquiries as to a an applicant's race, sex, national origin, religion, or age. However, as asking applicants to state age or date of birth deters older workers, the inquiry should be accompanied by a notice of ADEA rights, with assurances of non-discrimination. 29 CFR 1625.5.

Employers can uniformly ask for references, educational credentials, and work histories from all applicants. However, as the statutes do proscribe applying neutral standards differently to protected classes, inquiries along such lines should be uniformly directed to all applicants. Inquiries into marital status, family plans, child care, or possible spousal objections, should be avoided, and when directed only at one gender, will support a finding of illegal motivation where the person asked the question is not selected. Inquiries into a woman's pregnancy plans are particularly suspect. *Barbano v. Madison County* (N.D.N.Y. 1988). Cf. *Bruno v. City of Crown Point* (7th Cir. 1991) (female applicant's responses not proved to have influenced decision). Inquiries directed solely to racial minorities on matters such as arrests, criminal convictions, credit records, family situation, or home ownership, likewise will support an inference that the employer relied on the answer, and thus engaged in illegal discrimination when it rejected a minority applicant. *Howard v. Roadway Exp.* (11th Cir. 1984). Inquires about even job related physical abilities of older applicants, when not asked of younger applicants, give rise to an inference of age discrimination if the younger worker is selected.

If information such as age, marital status, pregnancy, number of dependents, etc. is necessary for insurance or other purposes, it should be asked of all persons and preferably only after an offer of employment has been tendered.

The Immigration Reform and Control Act requires employers to verify the eligibility of applicants to work under U.S. immigration law. The employer must demand work eligibility documentation from the applicant, and must refuse employment to alien applicants who fail to supply the required documentation.

III—12.02 Americans with Disabilities Act

a. Pre–Employment Inquiries

The ADA prohibits pre-employment medical examinations and prohibits written or oral inquires as to whether the individual considers himself to have a disability. It prohibits questions concerning conditions that might disclose a disability, such as medications being taken, records of hospitalization, or workers' compensation and insurance claims. *Griffin v. Steeltek, Inc.* (10th Cir. 2001). The prohibition is applicable to *all applicants*, not just individuals with disabilities. 42 U.S.C.A. 12112(d); *Roe v. Cheyenne Mountain Conf. Resort* (10th Cir. 1997).

The employer may describe to applicants the essential job duties and make inquires as to whether the applicant possesses the credentials and ability to perform those duties. For example, if the job requires driving a motor vehicle, the employer may ask: "Do you have a valid driver's license, and are you willing to drive?"

Individuals who are hired notwithstanding being asked illegal questions are not likely to have suffered monetary damage. *Griffin v. Steeltek, Inc.* (10th Cir. 2001). However, if the employee who is asked forbidden questions is not hired, it is presumed that the answers—or refusal to answer—played a role in the employer's decision. In such a case, to avoid liability the employer must establish that it would have made the same decision based on legitimate grounds.

An employee who provides false information to questions that an employer may not legally ask, may not be subsequently terminated because he/she supplied false information. *Downs v. Massachusetts Bay Transp. Auth.* (D. Mass. 1998).

b. *Post–Offer Examinations*

Employers may require a medical examination *after an offer* of employment has been made, but before the commencement of actual employment, if: 1) all new employees are subject to the examination, 2) the results and information are kept confidential, and 3) the information is not thereafter used in a manner inconsistent with the ADA.

A job offer may be revoked if the examination discloses lack of qualifications to perform essential job duties. Thus, an individual was conditionally hired as a pipe fitter and subjected to a physical examination. The examination disclosed that he could not lift 100 lbs. Because the job required that level of lifting, the offer was revoked. As it was "job related" the examination was justified, and the revocation of the offer was proper. *Fuzy v. S & B Engineers & Constructors, Ltd.* (5th Cir. 2003).

Drug testing is *not* an examination. Thus, an employer may give pre-employment or post-offer drug tests without liability, and may require more frequent drug tests of recovering addicts than of other employees. *Buckley v. Consolidated Edison Co.* (2d Cir. 1997).

c. *Post–Employment Examinations*

Employers may encourage employees to have *voluntary* physical examinations as part of a wellness program. It may *require* examinations only if the examination focuses on the ability of the employee to perform necessary job functions, such as eye and hearing tests for drivers or pilots or cardiovascular examinations for strenuous or high risk jobs such as police officers and firefighters. 42 U.S.C.A. 12112(d)(4)(B). If the job involves high risks to others, employers may test for specific infectious diseases. Thus, employees involved in food handling may be tested for HIV, hepatitis, and similar conditions. *EEOC v. Prevo's Family Market* (6th Cir. 1998). *Tice v. Centre Area Transp. Auth.* (3d Cir. 2001) allowed a physical examination of a bus driver who had complained of pain and walking difficulty and there were complaints about his driving, even though other drivers were not routinely examined.

An employer may pre-condition return to work of an injured or previously disabled employee on passing a job related physical examination or test given for the purpose of determining the employee's fitness for essential job duties. *Porter v. U.S. Alumoweld Co.* (4th Cir. 1997). An employer may not test for the ability to perform non-essential duties or limit return to work only if employees are 100% recovered.

III—12.03 Polygraphs

The Employee Polygraph Protection Act of 1988, (29 U.S.C.A. 2001) prohibits private employers from using lie detectors or polygraphs to select employees. The Act does not apply to government employers nor to private employers engaged in security work or the manufacture or distribution of controlled substances. An otherwise subject employer may use a polygraph pursuant to an ongoing investigation involving economic loss if the employee had access to the missing property, the employer has a reasonable suspicion that the employee was involved, and the employee is supplied with a statement as to the loss and the basis for the employer's suspicion. The employee must be informed of his rights under the statute. A test lawfully given may not inquire into sexual matters, political beliefs, or union activity. The employee has a right to counsel, to an advance copy of the questions, may terminate the test, and may secure at its end, the test papers and markings.

Employees may enforce the Act through judicial actions, and if successful they are entitled to reinstatement, promotion, lost wages, compensatory damages and attorneys' fees. *Mennen v. Easter Stores* (N.D. Iowa 1997).

*

PART IV

"TERMS AND CONDITIONS OF EMPLOYMENT"

CHAPTER 13

COMPENSATION

IV—13.01 Generally

The Equal Pay Act of 1963 (29 U.S.C.A. 206(d)), which predated Title VII, requires employers to provide male and female employees "equal pay" for "equal work." Title VII, the ADEA, and the ADA prohibit discrimination with "respect to compensation, terms, conditions, or privileges of employment" "because of" race, color, national origin, religion, age, disability, and sex. The 1866 Civil Rights Act (42 U.S.C.A. 1981) prohibits race discrimination in the "performance, modification and termination" as well as "enjoyment of all benefits, privileges, terms and conditions of the contractual relationship," and by this prohibits racially based pay discrimination. In determining when a pay distinction violates Title VII, courts look to analysis developed under the Equal Pay Act.

"Compensation" includes all compensatory benefits such as bonuses, insurance, vacations, sick leave, clothing allowances, and transportation. It reaches employer sponsored retirement and pension plans even though the benefits are not paid until after the employment relationship is terminated and are made by underwriters distinct from the employer. *Arizona Governing Comm. v. Norris* (S.Ct. 1983).

IV—13.02   The Equal Pay Act of 1963 (EPA)

a. Generally

Coverage of the Equal Pay Act is set by the Fair Labor Standards Act, (29 U.S.C.A. 201). Coverage is determined by whether the employee seeking equal pay is "engaged in commerce," "engaged in the production of goods for commerce," or employed by an "enterprise engaged in commerce." While virtually all employers covered by Title VII are subject to the EPA, the employee-centered basis for coverage of the EPA makes it applicable to small employers not covered by Title VII. The EEOC administers and may judicially enforce the EPA. Private suits may be filed without invoking administrative procedures.

The Equal Pay Act sets an objective standard for determining an employer's obligation. Plaintiff must prove that: 1) the work of the plaintiff was "equal" to the work of an employee of the opposite sex; 2) the "rate" of plaintiff's pay was less than the "rate" of the employee of the opposite sex, and 3) the work of the two employees was performed in the same "establishment." *Plaintiff need not prove gender motivation for the pay difference.* EPA obligations apply regardless of which gender is the victim of the pay difference, thus protecting men as well as women. It does *not* reach pay differences between races, ethnic groups, or those based on age or disability.

If plaintiff establishes these three objective elements, (equal work, unequal pay, same establishment) the burden shifts to the employer to prove that the pay difference was based on (i) a seniority system, (ii) a merit system, (iii) a system that measures the quantity or quality of production, or (iv) "any other factor other than sex."

Compliance with the EPA cannot be accomplished by lowering the wage of the higher paid employee (29 U.S.C.A. 206(d)(1)) or by transferring employees to other jobs. *Hodgson v. Miller Brewing Co.* (7th Cir. 1972). The wage rate of the lower paid employee must be raised, and the past difference in wages is considered unpaid back wages.

b. "Equal Work"

"Equal work" involves jobs, the performance of which requires *equal:* 1) skill, 2) effort, and 3) responsibility; performed under working conditions that are *"similar."* 29 U.S.C.A. 206(d)(1). "Equal" does not mean "identical." Work is "equal" when job duties are *"substantially* equal." *Hein v. Oregon College of Educ.* (9th Cir. 1983). Work is not "equal" when duties are merely similar or comparable. Actual duties performed, not job descriptions or hypothetical assignments, are determinative.

Discriminatory job assignments, or workload discrimination, will violate Title VII, but if the work actually being performed by men and women is not "substantially equal" there is no EPA violation. *Waters v. Turner, Wood & Smith Ins. Agency, Inc.* (11th Cir. 1989).

—*"Effort"* is the physical or mental exertion expended. Work of a qualitatively different nature is not "equal," even if the two jobs require the same level of exertion. For example, a janitorial job that required dusting and light mopping of a large area, was not equal to a janitorial job that required heavy wet mopping of smaller areas simply because the two jobs were outwardly similar and may have been equal in terms of calories expended at the end of the day. *Usery v. Columbia Univ.* (2d Cir. 1977). A male academic's primary duty was to save a flagging academic program and create a graduate course of study. The female administrator's primary duty was to improve outside funding. Because the nature of their effort was not equal, the work was not equal. *Cullen v. Indiana University Bd. of Trustees* (7th Cir. 2003)

—*"Skill"* is the ability or dexterity to perform regular job duties, not abstract skill or unused potential. The jobs of a carpenter and a plumber involve different, and thus unequal skills.

—*"Responsibility"* is the degree of accountability required. It can involve supervisory responsibility, ultimate decision-making authority, or the accountability for consequences attributable to performance. If one bank teller handles small deposits, and another teller manages large interbank transactions, responsibility is different. A coach of the male basketball team may have more responsibility than the coach of the female team in that the male team's coach has more visible public duties and the men's team generates more revenue. *Stanley v. University of Southern Cal.* (9th Cir. 1994). A male academic administrator will have more responsibility than a similarly situated female administrator in a different department where he supervises more employees and his department enrolls more students. *Cullen v. Indiana University Bd. of Trustees, supra* (7th Cir. 2003).

—"*Working conditions*,"—which need only be "*similar*"—is an industrial term of art, meaning conditions that industrial relations experts use to set salary differences. If the condition is not used by such experts to measure salaries, the condition is not within the statutory term. Thus narrowed, "working conditions" encompass the physical surroundings and hazards of the job, such as inside vs. outside work, exposure to extreme temperatures, wetness, noise, fumes, toxic conditions, dust, vibrations, risk of injury, or poor ventilation. "Working conditions" do not include the time of day or shift in which the work is performed. Thus, men doing jobs at night that women perform during the day were working under "similar" conditions. *Corning Glass Works v. Brennan* (S.Ct. 1974).

If plaintiff proves that the two jobs share a "common core of tasks," rendering them largely identical, the employer may identify additional secondary duties that may render the two jobs unequal. Five conditions must be met: 1) The additional duties must actually be performed in the pay period by the employee receiving the extra pay. 2) The extra duties must be regular and recurring. 3) Extra duties must be substantial. Inconsequential chores, such as turning off the lights, starting the morning coffee, or answering infrequent telephone calls do not make otherwise identical jobs unequal. 4) Additional duties of a comparable nature must not be assigned to the lower paid employees. Thus, an additional duty of stocking a soft drink machine at the end of the shift may be set off against the extra duty of the other employee carrying out trash. 5) Extra duties must be rationally related to the pay differential. An employer cannot distinguish otherwise equal jobs by assigning alternative duties to a higher paid employee when such duties normally are compensated at a rate lower than the primary duties. *Shultz v. Wheaton Glass Co.* (3d Cir. 1970).

c. *"Unequal Wage Rate"*

1. "Rate": The *"rate"* of pay between male and females doing equal work must be unequal. "Rate"—not gross salary—is calculated. A female manager of the female portion of a health club was paid a commission rate of 5% of the female membership dues. The male manager of the male portion was paid a commission of 7.5% of male membership dues. Because more females than males were club members, the gross income of the two

managers was nearly the same. Nonetheless, as the wage "rate" was the commission, and this "rate" was different for the male and female managers, the EPA was violated. *Bence v. Detroit Health Corp.* (6th Cir. 1983).

If employees are paid a fixed sum based on relatively short time periods, such as a week or month, gross wages should be translated into an hourly rate. Thus, allowing males to work 40 hours a week and paying them the same weekly wage as females who are assigned to work 48 hours per week would be paying a lesser hourly "rate" to the female employees. *Hein v. Oregon College of Educ.* (9th Cir. 1983). When compensation is set by reference to a longer period (e.g., year), even if distributed at shorter intervals (e.g., monthly), as in the case of professionals or executives, gross salaries would not be translated into an hourly rate. Thus, if two attorneys were paid $100,000 per year, an EPA claim will not be established by showing that the female attorney worked more hours during the year than the male attorney. *Berry v. Bd. of Supervisors of L.S.U.* (5th Cir. 1983)(heavier teaching load of female teacher not an equal pay violation).

2. Inequality: Comparisons and Comparators: Plaintiff must compare her wage rate to that of a male performing equal work. The comparison is not limited to jobs held simultaneously, but can be made with those held in succession. A female's work and pay thus may be compared to her male predecessor or to the male employee who succeeded her.

Lawrence v. CNF Transp., Inc. (8th Cir. 2003). Jobs need not be held in immediate succession. A female employee was paid the same as her immediate male predecessor, but a male employee who preceded them both was paid more. When plaintiff's background more closely resembled the remote predecessor than her immediate predecessor, she may compare her rate of pay to the remote predecessor. *Clymore v. Far–Mar–Co.* (8th Cir. 1983).

Simply because a plaintiff can identify a single employee of the opposite sex doing equal work at a higher rate of pay will not insure plaintiff's recovery if other employees of the opposite sex who perform the same job earn the same or less than plaintiff. In such cases, plaintiff must identify a comparator of the opposite sex whose background and credentials are similar to plaintiff's, but whose pay is greater. *Houck v. VPI* (4th Cir. 1993). An alternative to the "best comparator" approach is to compare plaintiff's wage rate to the *average* wage rate of members of the opposite sex in the establishment performing equal work. If the average rate of the opposite sex is higher than plaintiff's wage rate, a prima facie violation exists. *Heymann v. Tetra Plastics Corp.* (8th Cir. 1981).

d. "Establishment"

The "equal work" of the two employees must be performed in the same "establishment". "Establishment" generally refers to a distinct physical location. It is narrower than "employer" but broader than "department" or "unit." For example, a retail enterprise may have five stores selling identical products, each in a different neighborhood. Presumably, each store would be a different "establishment." Departments within the store, such as women's clothing and men's clothing departments in a single store, would be within the same "establishment." Separate physical locations may be within the same "establishment" if: 1) there is central authority for hiring and maintaining employee relations, 2) records are centrally maintained, and 3) there is regular movement of employees between the distinct locations. 29 CFR 1620.9.

e. Defenses

If plaintiff establishes equal work and unequal pay between the sexes in the same establishment, the employer avoids liability only by establishing that the pay difference was attributable to systems of: 1) seniority, 2) merit, 3) quality or quantity of work, or 4) any other "factor other than sex." The employer's burden is to establish the existence of such a "system," that it was imposed in good faith, and that it is gender neutral. Merely because a facially neutral system disadvantages one gender will not deprive the system of its bona fides. Thus, an employer may use seniority as a wage setting factor even though the more senior, and thus higher paid workers, are men.

Systems of merit or seniority need not be formalized, but they must be objective, rational, and uniformly applied. Haphazard, idiosyncratic pay patterns are not justified by subjective, ad hoc, or post facto conclusions that in one case that the higher paid employee had more "seniority" and in the next case possessed more "merit." Such distinctions are not the product of a "system," and do not carry the employer's burden. *Brock v. Georgia Southwestern College* (11th Cir. 1985).

"Other than sex" requires the "factor" to be gender neutral. Gender distinctions in actuarial tables upon which different pension deductions were based, was not based on "any other factor other than sex;" "sex is exactly what [the actuarial table] is based on." *Los Angeles Dep't of Water & Power v. Manhart* (S.Ct. 1978). Even a factor neutral on its face is not "other than sex" if it perpetuates the employer's past sex discrimination or segregation. Thus, "night shift" could not be a "factor other than sex" if the employer denies women the opportunity to work in the night shift. *Corning Glass Works v. Brennan* (S.Ct. 1974). A training program that excluded women was not a "factor other than sex." *Shultz v. First Victoria Nat. Bank* (5th Cir. 1969). If defendant previously set salaries because of sex, and continues to base current salaries on its past rates, this perpetuates past sex discrimination by *this* employer and deprives the "factor"—past salary—of its gender neutrality. *Bazemore v. Friday* (S.Ct. 1986). However, simply because a "factor" results in statistically lower salaries for one gender does not preclude the factor from being "other than sex." Thus, where the employer based its starting salaries on the past salary *at another employer*, this factor did not perpetuate *defendant*'s past discrimination, and could be a "factor other than sex." *Kouba v. Allstate Ins. Co.* (9th Cir. 1982).

"Factor" presupposes a level of rationality weightier than the "legitimate, non-discriminatory reason" but less burdensome than "business necessity." While some informality and subjectivity are not fatal (*Taylor v. White* (8th Cir. 2003)), a reason will not be a "factor other than sex" if it is so unpredictable and erratic that it reflects little more than the employer's day-to-day personnel needs. *Shultz v. First Victoria Nat. Bank* (5th Cir. 1969). (erratic, ill defined "training program" not "factor other than sex."). Some authority holds that the "factor" must derive from unique characteristics of the same job; from the individual's training, experience, or ability; or from special circumstances connected with the employer's business. *Glenn v. General Motors, Corp.* (11th Cir. 1988). Under this standard, premium pay to male employees because they were the "head of household" would not be a "factor" because it did not relate to employee job performance or to the employer's *business* needs. 29 CFR 1620.21. Other courts hold that so long as it is *rational,* the "factor" need not be connected to employee performance or serve business needs. *Kouba v. Allstate Ins. Co.* (9th Cir. 1982). Under this standard a program which paid a premium to employees who were the "head of the household" would be a legitimate "factor" even though it had no *business* purpose. *EEOC v. J.C. Penney Co.* (6th Cir. 1988).

There are a wide range of gender neutral and rationally applied factors that meet the requirements for the defense: 1) shifts: day vs. evening; holiday pay; weekend work; 2) temporary or part time vs. full time or permanent; 3) training programs whereby trainees receive more (or less) than incumbent workers, 4) education premiums; 5) differences in background or experience, 6) past work record or performance; 7) "red circling" or temporarily maintaining a higher rate of pay while performing a lower level job; 8) salary matching to attract or retain a worker. *Taylor v. White* (8th Cir. 2003).

IV—13.03   Title VII

a.   *Reconciliation with the EPA: The "Bennett Amendment"*

Title VII liability requires proof that the difference in compensation was "because of" plaintiff's membership in a protected class. The employer's motive is key. Although the standards are different, pay distinctions between genders can thus violate both Title VII and the Equal Pay Act. Title VII attempts a reconciliation with a provision known as the "Bennett Amendment" that allows employers to make pay distinctions "if such differentiation is authorized by [the Equal Pay Act.]" 42 U.S.C.A. 2000e–2(h).

County of Washington v. Gunther (S.Ct. 1981) accepted that the work of male prison guards and female guards was not "equal" within the meaning

of the Equal Pay Act, and thus could not violate the
EPA. The employer argued that under the "Bennett
Amendment," a finding that the EPA was not violated precluded a sex-based pay discrimination complaint under Title VII. The Court disagreed, holding
that a pay difference is "authorized" by the EPA
only when it is based on one of the four statutory
defenses in the EPA (seniority, merit, quality or
quantity of work, or "any other factor other than
sex."). Title VII liability is premised on motive. A
finding that work of male and female prison guards
was unequal, did not preclude plaintiff from proving
that the pay difference was *motivated* by sex in
violation of Title VII. Thus, the "Bennett Amendment" simply makes the EPA defenses applicable to
Title VII claims of sex based pay discrimination.

b. *Proving Motive*

Facial gender distinctions, such as different salary scales drawn along racial or gender lines, carry
their own indicia of illegal motive. Basing raises on
prior discriminatory salaries perpetuates the race or
gender motivation originally used by this employer
to set base salaries. *Bazemore v. Friday* (S.Ct.
1986). Illegal motive is not established, however,
simply because an employer is aware that a neutral
factor is producing lower wages in job categories
occupied by women or minorities, even if there is an
acknowledgment that such differences are "unfair."
AFSCME v. Washington (9th Cir. 1985). Ostensibly
neutral distinctions, such as seniority, will violate
Title VII only if plaintiff proves that defendant

adopted the system to disadvantage a protected class.

Statistics can be used to prove motive. However, a demonstration that on the average one class of employees earns less than another class of employees in comparable jobs does not, standing alone, create an inference that individual salary differences were the product of illegal motivation. Salary differences between *classes* often are attributable to legitimate independent variables such experience, education, seniority, and performance evaluations. Merely eliminating chance as an hypothesis for an observed average difference in pay does not create an inference that the difference was "because of" race or sex. *Coble v. Hot Springs School Dist. No. 6* (8th Cir. 1982). Nonetheless, a statistical technique known as multiple regression analysis holds constant identified independent variables such as experience, education, seniority, and past performance, and evaluates whether the illegal, dependent factor mathematically is the most likely explanation for the salary pattern. Such a technique can establish illegal motive. Failure of plaintiff's analysis to account for all possible variables is not fatal if the analysis allows a fact finder to conclude that it is more likely than not that impermissible discrimination accounts for the salary differences. That some possible variables were not included in the study goes to the weight of plaintiff's evidence, not to its admissibility. *Bazemore v. Friday, supra* (S.Ct. 1986).

Plaintiff can prove motive through unexplained disparate treatment:

1. Plaintiff's Prima Facie Case: Plaintiff must prove that as a member of a protected class he/she is paid less than individuals in a different class, and that there is significant similarity in their jobs. Simply because two different jobs have an abstract "comparable worth" and receive non-comparable pay, is not sufficient to establish improperly motivated pay discrimination. *AFSCME v. Washington, supra* (9th Cir. 1985). Some courts require plaintiffs to carry the relatively heavy burden of proving that the work of plaintiff and an appropriate comparator are *"equal"* under standards of the Equal Pay Act. *Tademe v. Saint Cloud State University* (8th Cir. 2003) (equal work standard applied even to claims of race discrimination). Other courts adapt a Title VII standard utilized in other contexts and require plaintiff to prove only that "similarly situated" individuals from different protected classes were "dissimilarly treated." Jobs must be more than "comparable," but need not be "substantially equal." *Miranda v. B & B Cash Grocery Store, Inc.* (11th Cir. 1992).

2. Defendant's Burden: Where plaintiff initially carries the relatively light burden of demonstrating "similar" work and dissimilar pay, the burden shifted to defendant is correspondingly light. Applying the Title VII model, defendant must "articulate" a reason for the pay difference that is "legitimate and non-discriminatory." *Miranda v. B & B Cash Grocery Stores. Inc., supra* (11th Cir. 1992). If defendant articulates such a reason, the burden re-shifts to plaintiff to present evidence indicating the pre-

text of the articulated reason, and ultimately to carry the burden of persuading the fact finder of defendant's illegal motive. *Supra,* 9.03. Courts adopting the Equal Pay Act model and thus impose on plaintiff the initial burden of proving "equal work," shift to defendant the heavier Equal Pay Act burden of proving that the pay difference was a consequence of a "factor other than sex." *Korte v. Diemer* (6th Cir. 1990).

c. *Impact Analysis*

Objective factors such as education or experience may be shown to have an adverse affect on classes that lack those credentials. However, the EPA specifically allows distinctions based on systems of seniority or merit, systems that measure quality or quantity of work, or on "any other factor other than sex." This defense is incorporated into Title VII at least for charges of sex based pay discrimination. In language similar to the Equal Pay Act, the ADEA allows "differentiation based on reasonable factors other than age." 29 U.S.C.A. 623(f)(1). Thus, employers may set salaries using seniority, merit systems, or *any other* legitimate factor (such as education or experience) regardless of the impact on a particular gender or age group. Business necessity of the "factor" need not be established.

CHAPTER 14

PENSION, LEAVE, AND BENEFIT PROGRAMS

IV—14.01   Title VII and Fringe Benefits

a.   Generally

The statutes reach discrimination in the operation of pension, health care, leave, retirement, and similar fringe benefits. There is no obligation on employers to provide particular benefits, but if provided, employers cannot allocate benefits using proscribed classifications. Thus, an employer's defined benefit retirement program violated Title VII when it made gender distinctions in the amount of contributions required of employees. *Los Angeles Dept. of Water and Power v. Manhart* (S.Ct. 1978). An employer sponsored defined contribution plan that allowed pay-out distinctions based on gender of the retirees also violates Title VII, even if participation in the plan was optional, it was administered by independent underwriters, and it allowed retirees to elect gender neutral options, such as lump sum payments or fixed year annuities. *Arizona Governing Committee v. Norris* (S.Ct. 1983). *Manhart* and *Norris* preclude employer sponsored pension programs that rely on mortality tables drawn along race or gender lines.

b. Pregnancy

Title VII defines "because of sex" to include "pregnancy, childbirth, or related medical conditions." This "definition" establishes an affirmative obligation. "Women affected by pregnancy, childbirth, or related medical conditions shall be treated the same for all employment related purposes, including receipt of benefits under fringe benefit programs, as other persons not so affected but similar in their ability or inability to work." 42 U.S.C.A. 2000e-(k).

Again, an employer with no health care benefits for employees need not provide benefits for pregnancy and childbirth. However, where the employer provides employee health care benefits, the benefit plan must include coverage for pregnancy, childbirth, and related medical conditions at parity with benefits provided for similar medical conditions. For example, a $100 deductible and a $100 co-pay obligation generally imposed in an employer's hospitalization plan, cannot require a $200 deductible or a $200 co-pay for pregnancy or childbirth hospitalization. It is permissible, however, for an employer to provide pregnancy benefits *greater* than those provided for other medical conditions. An employer does not violate Title VII by having no deductible for pregnancy while imposing a deductible on other medical conditions. *California Fed. Sav. & Loan Ass'n v. Guerra* (S.Ct. 1987).

Health benefits given to employees need not cover *dependents* of employees, and if provided, those benefits may differ from benefits provided employees. However, when dependents are eligible to receive health benefits, the plan must cover the pregnancy and childbirth of employee spouses at the same level of other benefits provided to *dependents*. Excluding pregnancy of dependent spouses from the dependent plan constitutes *sex* discrimination against male employees in that female employees would have family pregnancy covered regardless of dependent coverage, while male employees would not receive a pregnancy benefit even though dependents generally were covered. Failure of the plan to include pregnancy of dependent *children* of employees, however, is not sex discrimination in that an exclusion of children affects male and female employees equally. *Newport News Shipbuilding & Dry Dock Co. v. EEOC* (S.Ct. 1983).

Title VII expressly provides that nothing shall *require* an employer to pay for health insurance benefits for abortion, except where the life of the mother would be endangered if the fetus were carried to term or except where medical complications have arisen from an abortion. An employer is free, however, to provide health care benefits for abortions. 42 U.S.C.A. 2000e-(k).

Leaves for pregnancy, childbirth, and related conditions must be granted under terms allowed those who have similar disabling conditions. Thus, if an employer formally or informally allows paid or unpaid leave for surgery or to recuperate from illnesses or injury the employer must grant similar sick leave rights for pregnancy and childbirth. If light duty assignments are granted generally to persons with medical conditions that preclude normal work, similar light duty assignments must be allowed pregnant employees. *Ensley-Gaines v. Runyon* (6th Cir. 1996). Cf. *Urbano v.Continental Airlines, Inc.* (5th Cir. 1998)(granting light duty only to workers who suffered *occupational injuries* was not discriminatory when light duty was denied a pregnant employee. Only if pregnancy was treated differently than other *off-duty* injuries or illnesses would denial to a pregnant worker be discriminatory).

It is neither sex nor pregnancy discrimination to refuse leave to care for a child. *Piantanida v. Wyman Ctr., Inc.* (8th Cir. 1997). (Such leave may be required under the Family and Medical Leave Act. *Infra,* 14.04) It is sex discrimination to grant parental leave to women not medically related to childbirth, while denying parental leave to similarly situated male employees. *Schafer v. Board of Pub. Educ., Pittsburgh* (3d Cir. 1990).

Treating pregnancy in benefit programs the same as other medical conditions may be shown to have an adverse impact on women, which, if so, must be justified by the employer as a "business necessity." Increased costs are not generally a "business necessity." *Nashville Gas Co. v. Satty* (S.Ct. 1977). A uniformly imposed one-year vesting period before an employee could claim sick leave may have an adverse impact on women who become pregnant. If so, it is not justified in terms of saving the employer costs or by an assumption that a delay in providing sick leave benefits encourages long term employment. *EEOC v. Warshawsky & Co.* (N.D.Ill. 1991). Nonetheless, an employer need not grant leave to pregnant workers when to do so would circumvent generally imposed performance standards or work rules. For example, an employer had a strict attendance policy for probationary employees, permitting only three absences during their first 90 days of employment. The pregnant employee was denied leave beyond the three days and was dismissed when she was absent because of her pregnancy. Though the rule adversely affected pregnant women, the employer was not required to demonstrate its business necessity. To hold otherwise, the court held, would virtually guarantee leave for all pregnant women, a special grant that Congress did not intend to make. *Stout v. Baxter Healthcare Corp.* (5th Cir. 2002).

IV—14.02   The Age Act

a.   *Benefit Distinctions*

The ADEA allows employers to observe actuarial premised age-based provisions of bona fide retirement, pension, and insurance plans. 29 U.S.C.A. 623(f)(2)(B). "No such employee benefit plan * * * shall excuse the failure to hire any individual, and no such * * * plan shall permit the involuntary retirement of any individual * * *." *Id.* Plans may reduce benefits paid to workers based on age where the amount of payment or cost incurred on behalf of the older worker is no less than the costs incurred on behalf of a younger worker. While benefits may be reduced based on actuarial costs associated with aging, forcing older workers to pay greater amounts to *maintain* benefits, even if based on increased costs, is not authorized. Employers may, however, offer *voluntary* participation in a plan that permits older workers to maintain the same benefit level by increasing employee contributions, if the increased contribution reflects actual increased costs associated with aging. The Act prohibits cessation of or reduction of the rate of retirement benefit accrual because of age, or cessation or reduction of allocations to an employee's retirement account because of age. A plan may, however, impose (without regard to age) a limitation on the amount of retirement benefits the plan provides or a limitation on the number of years of participation which are taken into account for determining benefits. 29 U.S.C.A. 623(i).

The employer has the burden of proving the lawfulness of plans. 29 U.S.C.A. 623(f)(2). A plan will be bona fide only if its terms have been accurately described in writing and actually provides the benefits in accordance with the terms. The Act has complex provisions stating with some exactness the content permitted in bona fide plans.

b. Early Retirement Incentives

Employers are authorized to offer "voluntary early retirement incentive plans." 29 U.S.C.A. 623(f)(2)(B)(ii). Such plans may not exclude or disadvantage older workers on the basis of age. The decision to accept an early retirement incentive must be voluntary in that an employer may not pressure employees to participate through suggestions of retaliation or indications that unless the employee participates she will be laid off without benefits. *Hebert v. Mohawk Rubber Co.* (1st Cir. 1989). The Act allows setting a minimum age as a condition of eligibility for normal or early retirement benefits (*e.g*, only available upon reaching age 60), but may not limit inducements to a younger age group (*e.g.*, only those age 50–55). 29 U.S.C.A. 623(*l*)(1)(a).

c. *Waiver*

Employees who retire may be asked to waive ADEA claims, and such waivers can be imposed as a condition of participation in an early retirement program. To be binding on the employee the waiver must be written and voluntarily executed. There are eight additional objective requirements: 1) the language must be in "plain English" understandable by an average person; 2) it must specifically refer to rights under the ADEA; 3) it may not attempt to waive future claims; 4) it must provide consideration beyond that which the employee is entitled to receive under existing pension or compensation schemes; 5) it must advise the employee to consult an attorney; 6) it must permit at least 21 days for the employee to review the proposed waiver, or 45 days if the waiver is requested in conjunction with an incentive program; 7) if it is part of an incentive program, all eligible employees must be informed about the program and its eligibility factors, along with ages of individuals not eligible; and 8) the agreement must provide 7 more days after execution in which the employee can revoke. 29 U.S.C.A. 626(f)(1). Failure of the waiver to meet these standards does not violate the Act. It merely prohibits the employer from interposing the waiver in defense of alleged ADEA violations. Prior to challenging the waiver, the employee need not return the consideration he was paid for its execution. *Oubre v. Entergy Operations, Inc.* (S.Ct. 1998).

IV—14.03 The Americans With Disabilities Act (ADA)

a. Leave and the Duty to Accommodate

The ADA imposes on employers an affirmative obligation to make "reasonable accommodations" to the known conditions of qualified individuals with disabilities. Even if leave or work rule adjustments are not normally allowed, the duty to make reasonable accommodations requires employers to grant individuals with disabilities reasonable periods of unpaid leave or modest schedule adjustments necessary to treat or adjust to the disability. *Ward v. Massachusetts Health Research Institute* (1st Cir. 2000). See, *infra,* 21.06.

b. Benefit Coverage

The ADA imposes no obligation to have insurance programs, even if the failure to do so has an adverse impact on persons with disabilities. *Alexander v. Choate* (S.Ct. 1985). If the employer has a benefit program, the employer may not refuse to hire an applicant with a disability, who is regarded as having a disability, or who has a record of having such a disability because of a perceived economic impact such a person might have on the employer's insurance or benefit program. 29 CFR 1630.16(f) Appendix. Nor may an employer exclude such a person from the general coverage of the benefit program because of the individual's condition. *Carparts Dist. Cent., Inc. v. Automotive Wholesaler's Ass'n* (1st Cir. 1994). Thus, an HIV patient or a person with a diabetes may not be refused employment because of such conditions, and once hired may not be denied health insurance coverage because of their condition. Nor may employers make such distinctions because a person with a relationship to the applicant has, is regarded as having, or has a record of having, a disability. Thus, an applicant could not be refused employment because a spouse or a child suffers from a debilitating condition.

c.   Benefit Distinctions

Similar to the Age Act, the ADA permits bona fide insurance and benefit plans to utilize underwriting standards to classify risks, and to administer risk-based plans consistent with state law. 42 U.S.C.A. 12201(c). While a person with a disability may not be denied participation in an employer's health care program, the program itself may limit or deny coverage for pre-existing conditions, and may utilize bona fide, actuarial distinctions that limit risks to categories that contain *both* disabled and non-disabled persons. For example, a plan may provide amounts for eye care that differ from amounts provided other medical conditions. The plan may have different caps based on actuarial distinctions between illnesses or conditions, such as a maximum benefit for physical therapy. Co-pay obligations may vary, for example, by imposing on patients greater obligations for prescriptions than for office visits.

The ADA's permission for plans to make bona fide actuarial distinctions between different types of illnesses that include both disabled and non-disabled persons, is qualified by the Mental Health Parity Act of 1996, 42 U.S.C.A. 300gg–5. Subject to a number of limiting qualifications, this Act requires health insurance that provides mental health benefits, to provide the same level of mental health benefits as is provided for physical conditions.

If a plan limits benefits for a particular type of disability (*e.g.*, blindness or deafness), the employer carries the burden of proving that the limitation is bona fide, and that it is not being used as a subterfuge to avoid obligations under the ADA. In such case, the mere fact that there are actuarial grounds for a distinction will not suffice.

IV—14.04 Family and Medical Leave Act of 1993 (FMLA)

a. *Leave Rights*

The Family and Medical Leave Act (FMLA) imposes on *covered* employers an affirmative duty to provide unpaid leave to *qualified* employees: 1) for the birth, adoption, or foster placement in order to care for the new child; 2) to care for a spouse, child, or parent with a "serious health condition" or 3) because a "serious health condition" renders the employee unable to work.

"Serious health condition" means illness, injury, or impairment that requires either inpatient care in a hospital or continuing treatment by a health care provider. For a child's medical condition to warrant the grant of leave to the parent, the child must be absent from school for at least three days. The FMLA does not require the grant of leave time for routine non-incapacitating conditions (e.g., strained knee), short term illnesses (e.g., flu), physical examinations, or routine dental work. *DuCharme v. Cape Indus., Inc.* (E.D.Mich. 2002).

While required leave is unpaid, the employer must maintain existing health care benefits with the caveat that should the employee not return to work, the employee may be liable for these costs. The employee taking FMLA mandated leave is entitled to return to the former position or its equivalent. Employers cannot ask employees to perform job duties during their leave and discipline them if they refuse. *Arban v. West Pub. Corp.* (6th Cir. 2003).

The leave may be as much as 12 weeks in a 12 month period. The employee is not entitled to these 12 weeks on an intermittent or reduced working schedule for the purpose of giving birth or for adopting or receiving a foster child. However, leave to care for one's own "serious health condition" or that of a spouse, child or parent may be taken on an intermittent or reduced leave schedule. If the employee requests an intermittent or reduced working schedule, the employer may require the employee to transfer temporarily to an available alternative position if that position better accommodates the need for intermittent leave.

If the employer provides *paid* leave the employee may elect, or the employer may require, the employee to substitute such accrued paid vacation or personal leave time to care for a new child, or use accrued paid sick leave to attend to his own serious health condition, or to care for a child, spouse, or parent with a serious medical condition.

b. Employee notice required

The employee must give the employer 30 days advance notice of the intention to take FMLA authorized leave. If the employee is seeking leave to care for a serious health condition or that of a spouse, child or parent, and the treatment is to begin in less than 30 days, the employee must provide such notice as is practicable. Failure of the employee to give proper notice warrants denial of the leave. Employees who simply absent themselves from work without giving notice, may be discharged even if the absence was caused by their health condition or that of family members. *Collins v. NTN–Bower Corp.* (7th Cir. 2001). Nonetheless, the employer may receive practical or constructive notice from the conduct of the employee, without the employee mentioning the statute or requesting its benefits. For example, where the worker collapses on the job and is taken to the hospital, no formal request for FMLA leave need be made. Where an employee was repeatedly found sleeping on job, left abruptly telling co-workers he was ill, and when his home was reached, his sister replied that he was "very sick," this may be sufficient notice to warrant the grant of leave, and prohibit retaliation against the employee for his absences. *Byrne v. Avon Products, Inc.* (7th Cir. 2003).

c. *Employer notice*

Ragsdale v. Wolverine World Wide, Inc. (S.Ct. 2002) addressed a Department of Labor regulation that required employers to notify employees in advance if FMLA authorized leave was to be deducted from the employer's more generous leave program. The employer provided 30 weeks of unpaid medical leave. To undergo cancer treatments the employee exhausted the 30 weeks, and requested the additional 12 weeks guaranteed by the FMLA (for a total of 42 weeks). The employer denied the request on the grounds that in granting the initial 30 weeks it had deducted the 12 weeks of leave required by the FMLA. Plaintiff was terminated when she did not return to work after 30 weeks of leave. The employer had failed to notify the employee, as required by Department of Labor regulations, of her rights under the FMLA and that her FMLA leave would be subsumed in the 30 weeks leave granted to her by the employer. The Court held that the notice obligation would unduly discourage employers from adopting leave provisions more generous than those required by the FMLA, and because of this, the regulation was inconsistent with the Act. The Court indicated, however, that employers may be required to notify the employee of their FMLA rights, particularly the right to take part time or intermittent leave to treat a medical condition, if the failure to do so might influence the employee's choices.

d. Non–Retaliation

An employee who claims FMLA leave may not be discriminated against because of that claim. Thus, an employee who is dismissed for "excessive absences" will have a claim under FMLA when the absences were authorized by FMLA. Whether the employer was motivated by the employee's exercise of FMLA rights or by legitimate reasons will be an issue of fact that will be addressed using Title VII models. Thus, where an employee was dismissed shortly after returning from FMLA leave, and the articulated reason for the dismissal was "lack of effectiveness," the court found from direct evidence that the articulated reason was a pretext. *Doebele v. Sprint/United Management Co.* (10th Cir. 2003) (complaints about "excessive absences" and the burden of the absence on other employees)

e. Coverage: Employees Protected

1. Employers Covered: The FMLA covers only employers that have *50* or more employees for 20 or

more calendar workweeks in the current or preceding year. The FMLA is applicable to state and local governments and, notwithstanding the Eleventh Amendment, it may be enforced against state entities by private litigants. *Nevada Dep't of Human Resources v. Hibbs* (S.Ct. 2003)

2. Employees Eligible: To be eligible for the leave the employee must have been employed by a covered employer for at least 12 months and during the previous 12 month period provided at least 1,250 hours of service.

The FMLA does not supersede State or local statutes that have broader coverage or impose on employers an obligation to grant more generous benefits.

IV—14.05 Employee Retirement Income Security Act (ERISA)

ERISA (29 U.S.C.A. 1001) sets minimum standards of fiscal responsibility for administrators of benefit and pension plans, a complex statute beyond the scope of this work. See, Conison, EMPLOYEE BENEFITS LAW IN A NUTSHELL (2d Ed. 1998). The Act makes it unlawful to discriminate against a covered individual because he may achieve a benefit under a covered plan. Thus, it violates the ERISA to dismiss an employee to deprive him of a retirement benefit. *Hazen Paper Co. v. Biggins* (S.Ct. 1993).

CHAPTER 15

WORKING ENVIRONMENT AND HARASSMENT

IV—15.01 Generally: "Adverse Action"

The statutes make it illegal to "limit, segregate, or classify employees in a way which would tend to deprive them of employment opportunities," because of membership in a protected class, or to discriminate in regard to "terms, conditions, privileges of employment." This language is "not limited to economic or tangible discrimination, * * * [but] strikes at the entire spectrum of disparate treatment." *Meritor Savings Bank, FSB v. Vinson* (S.Ct. 1986). The Court cautioned, however, that the statutes "do not reach genuine but innocuous differences." *Oncale v. Sundowner Offshore Services* (S.Ct. 1998). Courts will not sit as super-personnel departments reviewing daily management directives, differences in office aesthetics, or criticism that results in no more than a bruised ego. *Harlston v. McDonnell Douglas Corp.* (8th Cir. 1994). A transfer to a different location that involves only minor changes in working conditions and no reduction in pay or benefits is not actionable simply because the new job site is less convenient for the employee. *Brown v. Lester E. Cox Med. Ctrs.* (8th Cir. 2002). Assignment of a teacher to a particular class, or even to a different school, does not affect a "a term and condition of employment." *Sanchez v. Denver Public Schools* (10th Cir. 1998). However, a transfer to a job with different stature or responsibility, making it less professionally fulfilling, does affect a "term and condition of employment" even if economic benefits are identical. *Stewart v. Ashcroft* (D.C.Cir. 2003).

IV—15.02   Segregation

Segregation in the workplace by race or national origin creates an oppressive, demeaning working environment and thus affects "conditions of employment." Employers may not allocate working areas, toilets, or eating areas by race or national origin, nor may they sponsor or organize social events or athletic competitions along racial or ethnic lines. *Firefighters Institute for Racial Equality v. St. Louis* (8th Cir. 1977). Segregation of customers by directing them to employees of a similar race or ethnic background creates an oppressive environment for employees. *Rogers v. EEOC* (5th Cir. 1971). However, the employer has no affirmative obligation to eliminate self-segregation of employees during non-working hours in eating areas or at social events. *Domingo v. New England Fish Co.* (9th Cir. 1984).

Unlike racial segregation, sex segregation of toilet facilities and changing rooms to preserve gender privacy is consistent with societal norms, and thus does not create an oppressive environment for women. Indeed, an employer's refusal to have distinct toilets and changing facilities for women may create, or contribute to, an oppressive environment. Allowing facilities to become so unsanitary that they present health hazzards unique to women can adversely affect working conditions of women.

Unions may not segregate hiring halls or administer bargaining units organized along gender or racial lines. *EEOC v. Int'l Longshoremen's Ass'n* (5th Cir. 1975). Employment agencies may not segregate their files, lists, or referral services. *Barnes v. Rourke* (M.D.Tenn. 1973).

IV—15.03   Grooming and Clothing

a.   Race and National Origin

Subjecting one race or ethnic group to a grooming standard not imposed on other races is sufficiently humiliating to create an oppressive environment. But, *uniformly* imposed grooming standards do not create an oppressive environment simply because a style that an employee prefers is identified with a particular race or ethnic group. Thus, prohibiting women from wearing "corn row" hairstyles is not race discrimination because the style had become associated with black women. Nor is it race discrimination to prohibit all male employees from having long sideburns or facial hair because men of one culture prefer such a style. *Smith v. Delta Air Lines, Inc.* (5th Cir. 1973).

Prohibiting facial hair might affect a immutable racial characteristic where genetic conditions make it painful and medically inadvisable for a disproportionate number of men of a particular race to shave. If so, defendant would have to prove a "business necessity" for the rule. Mere desire to maintain an image or comply with customer expectations is not a "business necessity." *Bradley v. Pizzaco of Nebraska, Inc.* (8th Cir. 1993).

b. Sex

Grooming requirements will create an offensive working environment only if they impose a significantly greater burden on one gender. Requiring men to wear short hair, while allowing women to have hair of any length or requiring employees to wear "business attire," which means jacket and tie for men and a "feminine suit" or dress for women, is not a difference in treatment that adversely affects conditions of employment. Requiring a T.V. newswoman to apply "feminine touches" is not actionable. *Craft v. Metromedia, Inc.* (8th Cir. 1985). Requiring all employees to have healthy weights is not discriminatory simply because the height/weight ratio differs for men and women, if those differences reflect natural weight differences between genders.

Grooming standards that impose a significantly greater burden on one gender do affect a condition of employment, as where female employees must remain svelte but male employees are permitted to become portly. *Laffey v. Northwest Airlines, Inc.* (D.C.Cir. 1976). Requiring women employees to wear provocative clothing may be humiliating itself, or if it provokes sexual advances from customers, it creates a working environment more burdensome for women. Even if the prescribed clothing is not provocative, it affects a term of employment when the required clothing places women in an inferior position, as where men were permitted to wear business attire of their choice, but women were required to wear a uniform ensemble selected by the employer. *Carroll v. Talman Fed. Sav. & Loan Ass'n* (7th Cir. 1979).

If an employer imposes a burdensome demand on a single gender workforce, such as a draconian maximum weight, this affects a term of employment. If it is imposed *"because of"* the sex of the employees, Title VII is violated. *Gerdom v. Continental Airlines, Inc.* (9th Cir. 1982).

c. *Religion*

Title VII prohibits discrimination "because of" religion, and defines "religion" to include "all aspects of religious observance and practice, as well as belief, unless the employer demonstrates that he is unable to reasonably accommodate an individual's religious observance or practice without undue hardship." 42 U.S.C.A. 2000e-(j). Religious "observances and practices" may call for particular grooming, such as facial hair for men, head covering, or a particular kind of clothing. An employer can enforce a dress or grooming standard that conflicts with a requested religious accommodation only if waiving the standard would impose on the employer an "undue hardship." *Infra,* 19.03.

IV—15.04   Language Rules

Discrimination against a person because she cannot speak English, or cannot speak it fluently, is not facial national origin discrimination. *Garcia v. Rush–Presbyterian–St.Luke's Medical Center* (7th Cir. 1981). Even if it were, the ability to communicate with the employer, fellow employees, or customers would make the ability to speak English with minimal fluency a Bona Fide Occupational Qualification. *Fragante v. Honolulu* (9th Cir. 1989). Distinguishing between applicants based on an *accent* deemed "foreign," is facial national origin discrimination. But speaking without a heavy accent can be a BFOQ, as in the case of teachers or radio announcers. *Bina v. Providence College* (1st Cir. 1994)(teacher)

At one time the EEOC asserted that prohibiting bi-lingual employees from speaking their native language at the work place necessarily created a hostile working environment for persons with non-U.S. national origins. The courts rejected this position. *Garcia v. Spun Steak Co.* (9th Cir. 1993). Nonetheless, prohibiting bi-lingual employees from speaking their native language at the work place might be shown to have an adverse impact on those of non-Anglo national origins, if a significant number of persons are disciplined for violating the rule. Such proof would require the employer to prove the rule's "business necessity." "Business necessity" may be established if speaking another language in public while on duty would be inappropriate. *Jurado v. Eleven–Fifty Corp.* (9th Cir. 1987)(radio announcer). However, it is unlikely that discomfort of the employer with employees speaking a different language would be a "business necessity."

Relative fluency standards will favor applicants from the nations where the preferred language is native. Data can probably be generated demonstrating the impact of English fluency tests on those whose origins are non-English speaking nations. If so, the employer will have to demonstrate the "business necessity" of a relative fluency standard. Only if the relative skill has a significant relationship to actual job duties (e.g., translator or teacher) will the test be sustained. *de la Cruz v. N.Y. City Human Resources Admin.* (2d Cir. 1996).

IV—15.05   Harassment

a.   Generally

When, "because of" an employee's class, an "employer" causes the "workplace [to be] permeated with discriminatory intimidation, ridicule, and insult that is sufficiently severe or pervasive to alter the conditions of the victim's employment" the employer will be in violation of the statutes. *Harris v. Forklift Sys., Inc.* (S.Ct. 1993). Plaintiff must establish three elements: 1) an oppressive atmosphere, 2) a causal link between the conduct and a protected class; and that 3) the conduct and motivation are attributable to a defined "employer." Harassment has three potential sources: a) Management—the alter ego of the employer, b) Supervisors—employees empowered by the "employer" to alter another employee's working conditions, and c) Co-workers of the plaintiff. The nature of plaintiff's proof will vary with the source of the harassment.

b. Tangible Benefits ("Quid Pro Quo")

An employee denied a tangible job benefit, (*e.g.*, promotion, dismissal, pay) because of his race, ethnic origin, religion, sex, age, or disability has a claim. The "employer" is liable for improperly motivated denial of tangible benefit even if the "employer" had an express policy proscribing discrimination and was unaware of the decision or of the supervisor's motivation. *Burlington Industries, Inc. v. Ellerth* (S.Ct. 1998).

An early issue was whether an employee (male or female) denied a tangible employment benefit because he/she refused to have a *sexual relationship* with a decisionmaker was a victim of sex discrimination or merely of a failed social relationship. The Court held that taking action against an employee because the employee rejected a supervisor's sexual advances is "because of sex." *Meritor Savings Bank, FSB v. Vinson* (S.Ct. 1986). A female employee also states a claim where she was threatened with a tangible loss if she did not have sex with her supervisor, and she complies with the demand. A threat may be implied if the words or conduct of the supervisor would communicate to a reasonable woman in plaintiff's position that her participation in a sexual relationship was a condition of her employment. *Jin v. Metropolitan Life Ins. Co.* (2d Cir. 2002). No claim will arise, however, where the sexual relationship was welcomed by the employee. *Holly D. v. California Inst. of Tech.* (9th Cir. 2003). Moreover, it is not sex discrimination for a supervisor to promote a willing paramour over another female in that favoring a paramour "disadvantages both sexes equally." *Ackel v. National Communications, Inc.* (5th Cir. 2003).

c.   *"Hostile Environment"*

1.   Hostile or Abusive Working Conditions: While minor job changes, increasing criticism, or assignments to slightly more inconvenient positions will not, in themselves, be considered "tangible employment actions," a coalescence of relatively minor job actions may create a hostile environment. "The environment must be both objectively and subjectively offensive, one that a reasonable person would find hostile and abusive, and one that the victim in fact did perceive to be so." *Harris v. Forklift Sys., Inc.* (S.Ct. 1993).

—*Unreasonableness, The Objective Element*: "Ordinary socializing in the work place—such as male-on-male horseplay or intersexual flirtation—[is not] discriminatory." *Oncale v. Sundowner Offshore Services, Inc.* (S.Ct. 1998). "Offhand comments and isolated incidents (unless extremely serious) will not amount to discriminatory changes in the 'terms and conditions of employment.'" *Clark County School Dist. v. Breeden* (S.Ct. 2001). A supervisor's "lack of sensitivity does not, alone, amount to actionable harassment." *Faragher v. City of Boca Raton* (S.Ct. 1998). On the other hand, to be hostile, the environ-

ment need not be "unendurable or intolerable," or
so severe that victim's mental or physical health is
affected. *Terry v. Ashcroft* (2d Cir. 2003). The standard is whether in the totality of the circumstances
a reasonable person in the employee's position
would find the conduct unwelcome and "severely
hostile or abusive." *Oncale v. Sundowner Offshore
Services, Inc., supra* (S.Ct. 1998). Key elements are
the frequency of conduct, its severity, whether it is
physically threatening or humiliating, and the extent it interferes with an employee's work. A single
sexually explicit comment followed by laughter of
male supervisors does not create a hostile atmosphere. *Clark County School Dist v. Breeden, supra*
(S.Ct. 2001). By contrast, where female employees
(and females generally) were routinely referred to
in derogatory terms, grabbed or fondled by co-
workers, and threatened with degrading duties if
they objected, a reasonable person could find that a
hostile working environment existed. *Faragher v.
City of Boca Raton, supra* (S.Ct. 1998). A single
request for a date does not create a hostile atmosphere; repeated requests for a sexual relationship
does, particularly if accompanied by threats of retaliation or acts of untoward behavior. *Burlington
Industries, Inc. v. Ellerth, supra* (S.Ct. 1998). A
single picture of a scantily clad woman at a man's
work station would not likely to be seen as creating
a hostile work place for women. Widespread posting
of sexually explicit pictures or graffiti does create an
abusive environment. *Robinson v. Jacksonville
Shipyards, Inc.* (M.D.Fla. 1991).

Repeated conduct is not required where the conduct involves significant physical contact or is particularly threatening or humiliating. Directing a racial epithet or threat of violence at the employee, or placing of a hangman's noose or a burning cross at a black employee's workstation may be sufficiently hurtful, standing alone, to create a hostile environment for that worker. *Rodgers v. Western–Southern Life Ins. Co.* (7th Cir. 1993). An attempt to kiss the employee and touching her thigh while refusing her requests to leave the room created an abusive environment. *Moring v. Arkansas Dep't of Correction* (8th Cir. 2001).

Harassment is more likely found where it is directed toward the plaintiff. Nonetheless, an atmosphere of racism or sexism can be sufficiently pervasive that employees of that race or sex may find the environment hostile, even if they were not the direct objects of the abuse.

—*Unwelcome, The Subjective Factor:* The victim must prove that objectively abusive conduct was personally—to her—offensive and "unwelcome." An employee who welcomed and joined in a ribald atmosphere that others might have found offensive, giving as good as she got, is not a victim of the abusive environment. While openly objecting, registering a complaint, or demonstrating disgust will establish the unwelcomeness of defendant's behavior, plaintiff's failure to object, her acquiescence, or even "voluntary" participation does not conclusively establish that the conduct was "welcomed" by her. In addressing the factual issue of whether plaintiff viewed the conduct as "unwelcome" defendant may present evidence of plaintiff's past ribald conduct, her sexual relationships with supervisors, and even her "sexual fantasies." *Meritor Savings Bank, FSB v. Vinson, supra* (S.Ct. 1986).

2. "Because of:" The unwelcome abusive working environment must be "because of" plaintiff's membership in a protected class. Hazing all new employees with unwanted touching and gross insults, inflicted evenhandedly and with no apparent antipathy toward a protected class, even if creating a hostile environment, is not discrimination "because of" race or sex.

Oncale v. Sundowner Offshore Services, Inc. supra (S.Ct. 1998) involved an all male workforce on an offshore oil platform. Plaintiff, a male employee, was subjected to ongoing physical abuse, some sexual in nature. Defendant contended that regardless of the offensiveness of the atmosphere, rough treatment of a male employee by other male employees in an all male workforce could not be discrimination "because of sex." The Court disagreed. Same sex harassment in a single sex work force can be actionable under Title VII if it was "because of sex."

Where a supervisor pursues the victim because of this sexual desire, it is easy to infer that the harassing acts were "because of" the victim's sex. *Harris v. Forklift Sys. Inc., supra* (S.Ct. 1993). This is true regardless of whether it was a same sex (homosexual) or opposite sex (heterosexual) pursuit. Conversely, when one displays hostility toward a gender or race in the work place, one may infer that the harassing atmosphere is "because of" the supervisor's hostility to plaintiff's class membership. Racist or sexist insults carry their own indicia of race or sex motivation. *Suders v. Easton* (3d Cir. 2003). Directing offensive or gross behavior at one gender or race only establishes hostile motivation behind the behavior. While hostility is more easily inferred when the harasser and victim are from different classes, the race or gender of the harasser vis-a-vis the victim is not critical. One could envision a male hospital director harassing male nurses because he believed men should not be nurses, or a female airline executive harassing female pilots because she believed that pilots should be men. And history is replete with examples of individuals treating members of their own race more harshly than they treat others. Where evidence indicates such hostility, the harassing behavior is "because of" a protected class.

It is discrimination to rely on stereotypes in making decisions, such as denying a woman a promotion because she is seen as not being sufficiently ladylike and feminine. Reliance on the stereotype placed a burden on plaintiff "because of" her sex not imposed on men. *Price Waterhouse v. Hopkins* (S.Ct. 1989). Accordingly, if a "masculine" acting woman were mocked and abused because she was not "feminine enough" this harassment would be "because of" her sex. Likewise, if a "feminine" acting man was belittled, mocked, and assaulted because he was not adequately "masculine," the harassment would be actionable sex discrimination. *Doe v. City of Belleville* (7th Cir. 1997). The gender or race of the harasser is not controlling. *Oncale v. Sundowner Offshore Services, Inc., supra* (S.Ct. 1998). A black employee who is abused because he was acting "too white" is being harassed "because of" race.

In *Rene v. MGM Grand Hotel, Inc.* (9th Cir. 2002) (en banc), an openly gay male employee was subjected to a barrage of harassing acts by male co-workers that included grabbing his crotch, poking his anus, and threatening him with rape. While a motive may have been hostility to plaintiff's perceived sexual orientation—not a hostility to the male gender—the sexual nature of the harassment itself was held to be "because of sex." Presumably, however, if the harassing acts consisted of badgering that was not sexual in nature, and the badgering was not premised on stereotyped gender assumptions, but motivated by the perceived sexual orientation of the victim, as sexual orientation is not protected by Title VII, such harassment is not "because of sex." *Hamm v. Weyauwega Milk Products, Inc.* (7th Cir. 2003).

d.   *"Employer"*

Title VII does not attach liability to individuals, but to "employers," and "employers" are not absolutely liable for all actions of their employees. "Employer" liability is determined by common law principles of agency, qualified by the remedial goals of the statutes. *Burlington Industries, Inc. v. Ellerth, supra* (S.Ct. 1998). The approach differs markedly according to the type of discrimination practiced (tangible benefits or hostile environment) and the level of the employee engaged in the behavior.

1.   Senior officers: Officers sufficiently senior in the management to control policies of the "employer" are the "employer." The "employer" is liable for their conduct even where there was an official policy prohibiting it. *Ackel v. National Communications, Inc.* (5th Cir. 2003).

2.   Mid-level supervisors: A "supervisor" is a non-management employee vested by the employer with power to promote, fire, or discipline the employee or effectively recommend such action. *Mikels v. City of Durham* (4th Cir. 1999). An employee charged with harassment may be a "supervisor" if he/she directs the daily work of the plaintiff. *Mack v. Otis Elevator Co.* (2d Cir. 2003).

—Tangible Benefits ("Quid Pro Quo"): When a supervisor fires, demotes, or reassigns an employee because of the employee's refusal to have a sexual relationship, this "quid pro quo" of sex for a benefit is attributable to the "employer" even if the employer had published policies against such behavior and management was unaware of the supervisor's actions. *Burlington Industries, Inc. v. Ellerth, supra* (S.Ct. 1998).

—Hostile Environment: *Faragher v. City of Boca Raton, supra* (S.Ct. 1998) held that when liability is premised on a supervisor creating a hostile environment—as opposed to denying a tangible benefit—the employer can avoid liability for this misconduct by establishing that: 1) it exercised reasonable care to prevent and correct promptly any sexually harassing behavior by having an explicit non-harassment policy in place, and 2) the plaintiff unreasonably failed to take advantage of the preventive or corrective opportunities provided. In *Faragher* the employer had a general non-harassment policy, but the policy was not widely disseminated nor brought to the attention of the victims. The policy did not include any assurance that the harassing supervisors could be bypassed in registering complaints. Finally, management made no attempt to monitor the conduct of supervisors. On these facts, the employer failed to establish the first element of the affirmative defense and was thus liable for the harassment committed by supervisors.

The required preventive policy, therefore, should contain a written prohibition of harassment that is brought to the attention of all employees. The policy should have clear and effective mechanisms for reporting and resolving harassment claims that do not subject the employee to undue risk, exposure, or expense, such as by requiring the complaint to be lodged with the supervisor responsible for the hostile environment. Finally, management must make ongoing and reasonable efforts to monitor the behavior of supervisors.

The second prong of the defense—the employee's obligation to invoke the processes—is satisfied where the employer proves that the employee unreasonably failed to avail herself of the employer's remedial apparatus. Thus, where the employee knew of her employer's anti-harassment policy, but failed to inform anyone in authority, including her immediate supervisor who was not involved in the harassment, the employee may have not acted reasonably. If so, the defense will have been established, and the employer will avoid liability for the supervisor's harassment. *Burlington Industries, Inc. v. Ellerth, supra* (S.Ct. 1998).

3. Co-worker harassment: Harassment by non-supervisory co-workers is *not* attributed to the "employer" by rules of agency. "Employer" liability is based on the employer's failure to take prompt and effective measures to remedy harassing behavior that it either knew, or in the exercise of due care, should have known was taking place. *Burlington Industries, Inc. v. Ellerth, supra* (S.Ct. 1998). Employers may not adopt a "see no evil, hear no evil" strategy, effectively condoning or ratifying an abusive atmosphere. Knowledge of harassment is imputed to the employer where a reasonable person intent on complying with Title VII would have known about the harassment, as where co-worker misbehavior was known to supervisors. Knowledge of harassment can be imputed also where a reasonably observant supervisor would have suspected that harassment may be taking place, such as by the presence of offensive graffiti or excessive "horseplay." *Ocheltree v. Scollon Productions, Inc.* (4th Cir. 2003)(en banc).

e. Employer's Remedial Response

Where the employer knows or reasonably should have known of the hostile environment, the employer must take prompt and effective measures to correct the harassment. The employer first must make a reasonable inquiry into the accuracy of any allegation. If a reasonable investigation would have reached a reasonable conclusion that the allegations were not true, the employer will not be liable even if it is later proved that the events took place. However, if a reasonable employer would have found a hostile environment, failure to take appropriate remedial action establishes employer liability.

Appropriateness of the response varies with the seriousness of the offense. That the harassing employee is too important to be disciplined does not justify an inadequate response. *Cadena v. Pacesetter Corp.* (10th Cir. 2000). Symbolic responses, such as unwritten, jocular reprimands or "suggestions" to the offender rarely are adequate. Some conduct can be so outrageous and damaging to the victim that discharge of the offender may be the only effective remedy. For less than outrageous or inadvertent first offenses, a formal reprimand, mandatory counseling, withholding of a pay increase, or a short suspension would be appropriate. Transfer, demotion, and ultimately dismissal may be required for repeat offenders. *Intlekofer v. Turnage* (9th Cir. 1992) Remedies cannot include transferring the victim. *Paroline v. Unisys* (4th Cir. 1989). Graffiti and offensive material must be promptly eradicated and steps taken to see that such displays are not repeated. *Daniels v. Essex Group, Inc.* (7th Cir. 1991).

f. Constructive Discharge

When an employee quits in response to an environment so abusive that a reasonable employee would have resigned rather than endure the abuse, particularly if the supervisor created the environment for the purpose of causing the employee to resign, the employee is "constructively discharged," and entitled to full remedial relief. *Jurgens v. EEOC* (5th Cir. 1990). *Infra*, 23.10. Some courts hold that when a supervisor constructively discharges the employee through creation of an intolerable environment, this is a denial of a tangible job benefit to which the employer has no reasonable care defense. *Suders v. Easton* (3d Cir. 2003). Others observe that when remedial mechanisms are available to an employee, it is difficult for the employee to argue that a reasonable person would have resigned prior to pursuing available avenues of relief. Accordingly, the failure of the employee to pursue these avenues prior to quitting means that the employee was not constructively discharged. The employer may thus assert a reasonable care 1998).defense to the supervisor's misconduct. *Lindale v. Tokheim Corp.* (7th Cir. 1998).

PART V

DEFINING PROTECTED CLASSES

CHAPTER 16

RACE AND COLOR

V—16.01 Title VII

Race and color discrimination reaches perceived racial origins of Africa, Asia, the Middle–East, or the Pacific Islands as well as indigenous Americans such as Eskimos and American Indians. Whites and those of European descent are protected under the same standards as applied to racial minorities. *McDonald v. Santa Fe Trail Transp. Co.* (S.Ct. 1976). Preferring a person based on relative skin complexion is proscribed "color" discrimination. *Walker v. Secretary of Treasury, IRS* (N.D.Ga. 1989).

Discrimination on the basis of interracial marriage is "race" discrimination. Defendant argued it was not the race of the employee, but the race of the spouse, that was the motivating factor. The court disagreed. As plaintiff would not have been discriminated against had he been of a different race, it was the race of the employee that motivated the employer. *Parr v. Woodmen of the World Life Ins. Co.* (11th Cir. 1986).

There is no statutory BFOQ defense for race or color discrimination. Moreover, "business necessity may not be used as a defense to a claim of intentional discrimination." 42 U.S.C.A. 2000e–2(k)(2). This raises the question of whether an employer could justify facial race or color discrimination that could serve legitimate employer needs, such as authenticity of actors or models, or where race of the employee might seem appropriate for the rehabilitation of troubled individuals served by the employer.

V—16.02 Civil Rights Act of 1866 (42 U.S.C.A. 1981)

The 1866 Civil Rights Act provides that "all persons" shall have the same right to make and enforce contracts, "as is enjoyed by white citizens." It was intended to proscribe only "race" discrimination. However, in the Nineteenth Century when the statute was enacted, the concept of "race" included "identifiable classes of persons * * * [based on] their ancestry or ethnic characteristics" (*e.g.*, the Irish race, the Jewish race, the German race). The Act thus reaches discrimination against Latinos, Filipinos, Middle Easterners, as well as the various "hyphenated-Americans" such as Irish–Americans or Polish–Americans. *St. Francis College v. Al-Khazraji* (S.Ct. 1987). It protects whites under standards applicable to racial minorities. *McDonald v. Santa Fe Trail Transp. Co.* (S.Ct. 1976).

Since the 1866 Act only proscribes race discrimination, it is imperative that plaintiff seeking relief under this Act define the alleged discrimination in racial terms. Thus, discrimination against a Jew alleged to be religious discrimination would not state an 1866 Act claim; if alleged to be "racial" discrimination, it would. Allegations of discrimination against a Latino, likewise, should be stated in terms of "race" not "national origin."

The 1866 Act is not applicable to neutral devices that have an adverse impact on a particular race; plaintiff must prove racial motivation. *General Bldg. Contractors Ass'n v. Pennsylvania* (S.Ct. 1982). There are a number of reasons why plaintiffs charging race discrimination would invoke the 1866 Act: 1) *Coverage*: there are no employer size requirements. Persons with as few as one employee are subject to the Act. Moreover, as the Act reaches all "contracts," it is not limited to the employment relationship. 2) *Procedures*: The 1866 Act imposes no administrative pre-requisites to suit. The statute of limitation for filing 1866 Act complaints is determined by the most appropriate state statute of limitation. *Burnett v. Grattan* (S.Ct. 1984); 3) *Remedies*: A successful plaintiff can recover, in addition to back wages and remedial seniority, compensatory and punitive damages that are not subject to the maximum recovery amounts imposed on Title VII. *Johnson v. Railway Exp. Agency* (S.Ct. 1975).

CHAPTER 17

NATIONAL ORIGIN

V—17.01   Title VII

"National origin" means "the country from which you or your forebearers came." *Espinoza v. Farah Mfg. Co.* (S.Ct. 1973). Discrimination against someone because of Italian, Mexican, or Polish family origins is proscribed. "National origin" also includes broader ethnic designations such as Latino or Middle–Eastern. It reaches distinct cultural heritages even if no current nation exists. Thus, discrimination against Gypsies, Cajuns, or Puerto Ricans is "national origin" discrimination. *Pejic v. Hughes Helicopters, Inc.* (9th Cir. 1988).

National origin is *not* the equivalent of citizenship, and thus, it is not a *per se* violation of Title VII for an employer to refuse to hire persons who are not U.S. citizens. *Espinoza v. Farah Mfg. Co., supra* (S.Ct. 1973). It is national origin discrimination, however, to make distinctions between aliens based on their citizenship in different nations, such as accepting Canadian citizens while rejecting Mexican citizens. Courts have assumed that discriminating against Americans based on their lack of citizenship in a foreign country is national origin discrimination. An employer thus violates Title VII by preferring Korean nationals over U.S. citizens. *MacNamara v. Korean Air Lines* (3d Cir. 1988).

Hoffman Plastic Compounds, Inc. v. NLRB (S.Ct. 2002), recognizing that immigration law precludes employment of undocumented aliens, held that an award of back pay to undocumented aliens was impermissible in that it "would unduly trench upon explicit statutory prohibitions critical to federal immigration policy." The Court left open the question of whether an undocumented alien could secure damages. *See, EEOC v. Tortilleria La Mejor* (E.D.Cal. 1991) (damages available for sexual harassment). The EEOC does not read *Hoffman* as precluding governmental investigative enforcement efforts on behalf of undocumented aliens not involving reinstatement or back pay.

V—17.02 The 1866 Civil Rights Act (42 U.S.C.A 1981)

The 1866 Civil Rights Act proscription against "race" discrimination does not proscribe "national origin" discrimination, but does reach discrimination based on "ancestry" and "ethnic characteristics." *Supra,* 16.02.

V—17.03 The Immigration Reform and Control Act (IRCA) (8 U.S.C.A. 1324a)

The IRCA mandates discrimination against undocumented aliens. It requires employers to verify the identity and employment eligibility under U.S. immigration law of all new hires by examining specified documents. Aliens unable to present this documentation cannot be hired. If the alien becomes unauthorized after being hired, the employer is compelled to discharge the worker. Violation of these obligations can subject the employer and the alien to criminal prosecution.

To guard against an employer overreacting by refusing to hire all non-citizens, including those authorized to work, or discriminating against "foreign appearing" applicants, the IRCA prohibits discrimination against a "protected individual" because of "national origin" or because of the individual's "citizenship status." 8 U.S.C.A. 1324b. "Protected individuals" include: 1) Citizens of the United States, and 2) lawfully admitted aliens who are: (a) permanent residents, (b) temporary residents under specified amnesty provisions, or (c) residents granted asylum. Non-citizen residents will lose "protected individual" status if they fail to apply for naturalization within six moths of becoming eligible to apply, or having applied on a timely basis, have not been naturalized within two years from the application, unless the alien can establish that he/she is actively pursuing naturalization. Thus, it is an unlawful "immigration related employment practice" for an employer to discriminate on the basis of national origin or citizenship against U.S. citizens and lawful residents who promptly apply for, and actively purse, U.S. citizenship.

The protection against national origin discrimination largely duplicates Title VII, but because IRCA covers employers of three or more employees, the IRCA reaches small employers not covered by Title VII. The IRCA is enforced by the aggrieved person filing administrative charges with the Special Counsel for immigration employment practices of the U.S. Department of Justice. If the Special Counsel fails to act within 120 days, the protected individual may file a complaint that will be referred to an administrative judge. The administrative judge may order as remedies for unlawful discrimination civil penalties of up to $2,000 in addition to back pay, reinstatement, and attorneys fees.

V—17.04   Language Distinctions

Discrimination against persons because they cannot speak English is not facial national origin discrimination. *Garcia v. Rush–Presbyterian–St.Luke's Medical Center* (7th Cir. 1981). Distinguishing between applicants based on an *accent* deemed "foreign," is national origin discrimination. Requiring bi-lingual employees to speak English at the work place does not invariably create a hostile working environment for employees with non-U.S. origins. *Garcia v. Spun Steak Co.* (9th Cir. 1993). *Supra,* 15.04

CHAPTER 18

SEX

V—18.01 "Sex" Defined

As "sex" was inserted as a class protected by Title VII through an amendment proposed by opponents of Title VII in an effort to defeat the bill, there is no meaningful legislative history. The courts have construed the word narrowly; "sex" refers to gender, not to sexuality, sexual preference, or sexual practices. *DeSantis v. Pacific Tel. & Tel. Co.* (9th Cir. 1979). Men, however, are protected against sex discrimination under the same standards as apply to women.

"Sex" includes relying on gender stereotypes. *Price Waterhouse v. Hopkins* (S.Ct. 1989), involved an employer that refused to promote a woman into a partnership stating that she was "too macho," "overcompensated for being a woman," and was a "lady using foul language," coupled with advice to "walk more femininely, dress more femininely, wear make-up, have your hair styled, and wear jewelry." This was sex discrimination because it measured performance by perceived proper roles and behaviors of the genders, with the consequence that the employer required women to meet standards not imposed on men.

It is sex discrimination to make gender distinctions against an *individual*, even though the employer is favorably disposed to the gender or treats the gender as *class* in a non-discriminatory fashion. *Los Angeles Dep't of Water and Power v. Manhart* (S.Ct. 1978)(pension distinctions based on sex-based actuarial tables is sex discrimination.). It is sex discrimination to impose different qualifications or performance standards on men and women. *Supra,* 8.01 and 14.01.

V—18.02 Pregnancy and Childbirth

A decision of the Supreme Court holding that discrimination the basis of pregnancy was not "sex" discrimination prompted the Pregnancy Discrimination Act amendments to Title VII in 1978. "Sex" is defined therein to include "pregnancy, childbirth, and related conditions." 42 U.S.C.A. 2000e-(k). It is sex discrimination to discriminate against a woman because she has secured an abortion, refuses to secure an abortion, or is contemplating an abortion. *Turic v. Holland Hospitality, Inc.* (6th Cir. 1996). Testing women applicants for pregnancy or fertility is sex discrimination. *Norman-Bloodsaw v. Lawrence Berkeley Laboratory* (9th Cir. 1998). Regularly inquiring about a woman's pregnancy, warning her about becoming pregnant again, making sarcastic comments about her childbearing, and denying her time off routinely granted other employees is pregnancy discrimination. *Walsh v. National Computer Systems, Inc.* (8th Cir. 2003).

While a woman may not be denied a job or dismissed because she is or was pregnant, pregnant employees enjoy no exemption from uniformly applied work rules or performance requirements. Thus, a pregnant employee may be discharged for excessive absenteeism or inability to work an established schedule, even if the absences or inability were caused by her pregnancy. *Maldonado v. U.S. Bank* (7th Cir. 1999). It is not "child birth" discrimination to refuse to accommodate a woman's working schedule so she can meet child rearing needs. *Walsh v. National Computer Systems* (8th Cir. 2003). (Such may be required under the Family and Medical Leave Act). Nonetheless, denying leave to a woman to care for children when leave is routinely granted to men for other reasons is "sex" discrimination. And if an employer has granted child care leave to mothers, it is sex discrimination to deny such leave to fathers.

The statutory definition of "sex" also requires that:

Women affected by pregnancy, childbirth, or related medical conditions shall be treated the same for all employment-related purposes, including receipt of benefits under fringe benefit programs, as other persons not so affected, but similar in their ability or inability to work.

Thus, if an employer has an employee health benefit plan, that plan must include pregnancy benefits equal to other similar conditions. If the employer provides health benefit plans for dependents of employees, failure of the plan to include pregnancy benefits for the spouse of the male employee is "sex" discrimination. *Supra,* 14.01(b).

Neutral requirements may be shown to have an adverse impact on pregnant women, and thus must be justified in terms of their "business necessity." *Supra* Chapt. 11. A woman was refused reinstatement following a medical leave taken during her pregnancy on the grounds that her condition precluded her from lifting 150 lbs. Plaintiff proved impact of the lifting rule through medical testimony that substantially all women recovering from childbirth would be advised not to lift such weights. The employer was unable to carry the burden of proving the "business necessity" of its lifting requirement. *Garcia v. Woman's Hospital of Texas* (5th Cir. 1996). However, a pregnant woman's challenge to a uniformly applied attendance policy that prohibited employees from missing more than three days of work during their first ninety days of employment was unsuccessful. Plaintiff provided medical testimony that virtually no woman who gave birth would be medically able to return to work three days after delivery. Nonetheless, the court refused to apply impact analysis to the attendance policy, reasoning that to do so would effectively require employers to grant leave to all pregnant employees, and by this treat absences caused by pregnancy more favorably than other absences, an outcome Congress did not intend. *Stout v. Baxter Healthcare Corp.* (5th Cir. 2002).

Employers occasionally are able to justify expressed limitations on pregnant employees by proving that non-pregnancy is a bona fide occupational qualification. *Supra,* 8.02

V—18.03 Marriage

"Sex" does *not* reach distinctions based on marriage or marital status. Thus, requiring *all* employees to be single, or to be married, or refusing to employee divorced *persons* is not engaging in sex discrimination. *Little v. Wuerl* (3d Cir. 1991)(if based on the employer's religious beliefs, it is "religious" discrimination). A marital status rule applied to one gender and not the other is sex discrimination. *Sprogis v. United Air Lines, Inc.* (7th Cir. 1971).

"Sex" does *not* reach nepotism rules. Accordingly, employers may have rule restricting the employment of the spouses or relatives. Nonetheless, such a rule might be shown to have an adverse impact on current women employees through data demonstrating that women employees, far more than men, are forced to resign when they marry a co-worker. If impact is proved, the employer will have to demonstrate the "business necessity" of its policy. Conflicting work schedules, supervisory responsibilities, and possible discipline issues may be sufficient to establish the "necessity" of prohibiting married employees from working in the same employment unit. *EEOC v. Rath Packing Co.* (8th Cir. 1986).

V—18.04 Sexual and Social Relationships

It is sex discrimination for a supervisor to discipline an employee for refusing a sexual relationship, to condition continued employment on maintaining such a relationship, or to harass an employee in an attempt to establish such a relationship. *Supra,* 15.05. It may be "sex" discrimination for a supervisor to promote a female worker with whom the supervisor is romantically involved over qualified *male* applicants. *King v. Palmer* (D.C.Cir. 1985). Cf. *DeCintio v. Westchester County Medical Center* (2d Cir. 1986)(favoritism of a paramour was not based on "sex" but upon a "personal relationship"). A *female* co-worker has no complaint when the employer promoted his female paramour in that such favoritism "disadvantaged both sexes equally." *Ackel v. National Communications, Inc.* (5th Cir. 2003).

Rules prohibiting intra-office dating between employees is not "sex" discrimination, nor is it "sex" discrimination to have policies regarding off-premises sexual behavior such as adultery or promiscuity. It is sex discrimination if such policies are enforced against one gender but not against the other. *Duchon v. Cajon Co.* (6th Cir. 1986). Cf *Platner v. Cash & Thomas Contractors, Inc.* (11th Cir. 1990)(dismissing female employee for suspected affair with owner's son who was also an employee, was not sex discrimination but lawful favoritism for a relative)

V—18.05 Sexual Orientation and Homosexuality

"Sex" does *not* refer to sexuality or sexual preferences. Thus, it is not sex discrimination to discriminate against someone because they are, or are perceived to be, homosexual, transsexual, or bisexual. *DeSantis v. Pacific Tel. & Tel. Co., Inc.* (9th Cir. 1979). Conversely, it is not sex discrimination for an employer to discriminate against heterosexuals. Homosexuality, bisexuality, transvestism, transsexualism, gender identity disorders, and sexual behavior disorders are specifically excluded from the protection of the Americans with Disabilities Act. 42 U.S.C.A. 12211. Discrimination along gender lines, such as refusing to employ gay men while taking no action against lesbians, is sex discrimination.

Numerous states and local governments prohibit discrimination based on sexual orientation. President Clinton issued an Executive Order 13087 which prohibited discrimination based on sexual orientation in the federal civilian workforce. Governmental discrimination on the basis of sexual orientation may violate the Constitution. *Supra,* 5.04.

As *Price Waterhouse v. Hopkins* (S.Ct. 1989) held that it was sex discrimination to deny a woman a promotion because she was "too macho" and should have presented herself more femininely, it would be sex discrimination to deny a male employment because he was seen as "too feminine." It is sex discrimination to harass an employee, regardless of the gender of the harasser, based on stereotyped perceptions as to how a man or woman should present themselves. *Nichols v. Azteca Restaurant Enterprises, Inc.* (9th Cir. 2001). Courts, thus, have drawn a fine line between discrimination based on stereotyped assumptions as to masculinity or femininity, which is "sex," and discrimination based on sexual orientation, which is not. *Hamm v. Weyauwega Milk Products, Inc.* (7th Cir. 2003).

The explicit sexual nature of the treatment may render it "sex" regardless of the motive behind the treatment. Thus, it was "sex" discrimination when an employee perceived to be homosexual was grabbed in the crotch, poked in the anus, and threatened with "rape." *Rene v. MGM Grand Hotel, Inc.* (9th Cir. 2002). *Supra,* 15.05(c)(2)

CHAPTER 19

RELIGION

V—19.01 "Religion" Defined

Title VII does not define "religion" except to provide that religion includes "all aspects of religious observances and practices as well as belief." 42 U.S.C.A. 2000e-(j). The EEOC and the courts define "religion" similar to that used when constitutional issues are addressed under the First Amendment. Thus defined, "religion" includes not only organized and established faiths such as Roman Catholic, Judaism, Islam, Mormon, Buddhism, but also:

> moral and ethical beliefs as to what is right and wrong which are sincerely held with the strength of traditional religious views. * * * The fact that no religious group espouses such beliefs or the fact that the religious group to which the individual professes to belong may not accept such belief will not determine whether the belief is a religious belief. 29 CFR 1605.1

Wicca (often thought of as "witchcraft") is protected as a religion (*Brown v. Woodland Joint Unified Sch. Dist.* (9th Cir. 1994)), as is Native American spirituality. Title VII protects atheists from discrimination based on their lack of religious belief. *Reed v. Great Lakes Companies, Inc.* (7th Cir. 2003). It is religious discrimination to require employees to participate in an employer's sponsored religious observance or practice (*EEOC v. Townley Engineering & Mfg. Co.* (9th Cir. 1988)), and to punish an employee's private activity because the activity conflicts with the employer's religious beliefs. *Little v. Wuerl* (3d Cir. 1991).

Protected "religion" must be distinguished from unprotected political association or belief, a line often difficult to draw. Strongly held views about military draft or reproductive choice are "religious." *Wilson v. U.S. West Communications* (8th Cir. 1995). Membership in the Ku Klux Klan or the Communist Party are political. *Bellamy v. Mason's Stores, Inc.* (E.D.Va. 1973) .

V—19.02 Religious "Observances and Practices"

Title VII defines religion to include religious "observances and practices." The practice need not be mandated by a formal religion; it will be protected if the individual considers it part of his personal religious duties or deeply held ethical commitments. Observation of the Sabbath, holy days, attending church conventions, or teaching Bible study classes are religious observances. Wearing testimonials to one's moral or ethical beliefs, such as anti-abortion or anti-war buttons or clothing or grooming standards expected by one's personal faith, such as head covers or facial hair, are religious practices.

Religious observances are distinguished from unprotected social or secular activity. Even if sponsored by a church, activity which is predominately social, such as sporting events, parties, or picnics, is not religious. Thus, an employer need not accommodate an employee's desire to play on a church league basketball team. *Wessling v. Kroger Co.* (E.D.Mich. 1982).

V—19.03 Failure to Accommodate Religious Practices

Employers have an affirmative duty to reasonably accommodate employees' religious observances and practices. 42 U.S.C.A. 2000e-(j). Plaintiff must establish the religious nature of the practice, distinguishing it from a personal, social, or political preference. *Vetter v. Farmland Indus., Inc.* (8th Cir. 1997) (desire for a transfer to a different town was more a personal desire than a religious need). Second, plaintiff must establish that the practice is based on a "sincerely held" belief. Third, plaintiff must inform the employer of the conflict between his/her religious practice and the employer's work rule and request an accommodation. Merely following the religious practice, without seeking an adjustment of the work rule, can subject the employee to discipline. *Goldmeier v. Allstate Ins. Co.* (6th Cir. 2003).

If plaintiff establishes these elements, the burden shifts to the employer to show that it initiated good faith efforts to accommodate the employee's practices or that it could not reasonably accommodate the practices without "undue hardship." The duty to make a *reasonable* accommodation does not require the employer to prove that the more sweeping accommodations suggested by plaintiff would constitute an "undue hardship." In *Ansonia Bd. of Educ. v. Philbrook* (S.Ct. 1986), the employer's policy of granting three days of paid leave for religious reasons and the right to take unpaid personal leave for religious holidays was held to be a reasonable accommodation. No more is required. The employer need not justify its refusal to expand its otherwise reasonable policy to allow the employee to pay the actual cost of the replacement (as opposed to taking unpaid leave), or to allow "business leave" to be allocated for the employee's religious practices. *Philbrook v. Ansonia Bd. Of Educ.* (2d Cir. 1991).

The accommodation obligation imposed on employers is relatively light. It may require minor adjustments to schedules by large employers, such as allowing non-essential employees to leave early on Friday evening to observe their Sabbath, or granting an employee unpaid leave to observe a religious holiday or to attend a religious convention. Reasonable accommodation requires modification of rules that prohibit employees from finding voluntary, temporary job exchanges. Accommodating employees who desire to wear an item of clothing or a symbol of their faith often may be reasonably accomplished. *Fraternal Order of Police v. City of Newark* (3d Cir. 1999) (wearing of beards). Minor additions to a requirement designed to do no more than promote "neatness" or create an esprit de corps do not impose an undue hardship. *Isaac v. Butler's Shoe Corp.* (N.D. Ga. 1980).

Trans World Airlines, Inc. v. Hardison (S.Ct. 1977) involved an employer that operated on a seven day, twenty-four hour schedule. Plaintiff's religion required observance of a Saturday Sabbath. Plaintiff's lack of seniority required him to work on Saturdays. The employer, which had already reduced week-end staffing to a minimum, tried unsuccessfully to secure a voluntary replacement for plaintiff on the Saturday shift. The employer refused, however, to offer premium pay to induce others to take plaintiff's Saturday shift, and, based on the union's objections, the employer refused to ignore the seniority provisions in the collective bargaining agreement and assign an employee senior to plaintiff to assume plaintiff's Saturday assignment. The Court held that the accommodation accorded plaintiff (*i.e.,* efforts to secure voluntary replacements) was reasonable. Reasonable accommodation did not require it to provide premium pay necessary to secure a replacement. Any cost beyond *de minimis* would be an "undue hardship." And, relying on the special protection accorded to seniority systems, "[The employer] is not required by Title VII to carve out a special exception to its seniority system in order to help [an employee] meet his religious obligations."

The employer need offer no accommodation where to do so would impose an "undue hardship." As *Hardison* held, imposition of more than *de min-*

imis economic costs on the employer or imposition of burdens on fellow employees are "undue hardships." Undue hardships occur when the employee's presence is needed for normal operations, such as Saturday work at a retail store, its busiest day (*Cooper v. Oak Rubber Co.* (6th Cir. 1994)), or where an employee refuses to serve certain clients or work with certain employees. *Endres v. Indiana State Police* (7th Cir. 2003)(police officer can be assigned to protect gambling casino even though he has sincere religious objections). An employer need not accommodate an employee's desire to impose his religious beliefs upon coworkers. Thus, an employee may be required to remove Biblical passages from his workstation that are perceived as attacks on homosexuals. *Peterson v. Hewlett–Packard Co.* (9th Cir. 2004).

Allowing an employee to disregard a uniform required for individual or product identification may constitute an undue hardship. Where facial hair or certain clothing present dangers to the employees and others, it would be an undue hardship to accommodate the employee's religious grooming obligations. *Bhatia v. Chevron USA, Inc.* (9th Cir. 1984) (beard would interfere with respirator). Moreover, certain expressive items of a religious/political nature such as anti-abortion or anti-war buttons may be sufficiently inflammatory that it would be an undue hardship to allow employees to wear them on the job. *Wilson v. U.S. West Communications* (8th Cir. 1995). As public employers are required to maintain religious neutrality, it may be an undue hardship to allow a postal worker who meets the public to present message-carrying buttons, to permit police officers to wear religious symbols such as crosses (*Daniels v. City of Arlington* (5th Cir. 2001)), or to allow public school teachers to wear patently religious clothing while in class. *United States v. Board of Educ., Philadelphia* (3d Cir. 1990). *Supra,* 15.03(c) .

V—19.04 "Religious Organizations"

Religious organizations and corporations are exempt from Title VII's prohibition against *religious* discrimination, an exemption applicable to both religious and *secular* activities of the religious organization. In *Corporation of Presiding Bishop v. Amos* (S.Ct. 1987), a church operated a secular gymnasium open to the public. The gym discharged the plaintiff for failing to maintain his church membership. Plaintiff had no Title VII claim as the discharge fell within the religious organization exemption. The statutory exemption for secular businesses of the religion does not violate the "establishment" of religion clause of the First Amendment.

An employer is a "religious organization" entitled to the exemption only if its purpose and character are *primarily* religious. *EEOC v. Townley Engineering & Mfg. Co.* (9th Cir. 1988). Ownership, management, church affiliation, and stated purposes (religious or secular) are evaluated. If the employer is a school, its history and mission, the religion of the faculty and students, religious activities expected of students, and the religious focus of the curriculum are examined. *EEOC v. Kamehameha Schools* (9th Cir. 1993)(although founded by Protestant missionaries and while retaining some religious references, the current purpose and character of the school were not *primarily* religious).

The exemption for religious organizations only allows religious discrimination. It does not, on its face, permit religious organizations to discriminate in employment based on race, color, sex, national origin, age, or disability. Nonetheless, the "free exercise" clause of the First Amendment may limit governmental intrusion into the selection, pay, assignment, or dismissal of those involved in the spiritual and pastoral mission of the church. *Combs v. Central Texas Ann. Conf. of United Methodist Church* (5th Cir. 1999). *Supra,* 7.01(e)(3).

V—19.05 Religion as a BFOQ

Secular employers can discriminate on the basis of religion where one's religion is a bona fide occupational qualification reasonably necessary to the operation of the business. *Supra,* 8.02(b). It is applicable only in limited situations where an employee's religion is necessary for the job, as, for example, where a pilot of a particular faith would not be allowed by the law of a foreign country to fly the aircraft he was employed to fly. *Kern v. Dynalectron Corp.* (N.D. Tex. 1983). By contrast, absence of Judaism was not a BFOQ for a job in an Arab country absent a showing that the hostility toward Jews in that country would render the employee unable to perform. *Abrams v. Baylor College of*

Medicine (5th Cir. 1986). Being a Protestant was not a BFOQ to teach traditionally academic subjects in a school founded by Protestants missionaries. *EEOC v. Kamehameha Schools, supra* (9th Cir. 1993). However, being a Jesuit was a BFOQ for a theology professor at a university founded by the Jesuits. *Pime v. Loyola University of Chicago* (7th Cir. 1986).

V—19.06 Proving Motive

As with other forms of discrimination, plaintiff must prove that an adverse action was "because of religion." It is often difficult to prove a religious motive. That an employer tolerated a vulgar, unprofessional environment which plaintiff found objectionable on religious grounds, did not establish that the conditions were created "because of religion." A claim would have been stated only if the vulgar behavior had been directed at the employee because of her religion. *Rivera v. Puerto Rico Aqueduct & Sewers Auth.* (1st Cir. 2003). Verbal references to religion, even if blasphemous, may be dismissed as non-evaluative stray comments. *EEOC v. Wiltel, Inc.* (10th Cir. 1996)("I don't like Ellie because she is into all that Jesus shit"). Absent "special circumstances," differences in treatment between persons of different religions does not alone carry an inference of religious motivation. *Supra,* 9.03(b)(1).

V—19.07 Labor Organizations

It is illegal for labor organizations to discriminate on the basis of religion, but the statutory obligation to make reasonable accommodation for religious practices is limited to "employers." Nonetheless, the courts impose on unions an implicit obligation to make accommodations similar to the explicit obligation imposed on employers. Employees with bona fide religious objections to payment of union dues imposed by collective bargaining agreements may not be discharged for refusing to pay those dues. Upon request, the union must either exempt the employee or provide a non-religious charitable alternative to dues. In such case the employee must pay any actual costs of union services provided the employee, such as processing his grievance. *International Ass'n of Machinists, Lodge 751 v. Boeing Co.* (9th Cir. 1987).

CHAPTER 20

AGE

V—20.01 "Age" Defined

The Age Discrimination in Employment Act of 1967 (ADEA) (29 U.S.C.A. 621), in language similar to Title VII, prohibits discrimination because of age. Only individuals *over the age of 40* are protected. Thus, a *minimum* hiring age of say, 18, 21, or even 35 does not violate the ADEA because no one in the protected "over 40" age group is excluded. However, a *maximum* hiring age, such as a refusal to hire persons over the age of 35, when applied to an applicant over age 40, is age discrimination. There is no upper age limit for protection. (The age 70 limit was repealed in 1986). Consequently, unless justified by an exemption or defense, mandatory retirement at any age is proscribed.

Hazen Paper Co. v. Biggins (S.Ct. 1993) construed "age" narrowly to mean the chronological age of the individual. It does not reach distinctions based on the passage of time. The employer had a pension plan which vested after ten years of service. A sixty-two year old employee had been working for the employer for nearly ten years when he was dismissed. The lower court found that while the employee was dismissed to avoid vesting of his pension, it nonetheless concluded that since vesting, like age, was based on passed of time, an employer

232

motivated by vesting, was motivated by age. The Supreme Court reversed. "[A]ge and years of service are analytically distinct * * * and it is incorrect to say that a decision based on years of service is necessarily age based." Thus, factors such as relative salary, greater experience, "excessive qualifications," even though related to time, are not facial forms of age discrimination. *Anderson v. Baxter Healthcare Corp.* (7th Cir. 1994) (replacing a higher paid older worker with a lower paid younger worker to reduce salary costs was not "age" discrimination).

Hazen Paper gave four caveats: 1) Dismissal of an employee to avoid pension obligations violates ERISA; 2) Plaintiff may prove that the employer's expression of "pension costs" was a pretext for the employer's concern over the employee's chronological age; 3) If the employer is motivated both by the employee's advancing age *and* by costs of a benefit program, such "mixed motivation" would require the employer to prove that it would have made the same decision based solely on pension costs. 4) If the pension plan vests because of the chronological age of the employee, discrimination because of vesting would be a form of age discrimination, as, for example, where a plan provides that pensions vest when employees reaches age 55, and to avoid having the pension vest, the employer dismisses the employee before his 55th birthday.

The EEOC had concluded that the broad prohibition of "age" discrimination reached all distinctions because of an individual's age; discrimination against younger workers (over age 40) in favor of older workers was proscribed. The EEOC position was rejected in General Dynamics Land Systems Inc. v. Cline (S.Ct. 2004). The employer there eliminated an obligation to provide health care benefits to employees who subsequently retired, except for current workers at least 50 years old. Thus, employees over age 50 would receive health benefits upon retirement; those under 50 would not. Workers between ages 40 and 50 sued. The Court of Appeals accepted the position of the EEOC. The Supreme Court reversed. The Court found that the statutory term "age" was ambiguous. It could refer to "older age" as well as chronological age. Based on legislative history pointing to an intent to protect only older workers against age discrimination, the Court concluded that the ADEA did not protect younger workers against chronological age distinctions that favored older workers. Accordingly, the employer's program that limited health benefits to workers over age 50 was sustained.

V—20.02   Proving Age Motivation

The proof models developed under Title VII have been adopted and applied under the ADEA. Direct or verbal evidence must be "evaluative" rather than merely "descriptive." Reference to a "good old boy network," "oldtimers," or "deadwood" are "descriptive" colloquialisms that will not support a finding of age motivation. *Pottenger v. Potlatch Corp.* (9th Cir. 2003). *Supra*, 9.02. Statistical evidence may be probative of motive behind selecting employees for layoff. *Supra*, 10.02(d).

An inference of illegally motivated disparate treatment can be created by showing that plaintiff was over age 40, was qualified for a vacancy and was not hired (or dismissed), and a person "substantially younger" than plaintiff was favored. *O'Connor v. Consolidated Coin Caterers* (S.Ct. 1996) involved a 56 year old plaintiff who had been dismissed and replaced by a person over 40 years old. The lower courts held that this created no initial inference of age motivation because *both* the plaintiff and his replacement were within the protected, "over 40" age class. The Court reversed. "[T]he fact that a replacement is *substantially younger* than the plaintiff is a far more reliable indicator of age discrimination than is the fact that the plaintiff was replaced by someone outside the protected class."

Once a prima facie case of disparate treatment based on age has been established, the employer must articulate a legitimate, non-discriminatory reason for plaintiff's treatment. *Supra,* 9.03(c). Subjective factors that may be code words for age, such as "potential" or "future," may not be legitimate. But objective factors "analytically distinct" from chronological age, such as relative output, absentee rates, education, or versatility, are legitimate even if they adversely affect older workers. *Hazen Paper v. Biggins, supra* (S.Ct. 1993). A wage difference between the younger and older worker is a legitimate reason for selecting the younger worker. *Marks v. Loral Corp.* (Cal. App. 1997).

Similar to Title VII, the ADEA specifically allows employers to observe bona fide seniority systems, with the proviso that such systems shall not require or permit involuntary retirement because of age. As seniority presupposes *increasing* benefits with length of service, a system would not be bona fide if benefits were *reduced* with length of service.

V—20.03 Defenses

Similar to Title VII, the ADEA allows the employer to justify age discrimination where age is a bona fide qualification for the position. *Supra,* 8.02(b). The ADEA contains two unique defenses based on the perceived need of certain employers to make age distinctions without carrying the burden of proving that age was a bona fide occupational qualification: 1) retirement of bona fide executives over age 65 and 2) hiring and retirement ages of firefighters and law enforcement officers. *Supra,* 8.02(b). Moreover, age requirements imposed by other federal laws and regulations having the force of law, such as mandatory retirement of air traffic controllers and age limits imposed on commercial air line pilots, have been upheld as indications of congressional intent to limit the scope of the ADEA. *Stewart v. Smith* (D.C.Cir. 1982). Finally, the ADEA allows benefit plans to make bona fide actuarial distinctions in the level of benefits provided employees based on relative risks attributable to age. *Supra,* 14.02.

V—20.04 Impact Analysis

Early authority uniformly held that impact analysis created in *Griggs v. Duke Power Co.* (S.Ct. 1971) could be applied under the ADEA. *Geller v. Markham* (2d Cir. 1980). *Hazen Paper Co. v. Biggins,* supra (S.Ct. 1993), holding that the ADEA reached only discrimination based on one's chronological age, and not on time-based factors, prompted many lower courts to reject liability based on the impact of a neutral factor on older workers. *Adams v. Florida Power Corp.* (11th Cir. 2001). Moreover, that the Civil Rights Act of 1991 codified impact analysis under Title VII, but made no codification into the ADEA, suggests that Congress did not intend for impact analysis to be used under the ADEA. Some courts, however, continue to recognize that use of neutral criteria that adversely impact the over 40 age class can be a basis for ADEA liability. *Pottenger v. Potlatch* (9th Cir. 2003).

Where impact analysis is recognized, plaintiff must prove the impact of a challenged device; impact will not be assumed to flow, even from the application of time measured factors. *Wooden v. Board of Educ. of Jefferson County* (6th Cir. 1991). The device must adversely affect the entire over—40 protected age group, not just sub-groups, such as those over age 60. *Lowe v. Commack Union Free School Dist.* (2d Cir. 1989). Cf., *Pottenger v. Potlatch Corp., supra.* ("older workers") Finally, the ADEA, unlike Title VII, specifically authorizes the use of "reasonable factors other than age." Thus even if impact is proved, the ADEA permits employers to avoid liability by proving that the neutral factor being challenged was "reasonable," a burden less onerous than the "business necessity" defense under Title VII.

CHAPTER 21

DISABILITY

V—21.01   Generally: An Overview

The Americans With Disabilities Act of 1990 (42 U.S.C.A. 1201)(ADA) has coverage coextensive with Title VII. (Except for the federal government. Disability discrimination against federal employers is proscribed in similar terms by the Rehabilitation Act of 1973, 29 U.S.C.A. 706, 791–794.) The ADA prohibits: 1) treating a qualified individual with a disability differently because of the disability, perceived disability, or record of a disability; 2) not making a reasonable accommodation to a known physical or mental limitation of an otherwise qualified individual with a disability, and 3) use of qualification standards or selection devices that tend to screen out individuals with disabilities.

Regardless of they type of discrimination plaintiffs must establish that they have: 1) a physical or mental impairment, 2) that "substantially limits" 3) a "major life activity," and 4) that they are "qualified" in that they can perform "essential job duties" with or without reasonable accommodation. "[T]hese terms need to be interpreted strictly to create a demanding standard for qualifying as disabled." *Toyota Motor Mfg., Ky., Inc. v. Williams*

(S.Ct. 2002). As the Act necessarily requires the employer to treat an employee with a disability differently, *i.e.*, preferentially, a non-disabled person does not have a claim under the ADA if an employer discriminates *in favor* of persons with disabilities. *US Airways, Inc. v. Barnett* (S.Ct. 2002).

V—21.02 "Record of"

The ADA prohibits discrimination because of an individual's "record of" having a disability even if the individual is not currently disabled, but that "record" must disclose a condition that reaches the level of being a "disability." Mere hospitalization or medical treatment records, such as cancer treatment or heart surgery, standing alone, do not create a "record of" a disability. *Burch v. Coca–Cola Co.* (5th Cir. 1997). See, *School Bd. Of Nassau County v. Arline* (S.Ct. 1987) where acute tuberculosis coupled with hospitalization created a "record" of disability.

V—21.03 "Regarded as Having"

The ADA prohibits discrimination against non-disabled individuals who are "regarded as having" a disability. *Sutton v. United Air Lines, Inc.* (S.Ct. 1999) held that the employer must subjectively have considered plaintiff's condition to be a defined "disability:"

By its terms the ADA allows employers to prefer some physical attributes over others and to establish physical criteria. An employer runs afoul of the ADA when it makes an employment decision based on a physical or mental impairment, real or imagined, that is regarded as substantially limiting a major life activity. Accordingly, an employer is free to decide that physical characteristics or medical conditions that do not rise to the level of an impairment—such as one's height, build, or singing voice—are preferable to others, just as it is free to decide that some limiting, but not substantially limiting, impairments make individuals less than ideally suited for a job.

Plaintiffs in *Sutton* were denied a position because of their acute myopia. The Court concluded that the employer did not "regard" corrected myopia as a condition that "substantially limited" plaintiffs' major life activities, only that the employer viewed plaintiffs' condition as precluding performance of a narrow range of jobs. Similarly, in *Murphy v. United Parcel Service, Inc.* (S.Ct. 1999), plaintiff was denied a mechanic position that required driving a truck because of his hypertension. Hypertension did not constitute a disability in that it did not impair a major life activity. Plaintiff was not "regarded as having a disability" because the employer only regarded plaintiff as being unable to perform the particular job he was denied.

An employee with a severely damaged hand was fired for using only one hand in securing a load to a truck in violation of a safety rule requiring use of both hands. The employee was not disabled because the injured hand did not substantially limit his

major life activities. Even though the employer described plaintiff as "crippled", "handicapped" and
"disabled," plaintiff failed to establish that the employer actually believed that plaintiff was substantially limited in performing major life activities.
Tockes v. Air–Land Transport Services, Inc. (7th
Cir. 2003). Nonetheless, an employer who requires
all injured or ill workers to establish that they are
"100% healed" before they are reinstated is regarding non-disabled persons as being disabled.
Henderson v. Ardco, Inc. (6th Cir. 2001).

V—21.04 "Disability" Defined

a.   "Impairment" vs. Characteristic

Plaintiff must suffer from a medically recognized
condition that reaches the level of impairing his/her
functions. General physical characteristics expected
within the normal range of the population, such as
height or weight differences, left vs. right handed-
ness, color of eyes or hair, baldness, or physical
attractiveness (not involving major disfigurement)
are not impairments. Obesity is not an impairment
until it reaches the extreme level of "morbidity."
Francis v. City of Meriden (2d Cir. 1997). Diseases,
even if contagious, such as tuberculosis and AIDS,
can be disabilities. *Bragdon v. Abbott* (S.Ct. 1998).

Mental impairment includes recognized mental or
psychological disorders including mental retarda-
tion, organic brain syndrome, emotional or mental
illness, and learning disabilities. Personality characteristics, variations in intelligence, aggressiveness,

excitability, or poor judgment are not mental impairments. Cultural or social status, including poverty or criminal proclivity, are not impairments. The ADA expressly excludes from the definition of disability homosexuality, bisexuality, transvestism, transsexualism, pedophilia, exhibitionism, gender identity disorders, sexual behavior disorders, compulsive gambling, kleptomania, and pyromania. Normal pregnancy is not a disability.

Addiction to alcohol or drugs, to be distinguished from a drinking or drug *problem*, is an impairment.

b.   *"Major Life Activity"*

The impairment must limit a "major life activity." *Toyota Motor Mfg., Ky., Inc. v. Williams* (S.Ct. 2002) held that severe carpal tunnel syndrome that prohibited a wide range of arm movement was not necessarily a disability. Plaintiff must prove that her impaired arm movement in fact prevented or severely restricted her "from doing activities that are of central importance to most people's lives" such eating, washing, dressing, and caring for one's self. Accordingly, severe medical conditions such as diabetes or epilepsy, as well as life endangering illnesses, such as multiple sclerosis, heart disease, or cancer, are not disabilities unless they limit the ability of the individual to engage in one or more "major life activities." *Ellison v. Software Spectrum, Inc.* (5th Cir. 1996)(cancer).

Hearing (*Davidson v. America Online* (10th Cir. 2003)), walking (*Belk v. Southwestern Bell Tel. Co.*

(8th Cir. 1999)), speaking, (*Stalter v. Board of Cooperative Educational Serv.* (S.D.N.Y. 2002)), seeing (*Shannon v. New York City Transit Authority* (2d Cir. 2003)(color blindness does not limit major life activity)), and breathing (*Rhoads v. FDIC* (4th Cir. 2001)) all are "major life activities" as are reproduction and sexual activity. *Bragdon v. Abbott, supra* (S.Ct. 1998) (HIV positive individual was restrained in her ability to engage in sex and bear healthy children). An insulin dependent "brittle" diabetic who had to assess blood sugar levels before eating anything, carefully time and measure the amount and nature of food taken, and have special food available at all times is limited in the major life activity of eating. *Lawson v. CSX Transp.* (7th Cir. 2001). By contrast, a person with dietary needs to attain or maintain a healthy life style, as where a person has moderate diabetes, is obese, or has a heart condition, is not impaired in the major life activity of eating. *Fraser v. Goodale* (9th Cir. 2003).

Major life activity includes the general ability to care for one's self by performing the basic chores needed to live in a healthy, sanitary environment. Thus, a person with missing fingers and an arm injury which required him to expend twice as much time to bathe, put on clothing, go to the toilet, and prepare a meal was impaired in the major life activity of caring for himself. *Fenny v. Dakota, Minnesota & Eastern R. Co.* (8th Cir. 2003). By contrast, general housework, shoveling snow, shopping, and playing recreational sports are not major life activities (*Marinelli v. City of Erie* (3d Cir.

2000)), nor is the ability to drive a vehicle. *Chenoweth v. Hillsborough Cty.* (11th Cir. 2001).

Where bipolar or ADD disorders cause an individual to have consistently high levels of abnormal hostility, social withdrawal, or inability to communicate, the major life activity of social intercourse is impaired. By contrast, aggressive, bashful, or difficult personalities are not impairments. *Doebele v. Sprint/United Management Co.* (10th Cir. 2003).

Working is a major life activity. However, "One must be precluded from more than one type of job, a specialized job, or a particular job of choice. If jobs utilizing an individual's skills (but perhaps not his or her unique talents) are available, one is not precluded from [working]." The courts must look to "the number and types of jobs using similar training, knowledge, skills, or abilities, within the geographical area, from which the individual is also disqualified." *Sutton v. United Air Lines, Inc., supra* (S.Ct. 1999). An employee with a lifting restriction was substantially limited in working where, given his education and work experience, he was precluded from 50% of the available jobs in the geographic area. *Burns v. Coca–Cola* (6th Cir. 2000). However, stress injuries that limited plaintiff's continuous keyboard use to 30 minutes a day, intermittent use to 60 minutes a day, continuous handwriting to five minutes a day, and intermittent writing to 60 minutes a day, while precluding certain jobs, did not substantially limit plaintiff in working. *Thornton v. McClatchy Newspapers, Inc.* (9th Cir. 2001).

c. *"Substantially Limit"*

The "major life activity" of the plaintiff must be *"substantially* limited." Courts look beyond a medical diagnosis and examine the plaintiff's own experience with the condition. *Toyota Motor Mfg., Ky., Inc. v. Williams, supra* (S.Ct. 2002). The point at which an impairment is "substantially limiting" is a matter of judgment and degree requiring evaluation of severity and duration. Non-severe impairments, such as anemia, trick knees, varicose veins, and simple pain in the back or legs, while annoying, painful, and somewhat limiting do not *"substantially"* limit major life activities. *Benoit v. Technical Mfg. Corp.* (1st Cir. 2003). Even severe, life threatening impairments such as asthma, allergies, hypertension, and heart disease, that limit life activities of eating and exertion, are not disabilities unless the individuals are substantially limited in their ability to care for themselves or cannot undertake meaningful employment. *Murphy v. United Parcel Service, Inc., supra* (S.Ct. 1999). A visual impairment that precluded plaintiff spending more than 50% of the day reading did not render plaintiff "substantially limited" in the major life activity of seeing. *Szmaj v. AT & T* (7th Cir. 2002).

To be "substantial" the limitation must occur with significant frequency. A person with epilepsy who suffered two or three seizures a month that lasted between 30 seconds and two minutes during which time she was unable to see, hear, speak, or walk was "substantially" limited in those life activities. *Otting v. J.C. Penney Co.* (8th Cir. 2000). By contrast a person with epilepsy who had only one seizure at work over a four year period was not "substantially" limited. *Brunke v. Goodyear Tire & Rubber Co.* (8th Cir. 2003).

"The impairment's impact must also be permanent or long term." *Toyota Motor Mfg. Ky., Inc., supra* (S.Ct. 2002). Temporarily disabling conditions such as broken bones, strained muscles, concussions, illnesses, and even the total incapacity following major surgery do not "substantially" limit major life activity. *McDonald v. Pennsylvania* (3d Cir. 1995). Note: The Family and Medical Leave Act requires covered employers to grant unpaid leave to qualified employees for the treatment of such serious medical conditions. *Supra* 14.04.

d. Correction and Control

Many conditions, if untreated, substantially limit major life activities, but while being treated are not substantially limiting. Diabetes, epilepsy, asthma, hypertension, depression, hearing and sight impediments are examples. The EEOC once asserted that an impairment is evaluated without regard to corrective or ameliorative measures. Persons with a disease or condition that substantially impaired critical bodily functions such as seeing, hearing, breathing, and walking *per se* were individuals with disabilities.

Sutton v. United Air Lines, Inc., supra (S.Ct. 1999), rejected the EEOC position. Plaintiffs suffered from severe myopia, having 20/400 vision uncorrected. As such, they were substantial impaired in the life activity of seeing. With corrective lenses, however, plaintiffs' vision was the normal 20/20. In this corrected state, no major life activity was substantially impaired. Defendant had a policy of not hiring individuals into airline pilot positions who had uncorrected vision of less than 20/100. On this basis plaintiffs' applications were rejected. The Court held that disability is to be determined with reference to corrective measures. Accordingly, plaintiffs' vision impairment, as corrected, did not substantially limit plaintiffs' major life activities of daily living or securing a wide range of employment. *Murphy v. United Parcel Service, supra* (S.Ct. 1999), decided along with *Sutton*, sustained a lower court holding that a mechanic dismissed from his job because of his hypertension stated no claim under the ADA in that his condition was controlled by his medication, and as controlled, the condition did not substantially limit plaintiff's major life activities. *Albertson's, Inc. v. Kirkingburg* (S.Ct. 1999), also decided along with *Sutton*, held that a plaintiff with sight in one eye only, and thus who had monocular vision, was not disabled because plaintiff's brain subconsciously adapted to the condition. "We see no principled basis for distinguishing between measures undertaken with artificial aids, like medications and devices, and measures undertaken, whether consciously or not, with the body's own systems."

Thus, a deaf person will not be substantially limited in a major life activity if hearing aids allow him hear. Diabetics, persons with epilepsy, bipolar disorder, or pancreatitis whose conditions are medically controlled to the point that while on medication they are not substantially limited in their major life activities are not individuals with disabilities. *Waldrip v. General Elec. Co.* (5th Cir. 2003).

Note: Some state statutes do not define disability to require "substantial" limitations. Others adopted the EEOC position and evaluate the plaintiff's condition without regard to ameliorating or corrective measures.

V—21.05 "Qualified Individual"

a. Generally

The individual with a defined "disability" is protected only if he/she establishes that he/she is "qualified." An individual with a disability is "qualified" if he/she possesses the "requisite skill, experience, and education requirements of the employment position," *and* "with or without reasonable accommodation can perform *essential* functions of such position." 42 U.S.C.A. 1211(8).

b. Job Prerequisites

Employers may establish levels of education, skill, experience, and other job related requirements. Individuals, including those with disabilities, who cannot meet established standards are not "qualified." 29 CFR 1630.2(m). A truck driver who could not meet visual acuity standards set by federal regulatory guidelines was not "qualified." *Albertson's, Inc. v. Kirkingburg, supra* (S.Ct. 1999).

c. *"Essential" vs. Non–Essential Job Functions*

If an individual with a disability possesses job prerequisites but cannot perform some aspect of the job because of the disability, it is critical to determine whether the aspect he cannot perform is "essential" or "non-essential." If the inability is limited to non-essential job functions, the individual is "qualified." To illustrate, when a power company employee who had both legs amputated and was fitted with prostheses that inhibited his ability to climb, the inquiry was whether climbing is an "essential" function of the job. If climbing was not "essential" to this job the individual was "qualified" and must be hired. *Lowe v. Alabama Power Co.* (11th Cir. 2001).

A duty is "essential" if removing it would fundamentally alter the nature of the position. *Davidson v. America Online, Inc.* (10th Cir. 2003). It involves a case-by-case balancing of a number of factors: 1) whether the particular task is the reason the position exists; 2) the number of employees capable of performing the task; 3) the level of expertise, skill, or training required to perform the task; 4) the time spent performing it; 5) the consequences of not requiring the employee to perform the function in terms of disruption of work assignments, burdens on other workers, and increased costs; and 6) whether all employees in the classification are required to perform the duty. The fact finder will also examine and give some consideration to four additional elements: 1) employer's stated judgement as to what tasks are essential, 2) the written job description, 3) collective bargaining agreements, and 4) past experience in the same or similar jobs. 29 CFR 1630.2(n). The following illustrate applications of this distinction:

* The ability to stay awake on the job *(Byrne v. Avon Products, Inc.* (7th Cir. 2003)) and the ability to arrive at work punctually and to work normal shifts usually are seen as "essential," and require the court to determine whether a variance would be a "reasonable" accommodation. *Halperin v. Abacus Technology Corp.* (4th Cir. 1997).

* A blind applicant for a school librarian position could perform all library duties, but could not perform hall and playground supervision of students. Duties of hall and playground supervision were nonessential; plaintiff was "qualified." *Norcross v. Sneed* (8th Cir. 1985). By contrast, the ability of an airline gate employee to lift and assist elderly or disabled passengers to and from airplanes was essential, even though infrequently required and other employees were available to perform the duty. *Summerville v. Trans World Airlines, Inc.* (8th Cir. 2000). Heavy lifting may be an essential aspect of a nurse's job. *Deane v. Pocono Med. Ctr.* (3d Cir. 1998) (en banc).

* The ability to inspect cars was not essential for a manager of a used car dealership. *Pals v. Schepel Buick & GMC Truck, Inc.* (7th Cir. 2000). However,

vacuuming was essential for a housekeeping supervisor. *Alexander v. The Northland Inn* (8th Cir. 2003).

* Where neatness and civility are not mandated by interaction with customers or fellow employees, such personal qualities are non-essential. *Den Hartog v. Wasatch Academy* (10th Cir. 1997). Where personal interaction is part of the job, the ability to act civilly toward customers or co-workers is essential. *Palmer v. Circuit Court, Cook County* (7th Cir. 1997).

* An applicant for assistant store manager was denied the position because her epilepsy prohibited her from obtaining a driver's license. Assistant managers were expected to make bank deposits, and usually drove themselves to the bank. The ability to drive was not "essential." Making deposits was essential, but an assistant manager could accomplish this task using alternative means of transportation or assigning this infrequent duty to others. *Lovejoy-Wilson v. NOCO Motor Fuel, Inc.* (2d Cir. 2001).

* The employer required prior "voice phone" experience for a position that did not itself require hearing. Because of her deafness plaintiff had no "voice phone" experience, and because of this lack of experience, she was denied the position. That deaf persons had filled the position until a policy change a few years early, coupled with the fact that persons with as little as two weeks "voice phone" experience had been transferred to it, suggested

that "voice phone" experience was not "essential." *Davidson v. America Online, Inc.* (10th Cir. 2003).

d. *"Direct Threat to Health or Safety"*

An individual is not "qualified" if he/she poses a "direct threat to the health or safety of other individuals in the work place" that cannot be eliminated or reduced to acceptable levels by reasonable accommodation. 29 CFR 1630.2(r). *School Bd. of Nassau County v. Arline* (S.Ct. 1987) held that an individual with tuberculosis was "qualified" to be a school teacher only if she did not pose a significant risk of transmitting the disease to others. That risk assessment should be based on reasonable medical judgments as to: a) the nature of the risk, in particularly how the disease is transmitted, b) the duration of the risk, that is, how long is the carrier infectious, and c) the probabilities the disease will be transmitted balanced against the degree of harm should it be transmitted. A teacher with AIDS was "qualified" in that she posed no significant risk to students or co-workers. *Chalk v. United States Dist. Court* (9th Cir. 1988). By contrast, an HIV-positive dental hygienist did pose a direct threat. Although the risk of transmittal was low, the risk of death in the event of a transmission warranted a finding that the threat was great enough to render the hygienist "unqualified." *Waddell v. Valley Forge Dental Assocs.* (11th Cir. 2001). An insulin dependent diabetic bus driver who presented a risk of collapsing was not "qualified." *Daugherty v. El Paso* (5th Cir. 1995).

Chevron U.S.A., Inc. v. Echazabal (S.Ct. 2002) addressed the validity of EEOC regulations authorizing the refusal of an employer to hire an individual because his condition presented a threat solely to the individual's *own* health. Plaintiff suffered from a liver condition that could be aggravated by continued exposure to toxins present at this employer's workplace. The Court rejected plaintiff's argument that concern for the employee's health that presented no risks to others, could not justify a finding that plaintiff was not "qualified." Deferring to the EEOC, the Court found legitimate employer concerns of lost time to sickness, excessive turnover from medical retirements, possible litigation under state tort law, and possible conflict with occupational safety legislation. Defendant must prove the actual threat to the health or safety of the employee through available objective scientific opinion of the medical profession. Good faith of the employer, even relying on an evaluation by its own non-expert physicians, does not establish the "defense" where defendant's non-expert opinion is not in accord with prevailing expert authority. *Eschazabal v. Chevron USA, Inc.* (9th Cir. 2003).

e. Accommodations that Permit Performance of "Essential" Duties

If an individual cannot perform an essential duty without accommodation, the inquiry becomes whether the individual could perform this duty if an accommodation were provided, and, if so, whether that accommodation would be "reasonable." If plaintiff could perform the essential function with an accommodation, *and* the necessary accommodation is reasonable, plaintiff is "qualified." Plaintiff must suggest the accommodation that would allow performance, and present evidence that the proposed accommodation, on its face, seems reasonable. If plaintiff makes this showing, the burden shifts to the employer to demonstrate the undue hardship of the proposed accommodation. *US Airways, Inc. v. Barnett* (S.Ct. 2002).

Reasonableness does not mean the best accommodation possible. "Reasonable" means, in the run of the cases, and on its face, feasible and plausible. *US Airways, Inc. v. Barnett, supra* (S.Ct. 2002) Nonetheless, "reasonable accommodation" under the ADA requires more from employers and may impose greater costs than the *de minimis* accommodation required for religious practices under Title VII. *Compare, supra,* 19.03. That a requested accommodation violates a neutral rule or gives the individual with a disability a preference over non-disabled persons will not, in itself, render the requested accommodation unreasonable.

In *US Airways, Inc. v. Barnett, supra* (S.Ct. 2002) plaintiff, who suffered a serious back injury, had been temporarily assigned to a less physically demanding mail room position. The employer's established seniority system permitted employees to bid for the position. Plaintiff sought an exception to the seniority system as an accommodation to his disability that would allow him to remain in the mail room. The employer refused to make an exception, and a non-disabled person with greater seniority was given the position. In a plurality opinion the Court assumed that absent a bona fide seniority system, plaintiff's proposed light work assignment would have been reasonable. However, if an accommodation requires ignoring seniority expectations of co-workers, *ordinarily* this would be unreasonable. "Hence a showing that the assignment would violate the rules of a seniority system warrants summary judgment for the employer—*unless there is more*." Plaintiff must present evidence of that "more", namely, special circumstances surrounding the particular case that demonstrate the assignment is nonetheless reasonable. Justice O'Connor concurred in the outcome, but disagreed with the analysis of the plurality. Justices Scalia and Thomas dissented, arguing that accommodations disregarding bona fide seniority are never reasonable.

Determining if an accommodation is "reasonable" rests on the unique facts of each case. To illustrate, the ability to work according to a schedule established by the employer is "essential." A disability makes it impossible for the employee to comply with the schedule. If the job involves office work and the accommodation requested is for short breaks or a slightly modified work schedule in order for the individual to rest or to take medication, the requested accommodation may be "reasonable", and if so, the individual is "qualified." Whereas, if the job is on an assembly line and a schedule

modification would require stopping the line or result in a chaotic substitution of another worker, the
requested modification might be "unreasonable;"
the individual would not be "qualified." Intermittent time off may be reasonable when a person with
arthritis or lupus occasionally is unable to come
work because of the pain. Granting an employee a
multi-month leave is unreasonable. *Byrne v. Avon
Products* (7th Cir. 2003)

That an employer has provided the accommodation in the past does not establish the reasonableness of an employee's request that it be continued.
An employer is free to discontinue accommodations
not required by law. *Watson v. Lithonia Lighting*
(7th Cir. 2002).

V—21.06 Failure to Accommodate and "Un-
due Hardship"

Once plaintiff makes an initial showing that a
suggested accommodation, on its face, appears reasonable, the individual with the disability has established that he/she is "qualified." The burden shifts
to the employer to demonstrate the "undue hardship" of the proposed accommodation. *US Airways,
Inc. v. Barnett, supra* (S.Ct. 2002). If the suggested
accommodation does not impose a hardship that is
"undue," the employer is required to undertake the
accommodation. Conversely, if the employer establishes the undue hardship of the requested accommodation, there is no obligation on the employer to
make the accommodation.

A hardship is "undue" when it imposes "significant difficulty or expense." 29 CFR 1630.2(p)(2). The factors to consider in determining "significant difficulty or expense" are: 1) nature and cost of the suggested accommodation, 2) financial resources of the particular facility, 3) overall financial resources of the employer, 4) type and operation of the entity, 5) impact of the accommodation on operations; whether the accommodation would fundamentally alter the duties of the position or change overall business operations, and 6) impact and burdens on other employees. The point at which the hardship of an accommodation is "undue" rests on the unique facts of each case. The EEOC has noted areas where accommodation should be *considered*.

—Accessibility: Employers must make the work place accessible such as providing wheelchair ramps and braille markers. Rest rooms and drinking fountains must be made accessible. *Marcano-Rivera v. Pueblo Int'l, Inc.* (1st Cir. 2000). However, lowering of a sink in a lunchroom to accommodate one wheelchair-bound employee imposed an undue hardship in light of the high costs and the presence of low sinks in rest rooms. *Vande Zande v. Wisconsin* (7th Cir. 1995). It is not an undue hardship on an employer with no pets and no trespassing rules to permit a blind employee to bring a guide dog or a personal assistant to work. *Johnson v. Gambrinus Co.* (5th Cir. 1997). Employers need not, however, provide "private" benefits that extend beyond an employee's unique work place needs, such as providing wheelchairs, eyeglasses, or prosthetic limbs. 29 CFR Part 1630, Appendix 1630.9.

—Equipment Modifications: Providing necessary work place equipment such as sound amplifiers on telephones, enlargers for monitors, and ergonomic furniture will not impose undue hardships even for small employers. *Crane v. Lewis* (D.D.C. 1982).

—Job Duty Realignments: An employer may have to reassign to other workers some essential aspects of the job the individual with the disability cannot perform, provided that the realignment does not redefine core job duties or assign significant, burdensome duties to other employees. *Alexander v. The Northland Inn* (8th Cir. 2003).

—Work Schedule Modification: Flexibility in work schedules to accommodate an employee's need to take medication or to rest, or to take reasonable amounts of unpaid leave often present no undue hardship. *Ward v. Massachusetts Health Research Institute* (1st Cir. 2000). (Such leave also may be required under the Family and Medical Leave Act). Grants of extended or extraordinary amounts of leave can be an undue hardship. *Walsh v. United Parcel Service* (6th Cir. 2000). Where an employer does not provide part-time work generally, it may constitute an undue hardship to allow an individual with a disability to work indefinitely at less than full time. *Terrell v. USAir* (11th Cir. 1998). Whether it is an undue hardship to allow disabled employees to telecommute—working at home rather than commuting to the place of business—depends on the nature of the employee's work. *Humphrey v. Memorial Hospitals Ass'n* (9th Cir. 2001).

—Readers, Interpreters, and Assistants: The obligation to provide an assistant varies with the size of the employer, the extent of the assistance needed, and the number of employees who could use the assistant. If providing an assistant would require full-time service used by one employee only, the expense may constitute an undue hardship; employers are not expected to hire two employees to perform a single job. On the other hand, if providing an assistant required only an occasional reassignment of another employee, or if a single assistant could be used by a number of disabled workers, the accommodation might impose no undue hardship on large employers.

—Transfer and Reassignment: If a lateral vacancy exists, and other accommodations are inadequate, the employer's duty requires more than merely allowing the employee with a disability to compete for the vacancy. Unless seniority rights direct otherwise, the general principle is that the employee with the disability should be reassigned to the vacancy. *Smith v. Midland Brake, Inc.* (10th Cir. 1999)(en banc). Nonetheless, reassignment is "an accommodation of the last resort," required only if necessary to enable the employee to continue working. *Burchett v. Target Corp.* (8th Cir. 2003). For a reassignment not to impose an undue hardship, there must be a vacancy. The employer need not create a new position (*Jay v. Intermet Wagner,*

Inc. (7th Cir. 2000)), and bumping an incumbent employee from the job imposes an undue hardship. *Hansen v. Henderson* (7th Cir. 2000). Second, the vacant position must be similar to the job the individual with a disability cannot perform. There is no obligation to promote the employee to a higher paying position, or to reassign the disabled employee to an entirely different class of job. *Lucas v. W.W. Grainger, Inc.* (11th Cir. 2001). Third, plaintiff must be qualified and able to perform. Some orientation for the new job does not impose an undue hardship; extensive re-training does. *Williams v. United Ins. Co. of America* (7th Cir. 2001). It may be an undue hardship to require reassignment of a minimally qualified disabled individual when other candidates have significantly greater qualifications. *EEOC v. Humiston–Keeling, Inc.* (7th Cir. 2000). Finally, disregarding seniority *usually* imposes an undue hardship. *US Airways, Inc. v. Barnett, supra* (S.Ct. 2002).

V—21.07 Alcoholism and Drug Addiction

Addiction to alcohol or drugs is a medical condition, to be distinguished from an alcohol or drug "problem." Addiction is a disability, however, only when the condition substantially limits the major life activity of being able to live independently and care for oneself. Inebriation resulting from alcoholism that resulted only in a temporary inability to walk, talk, think, and sleep, did not substantially limit those activities. *Burch v. Coca–Cola Co.* (5th Cir. 1997). Nonetheless, an across-the-board refusal to employ alcoholics or rehabilitated drug addicts, or those perceived to be addicted or who have a record of such addiction, is proscribed. *Miners v. Cargill Communications* (8th Cir. 1997). An individual cannot be discriminated against because he has completed or is currently participating in an alcohol or drug rehabilitation program. 42 U.S.C.A. 12114(b). There are three caveats:

1) Current use of illegal drugs is not protected. This is true even if the illegal activity is caused by the addiction, and even if the addiction or drug use does not directly interfere with the employee's job performance. *Shafer v. Preston Memorial Hosp.* (4th Cir. 1997). "Current use" of illegal drugs is defined by the EEOC as having occurred recently enough to justify an employer's reasonable belief that involvement is an ongoing problem. Thus, an employee who had recently used cocaine and had been notified that dismissal proceedings would begin, is not protected even though he had ceased illegal use by the time termination proceedings were completed. *Zenor v. El Paso Healthcare System, Ltd.* (5th Cir. 1999). As drug testing is not considered a "medical examination," employers are free to test applicants or employees for illegal use of drugs and to make employment decisions based on the results of such tests. 42 U.S.C.A. 12114(d).

2) The individual must be able to come to work, conform to attendance policies, secure necessary licenses, and perform job duties. Inability to per-

form because of addiction is not protected. *Maddox v. University of Tenn.* (6th Cir. 1995).

3) Employers may restrict possession or use of alcohol at the work place or during working hours, and may dismiss employees, even alcoholics, who violate such policies. 42 U.S.C.A. 12114(c). In *Raytheon Co. v. Hernandez* (S.Ct. 2003) plaintiff, while an employee, was forced to resign for inappropriate use of alcohol on the employer's premises. Thereafter, plaintiff completed rehabilitation treatments and applied for re-employment. The employer refused to hire plaintiff based on its broad policy of not rehiring former employees who had been dismissed for misconduct. The Court held that such a policy was a "legitimate non-discriminatory" reason for rejecting the former employee. That such a policy might have an adverse impact on disabled persons did not deprive the "no-rehire" policy of its legitimacy. The Court did not address the issue of whether such a policy would be valid under an adverse impact theory of liability.

V—21.08   The "Interactive Process"

Plaintiff who cannot perform essential duties without an accommodation must disclose and document the nature of the disability (even if it is embarrassing) and suggest with some specificity the accommodation that would allow performance. *Conneen v. MBNA America Bank, N.A.* (3d Cir. 2003). Once an apparently reasonable accommodation is suggested, the employer has an obligation to make the accommodation, or, if not, to engage in an "interactive process" that explores with the disabled individual the reasonableness of the request and suggest alternatives that might meet the individual's needs with less of a hardship on the employer. 29 CFR 1630.2(*o*). The obligation might include exploring job realignment or identifying alternative jobs. The employer may not sit back passively, offer nothing, and then in post-termination litigation, try to knock down each possible accommodation as unduly burdensome. *Taylor v. Phoenixville School Dist.* (3d Cir. 1999).

Defendant's failure to engage in good faith in the process creates an assumption that plaintiff's suggested accommodation was reasonable, and thus makes summary judgement in favor of defendant unlikely. *Shapiro v. Twsp. of Lakewood* (3d Cir. 2002). Moreover, good faith interactive efforts may allow an employer ultimately held liable to avoid compensatory or punitive damages. 42 U.S.C.A. 1981A(a)(3).

The employee has a reciprocal obligation to respond to employer suggestions. The employee may not insist on her proposed accommodation while rejecting out of hand rational employer proposals. Failure of the employee to engage in the interactive process may relieve the employer of further attempts to accommodate and will make the employee's suggested accommodation presumptively unreasonable, thus increasing the chance of summary judgment for the employer. *Steffes v. Stepan Co.* (7th Cir. 1998).

V—21.09 Proof of Motive

The employer's motivation frequently is not at issue; the employer admits that it was plaintiff's perceived inability to perform that prompted its decision. Only when the employer denies that plaintiff's disability motivated its action, does the court have to address defendant's motive. Models of proof developed under Title VII are applied. Plaintiff may present verbal evidence, *(Supra,* 9.02), or may proceed using the *McDonnell Douglas* model, creating an inference of illegal motivation by demonstrating that: 1) he/she is a "qualified individual with a disability," 2) he/she was subjected to an adverse employment action, and 3) similarly situated individuals without disabilities were more favorably treated. If plaintiff establishes such a prima facie case, the employer's burden is to "articulate a legitimate non-discriminatory reason" for its treatment of plaintiff. *Supra,* 9.03 (c). That the articulated reason might have an adverse impact on persons with disabilities does not deprive it of legitimacy. If the employer carries this modest evidentiary burden, plaintiff must present additional evidence that the articulated reason was pretext, and carry the ultimate burden of persuading the fact finder of the employer's illegal motive. Absent proof by plaintiff that the employer's neutral reason or policy was a pretext, defendant must prevail. *Raytheon Co. v. Hernandez, supra* (S.Ct. 2003).

V—21.10   "Qualifications" That Have an Adverse Impact

a. Generally

The ADA adopts impact analysis as codified in Title VII. It is illegal discrimination to use:

> qualification standards, employment tests, or other selection criteria that screen out or tend to screen out an individual with a disability or a class of individuals with disabilities unless the standard, test, or other selection criteria * * * is shown to be job related for the position in question and is consistent with business necessity. 42 U.S.C.A. 12112(b)(6).

Plaintiff must prove the adverse impact of the qualification on either the individual or the class. *McWright v. Alexander* (7th Cir. 1992). If impact is established, the burden shifts to the defendant to prove that the qualification was both "job related" and "consistent with business necessity." *Supra* 11.05.

In *Albertson's, Inc. v. Kirkingburg, supra* (S.Ct. 1999), the employer enforced a qualification that drivers meet applicable federal safety regulations. The federal regulation required certain vision acuity in each eye. Plaintiff failed to meet that standard. Nonetheless, while the regulation allowed waiver of the standard, the employer refused to seek such a waiver. Plaintiff thereafter himself secured a waiver, but defendant continued to refuse to hire him. The Court held that the employer was not in violation of the ADA solely because it refused to seek or recognize the waiver of the credential. The Court refused to impose on the employer the burden of showing the business necessity of a generally applicable governmentally imposed safety regulation.

b. Tests

The Act also specifically makes it illegal for employers to fail:

> to select and administer tests concerning employment in the most effective manner to insure that a job applicant or employee who has a disability that impairs sensory, manual or speaking skills, that such test results accurately reflect * * * whatever factor that such test purports to measure, rather than reflecting the impaired sensory, manual, or speaking skills of such employee or applicant (except where such skills are the factors that the test purports to measure). 42 U.S.C.A. 12112(b)(7).

Tests cannot be challenged by non-disabled persons. A plaintiff who could not lift the required 100 lbs because of a medical condition—but who was not "disabled" in that he was not "substantially limited" in a "major life activity"—could not challenge the employer's lifting standard. *Fuzy v. S & B Engineers & Constructors, Ltd.* (5th Cir. 2003).

V—21.11 Disability Claims Made Elsewhere

Persons with disabilities may have applied for or received state or federal benefits based on assertions and/or adjudications that they were totally or substantially disabled, and thus not "qualified" for continued employment. *Cleveland v. Policy Management Systems Corp.* (S.Ct. 1999), recognized that "plaintiff's sworn statement that she is * * * 'unable to work' will appear to negate an essential element of her ADA case. * * * For that reason * * * an ADA plaintiff cannot simply ignore the apparent contradiction that arises out of the earlier [social security] total disability claim. * * * When faced with a plaintiff's previous sworn statement asserting 'total disability' or the like, the court should require an explanation of any apparent inconsistency with the necessary elements of an ADA claim." In the absence of such an explanation, defendant will prevail.

CHAPTER 22

RETALIATION

V—22.01 Generally

Title VII, the ADEA, and the ADA, in similar language protect individuals against retaliation because of their "participation" in proceedings under the Acts or who have "opposed any practice made unlawful" by the Acts. 42 U.S.C.A. 2000e–3(a). Federal employees are protected against retaliation by regulation. 29 CFR 1614.101. Protection extends to employees or applicants based on the "participation" or "opposition" of a spouse or relative. *Aquino v. Sommer Maid Creamery* (E.D. Pa. 1987). The statutes implicitly protect former employees. A defined "employer" may not give bad references to prospective employers based on the fact that the individual had participated in EEO proceedings or had "opposed" illegal practices of the employer. *Robinson v. Shell Oil Co.* (S.Ct. 1997).

V—22.02 "Participation"

"Participation in proceedings" is absolutely protected in that an employer may not retaliate against an employee, even for false and malicious statements made as part of "proceedings." *Pettway v. American Cast Iron Pipe Co.* (5th Cir. 1969). An employer may sue an employee under state defamation law for statements made by the employee during non-judicial proceedings if: 1) recovery under state law requires proof of malice, 2) the employer has a reasonable basis for eventual recovery, and 3) the suit has been initiated for the purpose of vindicating the employer's good name and not to retaliate against the employee or to deter others from asserting their rights. *Bill Johnson's Restaurants v. NLRB* (S.Ct. 1983).

"Participation" includes charges with the EEOC or state enforcement agencies, evidence or testimony given during the investigation by enforcement agencies, judicial actions, and testimony given as part of those proceedings, including discovery. *Deravin v. Kerik* (2d Cir. 2003) (non-party testimony). Writing a letter to the EEOC complaining about the agency's failure to find "reasonable cause" that also asserted employer corruption was considered a motion for reconsideration and thus protected "participation." *Pettway v. American Cast Iron Pipe Co., supra* (5th Cir. 1969). Participation also includes reasonable gathering of non-confidential evidence in anticipation of a formal proceeding. *Grant v. Hazelett Strip–Casting Corp.* (2d Cir. 1989). Statements made outside the statutory processes are *not* "participation" even if the same statement was made during a proceeding. Thus, when an employer discharged an employee for lying during an employer's internal investigation, the employee was as not discharged for "participation." *EEOC v. Total Sys. Servs., Inc.* (11th Cir. 2000).

V—22.03 "Opposition"

a. Employee Conduct: "Reasonableness"

"Opposition" to employer practices include making internal complaints about the treatment being accorded plaintiff or other individuals, (*Fine v. Ryan Intern. Airlines* (7th Cir. 2002)), filing grievances with private civil rights or labor organizations, circulating petitions, writing letters to legislators, publishing advertisements, making statements to the media, or engaging in lawful concerted activity such as striking, picketing, or encouraging consumer boycotts. "Opposition" is protected only if the acts of the employee are lawful and reasonable. Trespass or violent behavior such as sit down strikes, blocking access to the premises, or inducing work stoppages that violate collective bargaining agreements or federal law are not protected "opposition." *Green v. McDonnell Douglas Corp.* (8th Cir. 1972).

Unlike the broad, perhaps absolute, protection given to "participation," false and malicious statements made as part of one's "opposition" are not protected. *Hicks v. ABT Associates, Inc.* (3rd Cir. 1978). Good faith belief by the employer that the employee lied to the employer on a material fact may justify the employee's discharge. Lies are not protected opposition. *EEOC v. Total System Services, Inc.* (11th Cir. 2000). Simple "disloyalty" to the employer is not a basis for retaliation based on the employee's public opposition. But if the employee maligns the product or services of the employer, this opposition is unprotected *Hochstadt v. Worcester Foundation for Experimental Biology* (1st Cir. 1976). Protected opposition does not extend to disrupting the work of other employees or to copying and distributing confidential documents. *Jennings v. Tinley Park Community Consolidated School Dist. No. 146* (7th Cir. 1988).

b. Practices Being Opposed: "Unlawful"

The language of the statute suggests that the employer's practice being opposed must be "unlawful." Nonetheless, if the employee believes in good faith that the practices being opposed were unlawful, and if there is a reasonable basis for reaching that conclusion, otherwise legitimate opposition is protected. Conversely, if a reasonable person would not believe that the practice opposed was illegal, the opposition, even if mild, is unprotected. In *Clark County School Dist. v. Breeden,* (S.Ct. 2001) the behavior plaintiff opposed consisted of a supervisor's sexual reference regarding an applicant followed by "chuckling." The Court concluded that no reasonable person could have believed that this one incident violated Title VII's prohibition against sexual harassment. Accordingly, plaintiff's opposition to the incident was not protected. Similarly, protesting an employer's failure to implement an affirmative action plan was unprotected in that the protesting employees could not reasonably have believed that the employer had acted illegally in not implementing a plan. *Holden v. Owens–Illinois, Inc.* (6th Cir. 1986). It is not reasonable for an employee to believe that Title VII prohibits discrimination based on sexual orientation. Therefore, objecting to discrimination against homosexuals was not protected "opposition." *Hamner v. St. Vincent Hosp. & Health Care Ctr., Inc.* (7th Cir. 2000).

Opposing employer practices outside the employment relationship is not protected. Thus objections to a *teacher's* alleged favoritism toward a Caucasian *student* was unprotected in that it was not an objection to a practice made illegal by Title VII. *Artis v. Francis Howell N. Band Booster Ass'n, Inc.* (8th Cir. 1998).

V—22.04 "Discriminate"

It is unlawful for an employer to "discriminate" against employees or applicants because of their participation or opposition, an obligation not qualified by "terms and conditions of employment." Accordingly, providing poor references because of a former employee's "participation" or "opposition" is prohibited even though a "term of employment" was not denied. *Robinson v. Shell Oil Co.* (S.Ct. 1997). An action is "discriminatory" if it is likely to deter plaintiff or other employees from engaging in the protected activity, and thus could include providing negative performance evaluations or inflicting petty indignities. Cf. *Ledergerber v. Stangler* (8th Cir. 1997)(retaliation must affect "term and condition of employment").

The ADA is even more explicit, making it unlawful to "coerce, intimidate, threaten, or interfere with any individual because they have exercised or enjoyed any right granted or protected by the Act." 42 U.S.C.A. 12203(b). The plaintiff, however, must show some injury flowing from a mere "threat" such as chilling the assertion of ADA rights. *Brown v. City of Tucson* (9th Cir. 2003).

"Discrimination" does not require an intent to punish the employee. If the action was in response to the participation, good faith is no defense. A union's refusal to process a grievance because a discrimination charge was pending with an enforcement agency is unlawful retaliation. *Johnson v. Palma* (2d Cir. 1991). Similarly, a provision in a collective bargaining agreement that terminates grievance proceedings once a lawsuit is filed, is retaliation for filing the suit, even though the contractual provision was designed to preserve resources and avoid duplicative proceedings. *EEOC v. Board of Gov., State Colleges & Universities* (7th Cir. 1992).

V—22.05　Causal Connection

Plaintiff must prove that the employer's action was "because of" protected employee activity. Notations in employment files such as "EEO action" and "pending complaint" will support a finding that a promotion was denied because of protected activity. *Terry v. Ashcroft* (2d Cir. 2003). A statement that plaintiff was a "problem employee" in the context of referring to an EEOC charge was direct evidence of retaliatory motive. *Fabela v. Socorro Ind. School Dist.* (5th Cir. 2003).

An inference of improper motivation also can be created by a "temporal proximity" between the protected activity and the adverse action. Plaintiff must prove that the decision maker was aware of plaintiff's protected activity, and that the time between the protected activity and the adverse action was "very close." Adverse action that followed plaintiff's protected activity by 20 months was too far removed in time to permit an inference of a causal connection. *Clark County School Dist. v. Breeden* (S.Ct. 2001). Lower courts have demanded even greater proximity. *Trammel v. Simmons First Bank of Searcy* (8th Cir. 2003)(two month interval is too long).

Plaintiff's demonstration of a "temporal proximity" between the protected activity and the employer's adverse treatment of plaintiff creates only a prima facie case of illegal retaliation. Defendant is free to "articulate legitimate, non-retaliatory reason" for its action. If defendant presents evidence of such a reason, plaintiff must carry the ultimate burden of persuading the fact finder of defendant's retaliatory motive. *Stone v. Indianapolis Pub. Util. Div.* (7th Cir. 2002).

Evidence may suggest that even if defendant harbored a retaliatory motive, it would have made the same decision on wholly legitimate grounds. For example, an employee who had filed an EEOC charge is soon thereafter transferred, and the evidence indicates that economic reasons, as well as the EEOC charge, may have played a role in the decision. Even if a retaliatory motive was present, the employer may avoid *liability* by convincing the fact finder that it would have transferred plaintiff *solely* on legitimate grounds. See, *supra* 9.04. The Civil Rights Act of 1991, which imposed liability for discrimination if *a* motive is discriminatory, subjecting the employer to injunctive relief and attorney's fees liability, may not be applicable to retaliation cases. *Tanca v. Nordberg* (1st Cir. 1996).

*

PART VI

ENFORCEMENT

CHAPTER 23

REMEDIES

VI—23.01 Introduction

a. The Statutes

Title VII and the ADA provide that when the defendant [h]as intentionally engaged in * * * an unlawful employment practice * * * the court may enjoin the * * * practice, and order such affirmative action as may be appropriate, which may include, but is not limited to reinstatement or hiring of employees, with or without back pay * * * or any other equitable relief as the court deems appropriate. 42 U.S.C.A. 2000e–5(g). Amendments in 1991 allow recovery of compensatory and punitive damages, but place dollar limits on recovery. 42 U.S.C.A. 1981A(a)(1). Compensatory, but not punitive, damages are recoverable against governmental employers.

As an amendment to the Fair Labor Standards Act, the Equal Pay Act incorporates the remedies of that Act. Illegal pay differences are collectable as unpaid back wages. A prevailing plaintiff is entitled to an additional amount equal to back wages as liquidated damages unless the employer can establish that it acted in good faith and with a reasonable basis for believing that it had not violated the Act.

The Age Discrimination in Employment Act also incorporates the remedial provisions of the Fair Labor Standards Act, as well as authorizing the grant of equitable relief in language similar to Title VII. 29 U.S.C.A. 626(b). By partially incorporating the Fair Labor Standards Act, the ADEA authorizes liquidated damages equal to unpaid wage liability. To recover liquidated damages under the ADEA, plaintiff must prove that defendant's violation was willful. Except for illegal retaliation, the ADEA does *not* authorize compensatory or punitive damages.

The Family and Medical Leave Act provides remedies of reinstatement and back wages as well as liquidated damages similar to the Equal Pay Act.

b. The "Make Whole" Directive

While the statutes allow remedies only for "intentional" violations, "intentional" means that the discriminatory act was not accidental. Remedial power is not dependent upon proof that defendant intentionally violated the law. Statutory terms "may" and "with our without back pay" suggest broad judicial discretion to deny relief. *Albemarle Paper Co. v. Moody* (S.Ct. 1975), however, found an overriding statutory purpose to "make whole" victims of discrimination: "The injured party must be placed, as near as may be, in the situation he would have occupied if the wrong had not been committed." Discretion does not extend to withholding remedies necessary to make a victim "whole."

VI—23.02 Hiring and Reinstatement

The statutes authorize courts to order "reinstatement or hiring." As they are necessary to "make whole" victims of discrimination, judicial discretion to withhold a hiring order is severely limited. That the victim has moved or is currently employed elsewhere does not warrant its denial. *EEOC v. General Lines, Inc.* (10th Cir. 1989). Personality conflicts or hard feelings engendered by the litigation generally do not justify denial of reinstatement (*Che v. Massachusetts Bay Transp. Auth.* (1st Cir. 2003)), unless the position involves a confidential relationship or the discord is so extreme that it precludes effective performance. *Price v. Marshall Erdman & Assoc., Inc.* (7th Cir. 1992).

To order the immediate hiring of a victim requires a vacancy. Courts will not order a current employee bumped from a position. Rather, the court will order "front pay" in lieu of reinstatement and require defendant to hire the plaintiff into the first available appropriate vacancy. If the discrimination was blatant, the position unique (such as a museum curator), and if there are viable alternatives for the incumbent employee, courts have ordered the immediate hiring of the victim even if the position is currently occupied. *Walters v. Atlanta* (11th Cir. 1986). A court cannot order the hiring of an alien not eligible for employment under U.S. immigration law. *Hoffman Plastics Compounds, Inc. v. NLRB* (S.Ct. 2002).

VI—23.03 Front Pay

Pollard v. E.I. duPont de Nemours & Co. (S.Ct. 2001), observed:

> [F]ront pay is simply money awarded for lost compensation during the period between judgment and reinstatement or in lieu of reinstatement. For instance, when an appropriate position for the plaintiff is not immediately available without displacing an incumbent employee * * * [or] is not viable because of continuing hostility between the employer or its workers, or because of psychological injuries suffered by the plaintiff as a result of the discrimination, courts have ordered front pay as a substitute for reinstatement.

When hiring or reinstatement is appropriate, defendant may not elect to pay wages as an alternative to hiring the plaintiff. *Blim v. Western Elec. Co.* (10th Cir. 1984). As front pay is equitable relief—as opposed to legal damages—the statutory caps placed on damages do not apply to front pay. Thus, the statutes do not limit the amount of front pay nor do amounts awarded as front pay count toward the statutory maximum set for damage recovery. *Pollard v. E.I. duPont de Nemours & Co., supra* (S.Ct. 2001)

Front pay may be made in the form of a lump sum that attempts to forecast future lost wages reduced to current value. That the amount is speculative is not grounds for denial. *Suggs v. Service-Master Educ. Food Management* (6th Cir. 1996). Alternatively, particularly if the plaintiff is a current employee, the employer may be ordered to make periodic wage payments in addition to current salary, until such time as the employee is offered substantially equivalent employment.

VI—23.04　Remedial Seniority

Franks v. Bowman Transp. Co. (S.Ct. 1976) read the "make whole" mandate to require an award of artificial, remedial seniority running from the date of the illegal discrimination, even though the grant to the victim would dilute the contractual seniority rights of innocent incumbent employees. "Complete relief" for victims required that they receive the seniority they would have earned had it not been for the employer's illegal act.

VI—23.05　Back Pay

a.　Discretion to Deny

"Given a finding of unlawful discrimination, back pay should be denied only for reasons which, if applied generally, would not frustrate the central statutory purposes of eradicating discrimination throughout the economy and making persons whole for injuries suffered through past discrimination." Back wages are denied only in the most extraordinary of circumstances. *Albemarle Paper Co. v. Moody* (S.Ct. 1975). Good faith of the employer, unsettled state of the law, reliance on general

EEOC guidelines, findings of no "reasonable cause," or ambiguity in the position of enforcement agencies all are insufficient. Uncertainty of the amount due does not justify denial or reduction of an award. On the contrary, doubts as to the amount are resolved against the employer. *Salinas v. Roadway Exp., Inc.* (5th Cir. 1984).

Where plaintiff proves that defendant was motivated by illegitimate reasons, but defendant can prove that it would have taken the same action in the absence of the impermissible motivating factor, back pay or damages may not be awarded. 42 U.S.C.A. 2000e–5(g)(2)(B). Back wages cannot be awarded to an alien not eligible for employment under U.S. immigration law at the time of the discrimination. *Hoffman Plastics Compounds, Inc. v. NLRB, supra* (S.Ct. 2002).

b. *Calculation*

Back pay liability shall not accrue from a date more than two years prior to the filing a charge of discrimination with the EEOC. 42 U.S.C.A. 2000e–5(g). The court will calculate the total amount of wages and benefits the victim would have earned from the date of discrimination to the date of judgement. Back pay includes gross salary, sick and vacation pay, health and pension benefits that would have accrued, bonuses, stock options, cost of living adjustments, and wage increases uniformly granted or reasonably expected.

Deducted from the gross amount of back pay due are *all* "interim earnings" received by plaintiff during the period. 42 U.S.C.A. 2000e–5(g)(1). Benefits coming from "collateral sources" such as social security, unemployment, welfare benefits, or income from the plaintiff's investments are not "interim earnings" that must be set off. *Gaworski v. ITT Commercial Finance Corp.* (8th Cir. 1994).

"Amounts earnable with reasonable diligence by the person discriminated against shall operate to reduce the back pay otherwise available." 42 U.S.C.A. 2000e–5(g)(1). The failure to mitigate is an affirmative defense that must be established by the defendant. It requires proof that: 1) positions are available in the geographical area that are *substantially equivalent* to the job denied plaintiff; and 2) plaintiff failed to exercise reasonable diligence in seeking out such positions. *Ford v. Nicks* (6th Cir. 1989). Merely because plaintiff is attending school, has moved from the community, started a business, or has accepted *significantly different* employment does not establish lack of plaintiff's due diligence. *EEOC v. Guardian Pools, Inc.* (11th Cir. 1987).

The calculation of back pay stops when the victim accepts *substantially equivalent* employment in terms of compensation, responsibilities, and stature. It is also tolled by defendant unconditionally *offering* the victim equivalent employment, even if defendant's offer did not include remedial seniority running from the date of the illegal treatment. *Ford Motor Co. v. EEOC* (S.Ct. 1982). Back pay is tolled during periods plaintiff is unavailable for work, as where he/she becomes disabled or has been incarcerated. Evidence of plaintiff's misconduct while employed by defendant, but discovered after the discriminatory treatment of the plaintiff, will limit back pay to the point that the misconduct was discovered, but only if the defendant can establish that it would have terminated plaintiff solely on the basis of this newly discovered evidence. *McKennon v. Nashville Banner Pub. Co.* (S.Ct. 1995).

Liability for back pay is both joint and several among defendants. Thus, where a union and employer are found liable, there is no right of contribution between them. *Northwest Airlines, Inc. v. Transport Workers Union* (S.Ct. 1981).

Interest on unpaid back wages is added to the award. The speculative amount of the back pay award is no basis to deny interest. *Barbour v. Merrill* (D.C. Cir. 1995).

VI—23.06 Compensatory Damages

Successful plaintiffs under Title VII and the ADA may recover compensatory damages. Damages compensate plaintiff for largely non-pecuniary and often imprecise injuries such as emotional distress, inconvenience, loss of enjoyment of life, injury to reputation or professional standing, loss of credit, and aggravation of pre-existing physical or emotional conditions. Damages are *not* presumed to flow simply from a violation. Plaintiff must prove actual injury with "competent evidence." *Carey v. Piphus* (S.Ct. 1978). If recovery is sought for emotional distress plaintiff must specify how the alleged distress manifested itself, and demonstrate a causal connection between the violation and the distress. While medical evidence is preferred, plaintiff's own testimony as to the manifestations of her distress can support a damage claim. *Bryant v. Aiken Regional Medical Centers, Inc.* (4th Cir. 2003) (frequent headaches, insomnia, nausea, anger).

Damages cannot be recovered when liability is based on adverse impact or, under the ADA, where defendant "demonstrates good faith efforts, in consultation with the person with the disability * * * to identify and make reasonable accommodation that would provide such individual with an equally effective opportunity." 42 U.S.C.A. 1981A(a)(3). Compensatory damages are *not* authorized under the ADEA.

The EEOC has authority to require federal agencies to pay compensatory damages. *West v. Gibson* (S.Ct. 1999).

VI—23.07   Punitive Damages

a. Entitlement

Punitive damages are available under Title VII and the ADA (but not under the ADEA). Punitive damages are designed to punish wrongdoing and to deter future illegal conduct. "Punitive damages are limited * * * to cases in which the employer has engaged in intentional discrimination and has done so with malice or with a reckless indifference to the federally protected rights of an aggrieved individual." *Kolstad v. American Dental Assoc.* (S.Ct. 1999). Punitive damages can only be used to punish behavior that bears a relationship to the plaintiff. Defendants cannot be punished simply for being unsavory characters. *State Farm Mutual Auto. Ins. Co. v. Campbell* (S.Ct. 2003).

Plaintiff must attribute the malice or recklessly indifferent conduct to a defined "employer" by the application of common law rules of agency. Punitive damages can be awarded only if: (a) the employer authorized the illegal act; (b) the agent who acted was unfit and the employer was reckless in employing him; (c) the agent was acting in a "managerial capacity;" or (d) the employer ratified the acts of the agent. *Kolstad v. American Dental Assoc., supra* (S.Ct. 1999). An employer with notice that a supervisor was acting in violation of the law and which takes no remedial steps can subjected to punitive damages for malicious conduct of the supervisor. "Turning a deaf ear to repeated complaints" warrants punitive damages. *Walsh v. National Computer Systems, Inc.* (8th Cir. 2003).

Kolstad added that an employer will not be liable for punitive damages for the discriminatory decisions by "managerial agents" where the manager's decisions were contrary to the employer's good faith efforts to comply with Title VII. Thus, where the employer had an extensive and well publicized EEO policy that contained effective grievance procedures, conducted EEO training sessions for supervisors, and monitored demographics for evidence of discrimination no award of punitive damages for discrimination by a supervisor was warranted. *Bryant v. Aiken Regional Medical Centers, Inc.* (4th Cir.

2003). Actions taken on advice of counsel usually preclude punitive damages. *Farias v. Instructional Systems* (2d Cir. 2001).

b. Amount

Factors considered in determining the *amount* of punitive damages are: 1) size and financial status of the defendant, 2) the degree the conduct is reprehensible, 3) the duration and frequency of the conduct, 4) the amount of actual damage suffered by plaintiff, and 5) awards in other cases for comparable misconduct. The amount awarded cannot exceed that which is necessary to punish and deter the misconduct and the amount awarded must have some relationship to the injury caused plaintiff. *BMW of North America, Inc. v. Gore* (S.Ct. 1996). Where defendant's conduct is particularly egregious and the period of plaintiff's employment relatively short—thus producing limited back wage liability— significant punitive damages are appropriate. *Corti v. Storage Tech. Corp.* (4th Cir. 2002). Traditionally, absent back wage liability and no injury sufficient to justify compensatory damages, punitive damages are denied. Most courts, however, allow punitive damages for egregious harassment even if no actual damages have been proved. *Cush-Crawford v. Adchem Corp.* (2d Cir. 2001).

VI—23.08 Damages: Statutory Limits

The statutes place dollar limits on the amount of compensatory and punitive damages that can be awarded, an amount that is tied on the number of defendant's employees: $300,000 maximum for employers of more than 500 employees; $200,000 for employers of 201–500 employees; $100,000 for employers of 101–200 employee and $50,00 for employers of fewer than 101 employees. Punitive and compensatory damage awards are aggregated to determine whether the cap has been exceeded. Front and back wage awards and interest are equitable remedies, and are *not* counted toward the maximum allowable damages. *Pollard v. E.I. duPont de Nemours & Co., supra* (S.Ct. 2001).

The jury, with proper instructions, assesses the amount of damages without being informed of the statutory limits. If the jury award exceeds the statutory caps, the court will reduce the amount to the appropriate limit. The court can order further remittitur of amounts awarded by the jury that are excessive in light of the evidence. *Lampley v. Onyx Acceptance Corp.* (7th Cir. 2003).

Damages can be awarded against state and local governments for violating the Constitution and against all non-federal employers for violation of the 1866 Civil Rights Act. These damages are *not* subject to the statutory caps. Bogle v. McClure (11th Cir. 2003) ($0.5 million in compensation for pain, suffering, and humiliation, and $2.0 million in punitive damages for each successful plaintiff).

VI—23.09   Liquidated Damages

a.   *Equal Pay Act and Family and Medical Leave Act*

A successful plaintiff under the Equal Pay Act is entitled to an additional amount equal to defendant's back wage liability. Trial courts have the discretion to reduce all or part of the liquidated damages—not the unpaid back wages—if the employer proves that it acted in good faith (*e.g.*, without discriminatory intent) and did so with reasonable grounds for believing that its action was lawful.

b. *The ADEA*

A successful plaintiff under the ADEA is entitled to liquidated damages in an amount equal to back pay liability, but only if *plaintiff* proves that the age discrimination was "willful." 29 U.S.C.A. 626(b). Discrimination is "willful" if age motivated a refusal to hire or the discharge of plaintiff. "The employee need not additionally demonstrate that the employer's conduct was outrageous, provide direct evidence of the employer's motivation, or prove that age was the predominant rather than a determinative factor in the employment decision." *Hazen Paper Co. v. Biggins* (S.Ct. 1993). However, when the discrimination is a consequence of a broad policy or where the employer was relying on age being a bona fide occupational qualification, liquidated damages cannot be imposed simply because the employer engaged in the act and knew of the potential applicability of the ADEA. In this context, "willful" means that the employer either knew the policy violated the Act or "showed reckless disregard for the matter." *Trans World Airlines, Inc. v. Thurston* (S.Ct. 1985).

Some have viewed liquidated damages as a substitute for all non-wage loses and where awarded have denied pre-judgement interest. *McCann v. Texas City Ref., Inc.* (5th Cir. 1993). Others see liquidated damages as punitive in nature, and thus award pre-judgement interest on the actual back wages even if liquidated damages are assessed. *Kelly v. American Standard, Inc.* (9th Cir. 1981). Where reinstatement is inappropriate, the possibility of liquidated damages under the ADEA does not preclude the grant of front wages. *Cassino v. Reichhold Chemicals, Inc.* (9th Cir. 1987). Liquidated damage calculation, however, may be limited to *back* wages, excluding amounts attributable to prospective front wages.

Liquidated damages cannot be collected against federal employers. *Smith v. Office of Personnel Management* (5th Cir. 1985). Title VII and the ADA do *not* provide for liquidated damages.

VI—23.10 Employees Who "Quit": "Constructive Discharge"

Employers may assert that a person who resigned is not entitled to reinstatement or to monetary remedies that extend beyond the date of the separation. However, when an employee resigns to escape treatment that is both illegal and *intolerable,* the employer has "constructively discharged" the employee. Such a plaintiff is entitled to the remedies accorded an illegally discharged worker. *Henson v. Dundee* (11th Cir. 1982). To establish a constructive discharge, plaintiff must prove that the conduct was so offensive that it would not have been tolerated by a reasonable person; that a reasonable person would have resigned rather than remain on the job. This requires a showing of especially severe harassment, assignment of particularly demeaning or dangerous jobs, or a dramatic and humiliating demotion. *Jurgens v. EEOC* (5th Cir. 1990). The employee's resignation must be caused by, or be in response to, the oppressive treatment. An employee who resigns for personal reasons unrelated to her treatment has not been constructively discharged.

Some authority requires plaintiff also to prove that the employer intended through its conduct to force the employee to quit. *Bristow v. Daily Press, Inc.* (4th Cir. 1985). Most courts either reject this requirement or circumvent it by reasoning that an employer will be held to intend foreseeable responses to intolerable treatment. *Goldmeier v. Allstate Ins. Co.* (6th Cir. 2003).

VI—23.11　"Affirmative Action"

Once a violation of the law has been found, the court may "order such affirmative action as may be appropriate." 42 U.S.C.A. 2000e–5(g). This provides courts with injunctive powers to require parties to post notices, expunge files, advertise non-discrimination, evaluate selection systems, and report ameliorative steps. It authorizes judicial orders directing employers who acted illegally to adopt racial, ethnic, or gender conscious affirmative action programs. Nonetheless, as arms of the government, courts are constrained in their use of this power by the Constitution. Governmental use of race and ethnicity classifications must be narrowly tailored to serve compelling governmental interests. Accordingly, employers can only be ordered to adopt affirmative action plans that use race, ethnicity, or gender in making hiring decisions for non-victims if the discrimination has been "persistent or egregious" and the affirmative action order is necessary to "dissipate the lingering effects of pervasive discrimination." *Local 28, Sheet Metal Workers' Intern. Ass'n v. EEOC* (S.Ct. 1986).

The tailoring of a judicial affirmative action remedy is similar to the discretion that must be observed by employers that voluntarily adopt affirmative action plans. *Supra,* 8.02(c). The affirmative action order must be reasonable in that it sets a remedial goal that reflects the appropriate labor pool of minority workers. The means of reaching that goal must not unduly trammel the interests of non-minority workers. *United States v. Paradise* (S.Ct. 1987), sustained an order of a 1–1 hiring ratio until 25% of the officer corps was black, a percentage roughly equivalent to the number of qualified black workers in the area. A plan will "unduly trammel" the rights of incumbent employees if it orders current employees fired, requires unqualified minority applicants to be hired, or directs that test scores or results to be altered. While individual victims of illegal discrimination are entitled to remedial seniority running from the date of their illegal treatment, an affirmative action remedy that benefits non-victims will not undercut contractual rights of non-parties created in collective bargaining agreements. *W.R. Grace & Co. v. Local Union 759* (S.Ct. 1983). Once the remedial goal is reached the affirmative action remedy must be discontinued. *Quinn v. City of Boston* (1st Cir. 2003).

Non-parties to the law suit that produced an affirmative action remedy may not later challenge the order if they had notice or otherwise had an opportunity to object or intervene in the litigation and failed to do so. Even if they had no opportunity to intervene, non-parties may not challenge an affirmative action order in subsequent litigation where a party in the original suit adequately represented non-party interests and challenged the order on the same legal ground. 42 U.S.C.A. 2000e–2(n).

VI—23.12   Attorneys' Fees and Costs

a. Discretion

Title VII and the ADA provide that "the court, in its discretion, may allow the *prevailing party*, other than the [EEOC] or the United States, a reasonable attorney's fee as part of the costs." 42 U.S.C.A. 2000e–5(k). The ADEA provides for fees for prevailing *plaintiffs* only.

Notwithstanding the apparent grant of discretion, trial courts, in fact, have very little. "A prevailing *plaintiff* ordinarily is to be awarded attorneys' fees in all but special circumstances." *Christiansburg Garment Co. v. EEOC* (S.Ct. 1978). Rarely are "special circumstances" found, and where they are, they involve a combination of extreme good faith by defendant and questionable, if not unethical, misconduct by the plaintiff.

By contrast, a prevailing *defendant,* is entitled to an award of attorneys' fees only upon a finding that "plaintiff's action was frivolous, unreasonable or without foundation." *Christiansburg Garment Co. v. EEOC, supra* (S.Ct. 1978). Rarely can a prevailing defendant prove "frivolousness." "Lack of foundation" is not established merely because plaintiff's case was dismissed on summary judgment. *Walker v. NationsBank of Fla.* (11th Cir. 1995).

Court costs are allowed the prevailing party as a matter of course. Rule 54(d), Fed.R.Civ.Proc. The award to a successful defendant is not dependent on proof that plaintiff acted without reasonable foundation. Prevailing party costs include filing, witness, and docket charges; fees for clerks and marshals; transcript and printing costs; and fees for court appointed experts and interpreters. 28 U.S.C.A. 1920.

To be a "prevailing party" plaintiff must secure a favorable judgement on the merits or secure a court approved consent decree. It is not enough that plaintiff achieved a desired result because the lawsuit stimulated a voluntary change in defendant's conduct. *Buckhannon Board & Care Home, Inc. v. West Va. Dept. of Health & Human Resources* (S.Ct. 2001). "A plaintiff prevails when actual relief on the merits of his claim materially alters the legal relationship between the parties by modifying the defendant's behavior in a way that directly benefits the plaintiff." *Texas State Teachers Ass'n v. Garland Independent School Dist.* (S.Ct. 1989). Thus, a judgment and an award of nominal damages makes the plaintiff a "prevailing party." Limited success, however, will warrant reduction of the amount of the award. *Farrar v. Hobby* (S.Ct. 1992).

A *pro se* plaintiff, even if an attorney, may not recover attorneys's fees. *Kay v. Ehrler* (S.Ct. 1991). Fee awards run against the party, and cannot be ordered against an attorney. *Roadway Exp., Inc. v. Piper* (S.Ct. 1980) However, courts have inherent power to assess litigation costs, including attorneys' fees, against an attorney who acts vexatiously.

b. Calculation

The statutes provide only that the attorneys' fee award be "reasonable." Calculation of "reasonableness" requires identifying an hourly rate for the attorney. Usually this is the "prevailing rate" charged by attorneys in the community who have experience and background similar to the party's attorney. Rates actually or normally charged by the attorney do not control. That plaintiff's attorney works for a legal aid or civil rights organization, and thus charges clients little if anything, will not reduce the fee award below the hourly rate that prevails in the community. *Blum v. Stenson* (S.Ct. 1984). If plaintiff could not secure competent local counsel, the court may use the prevailing rate of the community where plaintiff's attorney normally practices. *Mathur v. Board of Trustees of Southern Ill. Univ.* (7th Cir. 2003). (Chicago attorney conducted Southern Illinois trial. Chicago prevailing rate is "reasonable".)

The prevailing hourly rate is multiplied by the number of hours the attorneys reasonably expended in pursuit of *successful* claims. Plaintiff may not include time spent on issues where the plaintiff did not prevail, unless plaintiff can show that unsuccessful and successful claims share a "common core of facts" or are "based on related legal theories." *Hensley v. Eckerhart* (S.Ct. 1983). Legal services provided at each stage of enforcement are entitled to compensation: preliminary state administrative proceedings (*New York Gaslight Club, Inc. v. Carey* (S.Ct. 1980)), preliminary relief, trial, appeal, post appeal monitoring of the degree, and hearings on the attorneys' fee award. *Pennsylvania v. Delaware Valley Citizens' Council* (S.Ct. 1986). The court may reduce the number of actual hours expended if it deems the number of attorneys involved in a task or the total time expended on an issue was excessive or unreasonable.

The "lodestar" sum produced by multiplying the appropriate number of hours by the prevailing rate presumptively is reasonable, but it can be adjusted. Long delay in securing a final award may warrant an upward adjustment. *Missouri v. Jenkins* (S.Ct. 1989). While an award is not capped by the amount of back wages or damages recovered (indeed, fee awards frequently exceed the amount of monetary relief), a very limited recovery such as nominal damages will justify a downward adjustment. *Farrar v. Hobby, supra* (S.Ct. 1992). Extraordinary performance of an attorney beyond that expected from peers may justify an upward adjustment, particularly if the performance expedited the proceedings. Conversely, a downward adjustment is possible where performance of the attorney was unusually poor and inflicted on the court and the opposing party unreasonable delay and unnecessary expenses. Strategy that resulted in a second trial or the rejection of a settlement offer that exceeded the amount eventually recovered may result in a reduction in the lodestar amount. *Shott v. Rush–Presbyterian–St. Luke's Med. Ctr.* (7th Cir. 2003).

An upward adjustment in the lodestar calculation is *not* warranted simply because the attorney was working on a contingency arrangement whereby the attorney would recover fees only if the plaintiff prevailed. That a higher rate may be necessary to attract competent attorneys and fairly compensate them for the risk of non-payment should plaintiff not prevail is not grounds for an upward adjustment of the prevailing hourly rate. *Burlington v. Dague* (S.Ct. 1992). On the other hand, an attorneys' fee award does not preclude the attorney for a successful plaintiff from collecting from the client a fee greater than that which the court awarded. *Venegas v. Mitchell* (S.Ct. 1990).

In addition to compensation for the attorney's time, a prevailing plaintiff is entitled to reimbursement for actual litigation expenses of the attorney, to be distinguished from the attorneys' normal overhead costs that traditionally are separately reimbursed by clients over and above the attorney's hourly rates (*e.g.*, long distance travel expenses, printing costs associated with the litigation, and compensation of para-legals who worked on the case). *Missouri v. Jenkins, supra* (S.Ct. 1989). The Civil Rights Act of 1991 allowing recovery of "expert fees" allows recovery of the costs for accountants, testing experts, statisticians, and health care professionals.

CHAPTER 24

PROCEDURES: NON–FEDERAL DEFENDANTS

VI—24.01 Introduction

Ultimately rights under all the statutes are enforced through lawsuits filed by individuals or government agencies. Title VII, the ADA, and the ADEA require victims to navigate complex pre-suit administrative procedures and comply with often confusing time limitations. Title VII and ADA procedures are identical. The ADEA is similar, but with important differences. There are distinct procedures for Federal employees.

The Equal Pay Act and the Reconstruction Era Civil Rights Acts impose no administrative prerequisites to suit. The Equal Pay Act has a two year statute of limitation for filing suits (3 years if the violation was "wilful"). The most appropriate state statutes of limitation govern the time to file actions under the Reconstruction Era Civil Rights Act.

VI—24.02 Pre–Suit: The "Charge"

a. Nature of the Charge

Enforcement is begun by the victim of discrimination filing an administrative "charge," a mandatory obligation, "impervious to judicial discretion." *Na-*

tional R.R. Passenger Corp. v. Morgan *(S.Ct. 2002)*. *"Charges shall be in writing under oath." 42 U.S.C.A. 2000e–5(b). Telephoned complaints or personal appearances with oral allegations at an EEOC office do suffice. The statutes provide that charges "shall contain such information * * * as the [EEOC] requires." By regulation the EEOC requires a charge to: 1) name the individual charging discrimination and the person or entity who allegedly discriminated, 2) outline the nature of the action taken (e.g., hiring, discharge, compensation, harassment), 3) state the nature of the discrimination (e.g., race, sex, national origin, religion, age, disability), and 4) set the time and place of the alleged discrimination. While charge forms are provided by the EEOC, no specific format is mandated. Letters to the EEOC or completion of an EEOC intake questionnaire that contains the requisite information will suffice.* Clark v. Coats & Clark, Inc. *(11th Cir. 1989).*

In *Edelman v. Lynchburg College* (S.Ct. 2002), plaintiff faxed a *timely* letter to the EEOC that contained the critical information, but the fax was not "under oath." The EEOC responded by asking plaintiff to complete a form that included the statutorily mandated oath. Plaintiff returned the verified charge *after* the statutory time for filing charges had expired. Pursuant to its regulations that permit amendments that remedy "technical defects" to relate back to the date of filing the original "charge," the EEOC determined that plaintiff's previously faxed letter was a timely filed "charge."

The lower court held that the EEOC regulation violated the statutory mandate that a charge be filed in a timely fashion, and that a document not "under oath" cannot not meet the statutory definition of a "charge." The Supreme Court reversed. As long as key written information is filed in a timely fashion, the technical defect of verification can relate back to the date of the original filing. However, amendments that raise new legal theories, such as adding a count of disability discrimination to an original charge alleging race discrimination, are not "technical" and do not relate back to the time of the initial filing of the charge. *Manning v. Chevron Chemical Co., LLC* (5th Cir. 2003).

It is important to frame the charge with care because the judicial complaint may allege only claims made in the charge or those so closely related that they reasonably could be expected to grow out of an EEOC investigation of the claims. *Infra,* 24.09.

b.   *Where the Charge Must Be Filed*

Charges must be filed with the appropriate district office of the EEOC. In jurisdictions which have equal employment legislation with administrative enforcement mechanisms recognized by the EEOC ("deferral agencies"), a charge also must be filed with the state agency.

Title VII and the ADA contemplate a two step, sequential filing. A charge *must* first be filed with the state agency. The EEOC charge, even if deposited with the EEOC, will not be considered "filed" with the EEOC until state agency procedures have been "exhausted." "Exhaustion" of state procedures occurs when the state agency waives state jurisdiction OR 60 days lapse from the filing of the state charge. Plaintiff may follow the envisioned system by first filing a charge with the state agency, awaiting the state outcome or the lapse of 60 days, and thereupon file a federal charge with the EEOC.

Agreements between the EEOC and local agencies utilize a system of referrals. A charge originally deposited with the EEOC will be referred by the EEOC to the state agency. The referred charge is deemed "filed" with the state agency upon such referral. After the state agency relinquishes jurisdiction of the referred charge, (which can take place at any time), or upon lapse of the 60–day period, the EEOC will "reactivate" the charge previously deposited with it. Only at the point of reactivation is the charge deemed "filed" with the EEOC. *Love v. Pullman Co.* (S.Ct. 1972).

The ADEA similarly requires the filing of a charge with both a state deferral agency and the EEOC. Under the ADEA a state charge of age discrimination may be filed prior to, simultaneously with, or after the filing of the federal EEOC charge. *Oscar Mayer & Co. v. Evans* (S.Ct. 1979).

c. *When the Charge Must Be Filed*

In those few jurisdictions that have no state or local enforcement agencies, charges must be filed with the EEOC within 180 days of the discriminatory act. In jurisdictions which have state enforcement agencies, charges must be filed with the EEOC within 300 days of the discriminatory act or 30 days from the date the state agency relinquishes its jurisdiction, whichever is *earlier*.

The charge is "filed" with the EEOC only upon a formal filing or a reactivation of a previously deposited charge, but only *after* required state procedures are "exhausted." In *Mohasco Corp. v. Silver* (S.Ct. 1980) a Title VII charge was deposited with the EEOC 291 days after the discriminatory act. No state charge had been filed. The EEOC promptly referred the charge to a state agency, which retained its jurisdiction for the full 60 days allowed by the statute. When the 60–day period of state jurisdiction expired, the EEOC reactivated the charge previously deposited with it. The Court held that charge was first "filed" with the EEOC upon this reactivation. As reactivation occurred 351 days after the discriminatory act, the filing of the charge was untimely. Accordingly, to allow timely filing in a deferral jurisdiction plaintiff should deposit the charge with a state agency or the EEOC within 240 days following the act of discrimination. This allows the required 60 days of state jurisdiction prior to the charge being reactivated and thus "filed" with the EEOC within the 300 day limit.

State agencies may relinquish or waive jurisdiction over a charge prior to the lapse of their 60 days of jurisdiction. Thus, if in *Mohasco* the state agency, having received the charge 291 after the discriminatory act, had waived its jurisdiction over the charge four days later, when the EEOC reactivated the charge, it would have been "filed" with the EEOC 295 days from the discriminatory act and would have been timely. This is true even if the state agency made no investigation and waived its jurisdiction for the sole purpose of allowing a charging party to pursue federal rights. *EEOC v. Commercial Office Products Co.* (S.Ct. 1988).

The charging party must also insure that a state charge resolved by a state agency is filed with the EEOC no later than 30 days following the state agency's release of its jurisdiction. To illustrate, assume a charging party filed a state charge of discrimination 40 days after the discriminatory act, but did not deposit a charge with the EEOC. Assume that the state agency relinquished its jurisdiction 50 days after the charge was filed with it (or 90 days from the discriminatory act). The charging party must file a charge with the EEOC within 30 days of being notified that the state had relinquished jurisdiction, even though only 120 days have lapsed since the discriminatory act.

VI—24.03   The Discriminatory Act: The Point From Which Timeliness is Measured

As the time to file suit under the 1866 Civil Rights Act, the Constitution, and the Equal Pay Act and the time in which to file charges under Title VII, the ADA, and the ADEA are measured from the point of the discriminatory act, that point must be identified. *National R.R. Passenger Corp. v. Mor-*

gan (S.Ct. 2002) held that refusal to hire and denial of access to a training program were discrete acts of discrimination that must be charged within the statutory period. A charge of harassment, however, may be brought if any discrete act of harassment occurred in the statutory period, and courts may evaluate events falling outside of the statutory period to determine whether a pattern of illegal harassment had occurred. In compensation cases a distinct act occurs each pay period. A timely charge following the last pay period allows plaintiff to challenge the pay system. The statute, however, limits recovery of underpayment of wages to the two year period prior to the filing of the charge. 42 U.S.C.A. 2000e–5(g).

The time begins to run when the charging party has unequivocal notice of the discrete act. In hiring or promotion cases the period does not commence until the applicant has unequivocal notice of the employer's action or has knowledge of facts which disclose that a decision rejecting plaintiff was been made. *Colgan v. Fisher Scientific Co.* (3d Cir. 1991). In discharge cases, it is the date the employee is told of his termination, not the employee's last day on the job or the day the employee receives the last pay check. In *Delaware State College v. Ricks* (S.Ct. 1980) a faculty member was notified by the college that he had been denied tenure, and accordingly that he would be terminated at the end of the next following academic year. Upon learning of the tenure denial, the employee filed an internal grievance which, if successful, could have resulted in the grant of tenure. The Court held that time for filing his charge began with the *notice* of his tenure denial, not his last day of employment, which would come a year later. Moreover, the period would not be extended pending the outcome of an internal grievance based on the possibility that the termination decision could be reversed.

The time limitation will not begin to run until plaintiff is aware of information that would put a reasonable person on notice that his/her rejection may have been for reasons outlawed by the statute. *Reeb v. Economic Opportunity Atlanta* (5th Cir. 1975). A plaintiff was discharged and told by his employer that his position had been eliminated. He later discovered that the employer was seeking applicants to fill the position, and learned still later that the position had been filled by someone substantially younger. There were three points from which the time limitation could be measured: 1) plaintiff's dismissal, 2) when the employer began seeking applicants, or 3) when a younger employee was hired. A court held that given the employer's representation, the point at which a reasonable person would have discerned a possible violation of the law did not arise until the employer filled the position with a younger worker. *Jones v. Dillard's, Inc.* (11th Cir. 2003).

VI—24.04 Extensions: Waiver, Estoppel, and Tolling

Time limits on filing charges are not jurisdictional. Statutory time limits may be set aside on grounds of estoppel, waiver, or equitable tolling. *Zipes v. Trans World Airlines, Inc.* (S.Ct. 1982). "Estoppel" involves misconduct by defendant that would make it inequitable for a defendant to demand strict compliance with time limits, as where defendant threatened or lulled the charging party into failing to make a timely charge, where defendant mislead the plaintiff as to the circumstances of the decision, or where defendant's attorney has provided plaintiff with misleading advice. *Coke v. General Adjustment Bureau, Inc.* (5th Cir. 1981). "Waiver" occurs when one relinquishes a known right, and another relies to their detriment on that relinquishment, as where an employer indicates that it will not hold plaintiff to the statutory limits. A time period may be tolled for periods when plaintiff suffers from incompetence or for delay resulting from erroneous advice from courts or enforcement agencies. *Canales v. Sullivan* (2d Cir. 1991). The time for filing an individual charge may be tolled during the period in which the individual was a member of a pending class for which a class action suit had been filed. *See, Crown, Cork & Seal Co. v. Parker* (S.Ct. 1983). Pursuing internal or collective bargaining grievances, including arbitration, or filing a lawsuit under another statute does *not* toll filing periods. *IUEW v. Robbins & Myers, Inc.* (S.Ct. 1976).

VI—24.05   Proceedings Before the EEOC

Once the charge is "filed" with the EEOC, the EEOC is directed by statute to notify the charged party, investigate the charge, and determine if there is "reasonable cause" to believe the statute has been violated. If it makes such a finding, the EEOC must attempt to eliminate such practices by "conference, conciliation and persuasion."

Under Title VII and the ADA, the EEOC has exclusive jurisdiction for 180 days in which to conduct its investigation and undertake conciliation. During this 180 days the EEOC has exclusive jurisdiction in which to file a lawsuit (if the charged party is a state or local government this power to sue is vested with the Attorney General). If the EEOC has not filed suit at the end of 180 days, charging parties have an option. They can wait for the EEOC to terminate its proceedings. When this takes place, the EEOC will notify the charging party with a "Notice of Right to Sue." Alternatively, any time after the lapse of 180 days from the date the charge was filed the charging party can terminate EEOC jurisdiction by demanding the "Notice of Right to Sue," which the EEOC must issue.

The ADEA is different. A party charging age discrimination must simply file timely charges with the EEOC and any state agency and allow both agencies 60 days to investigate the charge and attempt conciliation. The 60 day waiting periods for both state and EEOC procedures can run concurrently. At the end of this 60 day period the plaintiff is free to file suit. No notice of right to sue or further administrative processes are required.

Where the defendant is a state or local government and the EEOC finds reasonable cause to believe a violation has occurred, the EEOC refers the matter to the Attorney General. If the EEOC finds no reasonable cause to believe a violation has occurred, its practice has been to so notify the charging party. Some authority has held, however, that the EEOC has no authority to issue such a notice, but must refer all charges to the Attorney General; the plaintiff's "right to sue" a government must come from the Attorney General. *Hiller v. Oklahoma ex rel. Used Motor Vehicle* (10th Cir. 2003).

VI—24.06   Timing the Judicial Action

a. Private Parties

The "Notice of Right to Sue" triggers the right of a private party to file a judicial action. The time in which suit must be filed is determined by the date the charging party *receives* the "Notice of Right to Sue." It is "received" when it is delivered to the charging party's mailing address supplied to the EEOC or to the charging party's attorney of record. *Suit must be filed within 90 days from the receipt of the EEOC notice!* A complaint *mailed* 90 days from the receipt of the EEOC notice, but received by the court five days later, was not timely. *Hallgren v. U.S. Dept. of Energy* (8th Cir. 2003).

The 90–day period in which to file a private judicial action is not jurisdictional, and thus, similar to the time for filing charges, can be extended by estoppel, waiver, or tolling. *Supra,* 24.04. Tolling *may* be permitted during the time plaintiff has pending before the court a motion for appointment of counsel or when plaintiff receives misleading advice from the clerk of the court. *Baldwin County Welcome Ctr. v. Brown* (S.Ct. 1984). Tolling requires reasonable diligence in pursuit of one's rights and the absence of prejudice to defendant, but does not extend to the "garden variety claim of excusable neglect" such as where the charging party's lawyer was absent from the office when the notice of right to sue was delivered. *Irwin v. Veterans Administration* (S.Ct. 1990).

The charging party need not request the "Notice of Right to Sue" within any particular time period, but may await the outcome of EEOC processes, and bring suit only after he/she receives the notice. However, excessive delay in requesting a right to sue notice that prejudices the defendant may preclude suit, or at the very least, limit the extent of plaintiff's back pay recovery. *National R.R. Passenger Corp. v. Morgan, supra* (S.Ct. 2002).

The charging party's right to file suit is not defeated by any EEOC failure to perform its statutory duties, such as notifying the defendant or attempting conciliation. *Russell v. American Tobacco Co.* (4th Cir. 1975).

b. Public Suit Time Constraints

There are no express limitations on the time in which the government must file suit. The EEOC is governed neither by the time limitations imposed on private plaintiffs nor by analogous state statutes of limitations. *Occidental Life Ins. Co. of Cal. v. EEOC* (S.Ct. 1977). However, where delay is inordinate and prejudices the defendant, the doctrine of laches will bar an EEOC suit. *EEOC v. Great Atlantic & Pacific Tea Co.* (3d Cir. 1984).

The EEOC may not sue until it has completed its statutory duties of notifying defendant of the charge and attempting conciliation. *EEOC v. Klingler Elec. Corp.* (5th Cir. 1981). The conciliation duty requires the EEOC to accord defendant a reasonable opportunity to reply to the charge and obligates it to respond to defendant's replies in a flexible way. The EEOC's conciliation duties were not satisfied by sending a letter of determination three years after a charge was filed, allowing 12 days for the employer to respond, denying extension requests without reason, and terminating contact at the end of the deadline. *EEOC v. Asplundh Tree Expert Co.* (11th Cir. 2003).

The EEOC (Attorney General if defendant is a state or local government) has the exclusive right to sue as long as it has jurisdiction over the charge. The government's power to sue is lost once the charging party files suit. Participation by the EEOC at this point is limited to intervention. Once a public suit is brought, the charging party's participation is limited to intervention.

VI—24.07   The Complaint

Private plaintiffs must file a judicial complaint within 90 days of the receipt of the Notice of Right

to Sue that satisfies the pleading requirement of
Rule 8(a)(2), Fed. R.Civ.Proc. ("a short plain statement of the claim showing that the pleader is
entitled to relief"). *Swierkiewicz v. Sorema N.A.*
(S.Ct. 2002), held that the general notice pleading
standard applies to employment discrimination
cases, rejecting a requirement imposed by the lower
court that plaintiff's complaint must set forth factual allegations that would establish a prima facie
case of discrimination. While legalistic formality is
not required, merely filing of the EEOC right to sue
notice or petitioning the court for the appointment
of counsel will not satisfy the obligation, unless
such papers satisfy the notice obligations of Rule
8(a)(2). *Baldwin County Welcome Center v. Brown,*
supra (S.Ct. 1984).

Both federal and state courts have subject matter
jurisdiction. *Yellow Freight System, Inc. v. Donnelly*
(S.Ct. 1990). State courts apply the federal statutes,
as well as claims arising under state law. A federal
court may consider under its pendent jurisdiction
any state law claims arising out of the same transaction. State courts do not have jurisdiction of
claims against the federal government.

VI—24.08 Appointment of Counsel

"Upon application by the complainant and in
cases the court may deem just, the court may appoint an attorney * * * and may authorize the
commencement of the action without the payment
of fees, costs or security." 42 U.S.C.A. 2000e–5(f)(1).
Exercise of this authority is discretionary and will

not be reversed on appeal except for an abuse of discretion. In determining whether to appoint counsel the trial court will examine the potential merit of the claim, plaintiff's financial resources, and plaintiff's documented but unsuccessful attempts to secure counsel.

VI—24.09   The Judicial Proceeding

Litigation of plaintiff's claims before the court is *de novo,* as opposed to a limited review of state or EEOC administrative findings. Any findings by the state or federal agencies such as a "reasonable cause" finding may, or may not, be admissible as evidence, depending on the nature of the finding and the degree of party participation. In no case do such findings restrict complete re-adjudication of plaintiff's claims. *McDonnell Douglas Corp. v. Green* (S.Ct. 1973). See, *Young v. James Green Mgt., Inc.* (7th Cir. 2003)(trial court may refuse to admit EEOC determination where prejudice would outweigh probative value).

There is a right to a trial by jury in all suits that claim money damages.

The parameters of the suit are set by the allegations in the EEOC charge. Only parties named in the original charge can be named as defendants, and only the discrimination alleged may be litigated, unless claims in the charge are so closely related to those in the suit that they would be expected to flow from an EEOC investigation. A lawsuit charging sex discrimination may not be premised on a charge asserting age discrimination. *Ajayi v. Aramark Business Services, Inc.* (7th Cir. 2003). However, a charge of national origin discrimination could support a suit alleging racial discrimination when the EEOC investigation of charge alleging preferential treatment for Irish–Americans could reasonably be expected to evaluate possible race discrimination. *Deravin v. Kerik* (2d Cir. 2003).

VI—24.10 Class Actions and "Pattern or Practice" Suits

a. Private Parties and Rule 23

A class actions is a procedural device governed by Rule 23, Fed.R.Civ.Proc., that permits a representative to sue on behalf of numerous similarly situated individuals and secure relief for all members of the defined "class." They are used in Title VII cases that involve a common issue of law and similar facts such as in cases alleging systemic motivation or challenging a selection device based on its adverse impact. A true class action under Rule 23(b)(2) binds all members of the defined class. That is, individuals who were in the class cannot file subsequent suits to litigate claims raised in the class action. *Cooper v. Federal Reserve Bank of Richmond* (S.Ct. 1984).

For a trial court to certify a class action, the petitioner must satisfy four elements: 1) Numerosity: The persons petitioner seeks to represent are so numerous that their joinder as named plaintiffs would be unruly and impracticable. 2) Commonality: Common questions of law and fact must exist, with common questions predominating over unique or individual claims. 3) Typicality: The claims, or the defenses against the claims, are typical of the claims existing in the class or defenses asserted against the class claim. 4) Representation: The named petitioner can fairly represent unnamed class members. Petitioner must demonstrate the competence of counsel and class representatives to present the claims, and show that no conflict of interest exists between the petitioner and class members. *General Tel. Co. of the Southwest v. Falcon* (S.Ct. 1982). To proceed under Title VII or the ADA, a named class representative must have filed a timely charge with the EEOC and must otherwise satisfy the pre-requisites to suit. Persons may be members of the class even if they have not filed individual charges.

There are no true class actions under the ADEA or EPA because the Fair Labor Standards Act, which applies to both, provides: "No employee shall be a party plaintiff to any such action unless he gives his consent in writing to become such a party and such consent is filed in the court in which such action is brought." 29 U.S.C.A. 216(b).

b. *Government "Pattern or Practice" Suits*

Title VII allows the EEOC (or Attorney General in the case of state or local governments) to challenge a "pattern or practice" of illegal conduct. This power does not permit the agency to proceed without satisfying the prerequisites of having a charge filed, notifying the charged party, and attempting conciliation. But the government may proceed with "pattern or practice" suits, in effect representing a large class of individuals with similar claims, without securing class certification pursuant to Rule 23. *General Tel. Co. of the Northwest* v. *EEOC* (S.Ct. 1980).

CHAPTER 25

FEDERAL EMPLOYEE PROCEDURES

VI—25.01 Introduction and Overview

Enforcement procedures available to federal executive department employees against their federal employers are dramatically different from those used in suits against other defendants. 29 CFR Part 1614. The essential difference is that the employing agency takes and investigates the initial complaint and ultimately renders a final decision. The first involvement of the EEOC is through its administrative judges who serve as neutral fact-finders where the complainant requests a hearing prior to the employing agency's final decision on the complaint. Time limitations are different from those applicable to non-federal complainants

Complaints of disability discrimination against federal employers are brought under the Rehabilitation Act of 1973, not the Americans with Disabilities Act, but using Title VII procedures. The ADEA makes administrative exhaustion optional. While the Equal Pay Act sets forth no administrative procedures, a complainant may invoke Title VII administrative complaint procedures.

VI—25.02 The Complaint and Agency Investigation

A federal employee or applicant must first contact an Equal Employment Opportunity (EEO) Counselor *at the agency where the alleged discrimination occurred.* This contact must be made within 45 days of the discriminatory act. The EEO Counselor conducts a preliminary investigation and attempts informal resolution. The parties are free to submit the matter to alternative dispute resolution. If the informal allegation is not resolved, the complainant is notified of his right to file a formal complaint with the employing agency. The complaint must be filed within 15 days from receipt of the notice. The agency may reject the complaint and issue a final order of dismissal. Alternatively, the agency may accept the complaint and conduct an investigation.

VI—25.03 EEOC Hearing and Agency Determination

At the conclusion of the agency investigation, the complainant may request either a hearing before an EEOC administrative judge or an immediate final decision by the employing agency. Upon a request for a hearing, an EEOC administrative judge in the geographical location where the complaint arose processes the complaint, rules on motions, oversees discovery, and if material issues of fact exist, conducts a formal, adversarial hearing. The EEOC judge renders a decision on liability and, if warranted, awards back wages, compensatory damages, and attorneys' fees. The agency head (or designee) must implement or decline to implement the judge's decision.

VI—25.04 Appeals to EEOC

A complainant who receives an unfavorable decision from the agency *may* appeal to the EEOC's Office of Federal Operations (OFO) in Washington, D.C. This appeal must be filed within 30 days of receipt of the agency's final decision. If the employing agency does not implement the decision of the administrative judge, the agency must, upon rejection, simultaneously file an appeal with the OFO.

The EEOC will examine the administrative judge's legal conclusions, such as the grant of a summary judgement, *de novo*, and the judge's factual conclusions under a "substantial evidence" standard. The EEOC will affirm, modify, or overturn the agency's final decision. A finding of discrimination against the agency will include ordering the agency to provide appropriate remedies: back pay, hiring, compensatory damages, and attorneys's fees. *West v. Gibson* (S.Ct. 1999).

VI—25.05 Judicial Complaint: Several Options

1) A complainant who receives an unfavorable decision from the agency, may file a lawsuit in federal district court without filing an appeal to the EEOC's OFO. That complaint must be filed within 90 days from the receipt of the agency's final decision.

2) If the complainant appealed the agency decision to the EEOC, the complainant must file suit within 90 days of the receipt of the EEOC's final decision on appeal.

3) While Title VII and the Rehabilitation Act require complaints to exhaust administrative procedures, this requires only that the complainant contact the EEO Counselor, file a formal complaint with the agency, and wait 180 days for the agency to complete its investigation. If the agency has not completed its investigation and issued a final decision within 180 days, the complainant may file a suit at this point. Suit terminates the administrative process.

Thus, in sum, the complainant may file suit: 1) any time after 180 days have passed since filing of a formal complaint with the employing agency, 2) within 90 days after the receipt of the final agency decision (if no appeal is filed with the EEOC), or 3) within 90 days of the receipt of the EEOC's decision on the appeal.

The agency head, not the agency itself, is the proper defendant, and must be named in the complaint. Notwithstanding the often extensive record compiled during the administrative process, the district court adjudicates the plaintiff's claim *de novo*. *Chandler v. Roudebush* (S.Ct. 1976). Under Title VII and the Rehabilitation Act, there is a right to a jury trial. *West v. Gibson, supra* (S.Ct. 1999).

The period in which the complaint must be filed runs from the date the notification is received by the complainant or her attorney of record. The time limitations are not jurisdictional, and thus are subject to equitable tolling. Tolling is not appropriate for a "garden variety claim of excusable neglect." *Irwin v. Veterans Administration* (S.Ct. 1990). *Supra,* 24.04 and 24.06.

VI—25.06 Age Discrimination in Employment Act (ADEA): Special Procedures

a. Notice of Intent to Sue

A federal employee or applicant is not required to exhaust agency or EEOC procedures. All that is required is notifying the EEOC of an intent to sue. Notice of intent to sue must be provided to the EEOC within 180 days of the alleged discriminatory act. The complainant must then wait at least 30 days before filing a lawsuit against the employing agency.

b. Administrative Procedures (Optional)

A federal employee or applicant alleging age discrimination *may* elect to use the administrative complaint process. If so, administrative processes and time limitations set forth *supra,* 25.02—25.04 will govern.

c. Judicial Action

The time in which a federal plaintiff must file suit under the ADEA is unclear. If complainant invoked the administrative process, it appears that suit must be filed within 90 days following notification of the completion of the process. The former two-year statute of limitations applicable to non-federal plaintiffs, apparently repealed by the Civil Rights Act of 1991, did not expressly apply to claims against federal defendants. If plaintiff did not invoke administrative processes, but rather notified the EEOC of its intent to sue, there are four possible periods in which the suit must be filed: 1) the former two-year statute of limitations, apparently repealed by the Civil Rights Act of 1991, and which did not expressly apply to claims against federal defendants; 2) The general six year limitation period for actions against the federal government (28 U.S.C.A. 2401(a)); 3) an appropriate state statute of limitation; 4) no precise limitation, but the equitable doctrine of laches would bar suits where undue delay prejudiced the defendant. Without resolving the issue, the Court has held that where notice of intent to sue had been filed with the EEOC within 180 days of the discriminatory act, a suit filed one year and six days after the discriminatory act was timely. *Stevens v. Secretary, Dep't of the Treasury* (S.Ct. 1991).

There is *no* right to a jury trial under the ADEA.

d. Remedies

Remedies available to federal ADEA plaintiffs are limited compared to private sector plaintiffs. They cannot recover liquidated damages. *Smith v. Office of Personnel Management* (5th Cir. 1985). They cannot recover compensatory damages for emotional distress arising from a claim of retaliation. *Villes-*

cas v. Secretary, Dept. of Energy (10th Cir. 2002). While attorneys' fees are not available under the ADEA, they may be recoverable under the Equal Access to Justice Act. *Boehms v. Crowell* (5th Cir. 1998). Because administrative procedures need not be invoked under the ADEA, attorneys' fees may not include time expended invoking these procedures. *Nowd v. Rubin* (1st Cir. 1996).

CHAPTER 26

ALTERNATIVE FORUMS
AND PRECLUSION

VI—26.01 State Litigation

Most states and numerous local governments have employment discrimination statutes similar to the federal legislation. All states regulate defamation and intentional infliction of emotional harm, and most provide some degree of protection against wrongful discharges. State judicial determinations must be given preclusive effect in subsequent actions filed in federal courts under standards the state courts would apply had the suit been brought in state courts. 28 U.S.C.A. 1738. Thus, if a plaintiff asserted in a state judicial proceeding that she was a victim of a wrongful discharge, unless a second suit would be permitted in state courts, she could not claim in a subsequent federal suit that the discharge violated Title VII. *Kremer v. Chemical Const. Corp.* (S.Ct. 1982).

VI—26.02 Administrative Determinations

Title VII, the ADA, and the ADEA require plaintiffs (other than those suing federal employers) to file both state and federal administrative charges. These proceedings tend to be informal and investigatory. Based on its inquiries, which may consist of *ex parte* communications, the EEOC will determine whether reasonable cause exists to believe defendant violated the Act. Such findings are not preclusive. The trial court will make its independent, *de novo* determination of the facts and law based on the evidence presented at the trial. *McDonnell Douglas Corp. v. Green* (S.Ct. 1973).

Similarly, determinations by state administrative agencies made pursuant to charges *required* by the federal statutes that are a pre-requisite for seeking federal judicial relief are not preclusive, even if the proceedings provided a full, fair, and complete adversarial hearing. *Astoria Fed. Sav. & Loan Ass'n v. Solimino* (S.Ct. 1991). However, if the state administrative determination was reviewed by a state court, and judicial confirmation of the administrative finding would preclude future litigation in state courts, the federal courts must give similar preclusive effect to the judicially confirmed agency determination, even if the state claim did not receive a full and complete review in the state court. *Kremer v. Chemical Const. Corp., supra* (S.Ct. 1982).

State agency resolutions of claims arising under state statutes that impose *no requirement* for a plaintiff to exhaust (such as an academic tenure review or a civil service hearing) may be preclusive in subsequent federal court litigation if the state agency made a full and fair resolution of the claim, and the resolution is binding under state law. *University of Tenn. v. Elliott* (S.Ct. 1986).

VI—26.03 Private Arbitration

a. Federal Arbitration Act

The Federal Arbitration Act of 1925 (FAA) provides that:

[a] written provision in any * * * contract evidencing a transaction involving commerce to settle by arbitration a controversy thereafter arising out of such contract * * * shall be valid, irrevocable and enforceable * * * 9 U.S.C.A. 2.

An award may be vacated only if procured by corruption, fraud, or undue means or where the arbitrators were guilty of misconduct or exceeded their powers. 9 U.S.C.A. 10(a)

b. Collective Bargaining Agreements

Alexander v. Gardner–Denver Co. (S.Ct. 1974) held that an individual filing a grievance under a collective bargaining contract had not "elected" remedies, and this filing did not preclude the individual's Title VII suit based on the same transaction. Moreover, the arbitrator's award was neither binding nor entitled to special deference in subsequent litigation. The court must make a *de novo* evaluation of plaintiff's statutory claim even if under state law arbitration awards are subject to limited judicial review. *McDonald v. West Branch* (S.Ct. 1984). Whether a union through a negotiated *collective bargaining* agreement has the power to waive an individual employee's right to seek individual judicial remedies for federal statutory violations has not been resolved. *Wright v. Universal*

Maritime Service Corp. (S.Ct. 1998)(agreement did not "contain a clear and unmistakable waiver" of the covered employees' rights to a judicial forum).

c. Individual Contracts

1. Compelling Arbitration: *Gilmer v. Interstate/Johnson Lane Corp.* (S.Ct. 1991) held that the Federal Arbitration Act was applicable to an *individual* who had personally contracted in a securities registration application to resolve all dispute between himself and his employer through arbitration. The employee was required to submit to private arbitration his federal statutory claim of age discrimination. *Circuit City Stores v. Adams* (S.Ct. 2001), expanded *Gilmer* by holding that the FAA's application to all arbitration agreements "evidencing a transaction involving interstate commerce," was not limited to "commercial contracts," as argued by the employee, but applied to contracts of employment. The Court held that the "workers engaged in commerce" exemption from FAA coverage applied only to workers actually engaged in interstate or foreign transportation. Finally, the Court reaffirmed its previous holding that the FAA pre-empted state law. Thus, employees who had contractually agreed to submit their employment claims to arbitration were not free to avoid arbitration and seek either federal or state judicial remedies, even if state law expressly allowed employees access to state courts. Because the EEOC implements public policy, it is not bound by an individual employment agreement to submit the employee's disputes to arbitration, and thus the EEOC may sue to recover victim-specific judicial relief for employ-

ees who have agreed to arbitration. *EEOC v. Waffle House* (S.Ct. 2002).

Whether a contract obligates the party to submit a dispute to arbitration is a question of state law. To determine if the agreement to arbitrate bound the employee, the waiver of the judicial remedy must be "express, knowing, voluntary," and perhaps even "unmistakable." *Wright v. Universal Maritime Serv. Corp., supra* (S.Ct. 1998). Arbitration clauses are not binding if they are obscure or hidden unnoticed in a voluminous employment manual. *Nelson v. Cyprus Bagdad Copper Corp.* (9th Cir. 1997). The agreement to arbitrate should clearly include claims arising under the statutes, as opposed to claims arising under the contract. *Paladino v. Avnet Computer Tech., Inc.* (11th Cir. 1998).

Basic contract law provides that contracts are not enforced if "unconscionable" *both* procedurally (*i.e.,* how the agreement was secured) *and* substantively (*i.e.,* unfair, one-sided terms). Some states aggressively apply this concept. Construing California law, the Ninth Circuit held that where employment is made conditional upon an employee agreeing to arbitrate employment disputes, the stark inequality in bargaining power makes the agreement procedurally unconscionable. *Ingle v. Circuit City Stores* (9th Cir. 2003). The employee must be accorded a meaningful opportunity to decline, which is not satisfied where the employee is told that he would have no future with the company if he elects to opt out of the agreement to arbitrate. *Circuit City Stores v. Mantor* (9th Cir. 2003). An agreement will

be substantively unconscionable—and thus unen-
forceable—when its terms unfairly deprive the employee of statutory rights. If the agreement to arbitrate does not bind the employer, prohibits class
actions, limits attorneys fees or damages below that
available under federal law, imposes draconian time
limits, or requires the employee to pay filing fees
and the cost of the arbitrator, such factors may
render the agreement unconscionable. *Circuit City
Stores, Inc. v. Mantor* (9th Cir. 2003).

Other states are less vigorous in their interpretation of unconscionability. Conditioning employment
upon acceptance of arbitration is not seen as procedurally unconscionable, and while clauses that are
contrary to federal law, such as damage limits, will
not be enforceable, they will be severed from the
agreement, leaving the agreement to arbitrate enforceable. *Hadnot v. Bay, Ltd.* (5th Cir. 2003). Mere
ambiguity as to which party shall bear fees and
costs of the arbitration will not preclude enforcement of the agreement. There must be some showing that possible shifting of costs to the employee
effectively precludes the employee from enforcing
statutory rights in the arbitration forum. *Green
Tree Financial Corp. v. Randolph* (S.Ct. 2000).
Plaintiffs seeking to avoid arbitration thus need to
demonstrate the amount of the costs and an inability to pay. *Musnick v. King Motor Co. Of Fort
Lauderdale* (11th Cir. 2003).

2. Enforcing the Award: The Federal Arbitration Act, which governs judicial enforcement of the
arbitrator's award, allows extremely limited judicial

review. Courts may refuse to enforce only those awards procured by corruption, fraud, or undue means, or where the arbitrators were guilty of misconduct or exceeded their powers. Courts have recognized an implicit limitation; they will not enforce awards that are "manifestly in disregard of the law." *First Options of Chicago, Inc. v. Kaplan* (S.Ct. 1995). Moreover, arbitration awards that violate public policy will not be enforced, but the Court narrowly construes this exception. *Eastern Associated Coal Corp. v. United Mine Workers* (S.Ct. 2000)(arbitration compelling reinstatement of truck driver who had twice failed random drug test did not violate public policy). Accordingly, on issues of fact (such as an employer's motivation) courts will not re-adjudicate an arbitrator's findings. On issues of law, for a court to refuse enforcement, plaintiff must prove that the arbitrator was corrupt, exceeded his/her contractual authority, or it was "manifest that the arbitrator acted contrary to applicable law" that resulted in "significant injustice." A mere mistake of law does not warrant refusal to enforce an award. *Williams v. Cigna Financial Advisors, Inc.* (5th Cir. 1999) (ADEA claim).

INDEX

331

†